Footsteps of Faith

Old Testament, Volume 4

Revised Edition

God Guides Us

by

Bernice Claire Jordan

BCM
BIBLE CENTERED
MINISTRIES
INTERNATIONAL

BCM International, Inc.

309 Colonial Drive, P.O. Box 249, Akron, PA 17501-0249
685 Main Street East, Hamilton, Ontario L8M 1K4 Canada
39a Swiss Road, Weston-super-Mare, N. Somerset BS23 3AY England

Footsteps of Faith is BCM's primary Bible teaching curriculum for children's Bible Clubs. This unique series has been revised for teaching God's Word in other settings, such as Sunday school, children's church, Christian school, and home schooling.

Revision Committee
Writer: Pamela Rowntree
Editor: Patricia Black
Copy Editor: Lois Haas
Contributors: David Haas
Esther Zimmerman

Cover design & book layout:
Bert VandenBos

This textbook is lovingly dedicated to
Donna J. Culver
who has served with distinction on the Revision Committee
as editor for four volumes of *Footsteps of Faith*.
Her unique skills in editing and her tenacity for correctness
have contributed significantly to the quality of these revisions.

Original title: *Following God's Trailblazers*

Copyright © 2005
BCM International, Inc. All rights reserved.

ISBN 978-0-86508-008-9

CONTENTS

Course Overview iv
Introduction v
    Understand Your Children vii
    Prepare Yourself to Be God's Channel viii
    Prepare Your Lesson ix
    Manage Your Class Effectively x
    Lead Your Children to Christ x
    Keep in Touch xi
    Important Information xii

Lesson 1   Elijah Demonstrates God's Power
            Elijah Tells God's Message to Ahab (Part One) 1
            Elijah Challenges the Prophets of Baal (Part Two) 12

Lesson 2   King Ahab Steals from Naboth 22
Lesson 3   Naaman Is Healed 31
Lesson 4   Jonah Runs Away from God 41
Lesson 5   Isaiah Prophesies to a Sinful Nation 51
Lesson 6   Josiah Repairs the Temple 61
Lesson 7   Jeremiah Delivers God's Warning 70
Lesson 8   God's People Are Taken Captive 80

Lesson 9   Daniel and His Friends Honor God
            Daniel Interprets the King's Dream (Part One) 90
            God Saves Daniel's Friends from Burning (Part Two) 100

Lesson 10   The Persians Conquer Babylon
            Daniel Reads the Writing on the Wall (Part One) 108
            God Saves Daniel from the Lions (Part Two) 116

Lesson 11   Esther Becomes Queen 125
Lesson 12   God Saves Esther and Her People 135
Lesson 13   Job Is Tested 144
Lesson 14   God Frees His People 154

Resource Section 165
Teaching Materials & Supplies 180

God Guides Us
Course Overview

No.	Title	Theme	Scripture	Verse
1-1	Elijah Tells God's Message to Ahab	The Righteous Way	1 Kings 16, 17	Psalm 1:6
1-2	Elijah Challenges the Prophets of Baal	The Righteous Way	1 Kings 18	Psalm 1:6
2	King Ahab Steals from Naboth	The Narrow Way	1 Kings 19, 20, 22; 2 Kings 9	Matthew 7:14
3	Naaman Is Healed	The Jesus Way	2 Kings 5	John 14:6
4	Jonah Runs Away from God	A Prepared Way	Jonah 1-4	Psalm 86:11
5	Isaiah Prophesies to a Sinful Nation	A Holy Way	2 Chronicles 26; Isaiah 6, 7, 9, 53, 61	1 Peter 1:15
6	Josiah Repairs the Temple	The Bible Way	2 Kings 21-23; 2 Chronicles 34, 35	Psalm 119:33
7	Jeremiah Delivers God's Warning	A Witnessing Way	Jeremiah 1, 5, 7, 20, 22, 25, 33, 36-39	Proverbs 3:6
8	God's People Are Taken Captive	The Way of Life	2 Kings 17, 23-25; Jeremiah 25, 29, 37-39	Jeremiah 21:8
9-1	Daniel Interprets the King's Dream	A Protected Way	2 Kings 24; Daniel 1, 2	Psalm 91:11
9-2	God Saves Daniel's Friends from Burning	A Protected Way	Daniel 3	Psalm 91:11
10-1	Daniel Reads the Writing on the Wall	An Obedient Way	Daniel 5	Psalm 37:34
10-2	God Saves Daniel from the Lions	An Obedient Way	Daniel 6	Psalm 37:34
11	Esther Becomes Queen	A God-Planned Way	Esther 1-4	Isaiah 55:9
12	God Saves Esther and Her People	A Courageous Way	Esther 5-10	Proverbs 10:29
13	Job Is Tested	A Tested Way	Job 1, 2, 38-42	Job 23:10
14	God Frees His People	A Rejoicing Way	Ezra 1-4, 6, 7; Nehemiah 1-6, 8, 9	Psalm 138:5

INTRODUCTION

Footsteps of Faith is an eight-volume Bible teaching curriculum that covers the Bible in basically chronological order. Its overall aim is to help children respond to the love of God in Christ and learn to walk in the footsteps of faith and obedience.

Each volume is complete in itself and centered around a theme that is carried through every lesson in that volume to provide for consistent learning as well as continual review and application of the Bible truths.

The course is non-graded and undated, written for teaching children ages 6-12, but adaptable to different age groups and many teaching situations. It has been used effectively in Bible Clubs, children's church programs, vacation Bible schools, and Sunday school classes, as well as in Christian schools and home school classes.

The series...
- shows God at work in the world. The Old Testament points ahead to Christ's coming, revealing man's fall into sin, God's promise of a Savior, and His program for accomplishing this. The New Testament records the actual fulfillment of God's program in the birth of Christ, His life, death, and resurrection, the birth of the Church, the establishing of a missionary program, and the yet-to-be-fulfilled promise of Christ's return!
- teaches Bible doctrine and history along with the principles of Christian living.
- emphasizes Scripture memorization and provides Bible study helps, which are coordinated with the lessons and may be used as work sheets or take-home devotionals.
- is both evangelistic and Christian-growth oriented, clearly presenting the plan of salvation and emphasizing practical Christian living.

The lessons...
- emphasize specific Bible truths.
- include practical, hands-on application of those truths for both Christian and non-Christian children.
- are structured with a teaching aim designed to help the teacher present the Bible truth and encourage the children to relate and apply that truth to their daily lives.

A unique review system...
- is built into each volume and visualizes the main theme of that course and the complementary lesson themes.
- relates the lessons logically to each other and to the central theme of the course.
- provides a framework for remembering biblical truth so that the children can apply it in their daily lives.
- enables the teacher to review and reinforce previous lessons and memory verses quickly, regularly, and in an interesting way.
- stimulates the children to *see, hear, verbalize,* and *do,* thus involving them in the learning process.

Correlated teaching aids enhance learning.
- Full-color flannelgraph figures enable children to focus attention and visualize scenes as you tell the Bible story.
- Flannel backgrounds provide a scenic backdrop for the figures. (Available from BCM Publications in black and white, with instructions for coloring.)

- The *Bible Verses Visualized* packet (available in King James Version only) furnishes colorful flannelgraph visuals for teaching the memory verses.
- The *God Guides Us* Resource CD-ROM contains the following:
  - *Bible Verses Visualized* (available in both King James and New International versions) furnishes visual pieces for teaching every memory verse in the course.
  - *Memory Verse Tokens* and *Token Holders* (adapted from the Review Chart and available in both King James and New International versions) are colorful review aids that encourage children to memorize the verses and that help to build links from week to week.
  - *Bible Study Helps* uses varied and interesting Bible questions and activities to encourage daily study of God's Word.
  - *Creative Idea Menus* provide a wealth of ideas to reinforce and extend learning in programs and learning centers.

God Guides Us, Old Testament Volume 4 of the *Footsteps of Faith* series, covers 2 Kings through Malachi. It continues the amazing story of God's chosen people, now divided into the two kingdoms of Israel and Judah. Israel continues its plunge into utter wickedness and rejection of God in spite of the marvelous ministries of two prophets, Elijah and Elisha. Judah's decline is slowed by the godly leadership of such outstanding kings as Jehoshaphat, Hezekiah, and Josiah.

On the backdrop of the utter darkness and doom of God's judgment falling on both kingdoms, God reveals His way to heaven through the lives of His special people—kings, prophets, and captives—who were willing to obey Him at any cost. *God Guides Us* issues a challenge for today's children to look to the living God of the ages to guide them safely and saintly through life.

The review system for *God Guides Us* is a pathway of stepping stones that blazes a trail to heaven. Each stone gives a description of God's Way, as illustrated by its corresponding lesson, and enables the teacher and students to interact with contemporary issues facing those committed to walking with God.

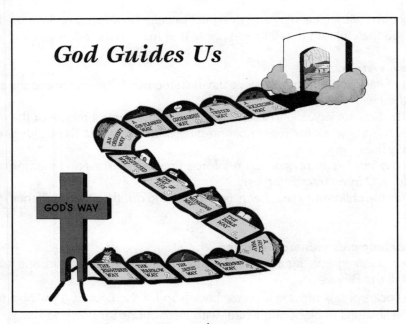

Understand Your Children

Today's children are different from previous generations. Growing up in a fast-paced, "instant-everything" society, accessing the world through computers and the Internet, they are bright, eager to learn, and well informed. They...
- receive much of their information in "sound bytes" (capsulized reports).
- are accustomed to seeing most problems solved within a 30- or 60-minute time slot in a television schedule.
- consequently, have short attention spans.
- expect great variety in all they see and hear.
- can be impatient with sitting still, being quiet, or waiting.

Children learn in many different ways:
- some by *seeing* what they're learning;
- others by *talking* about it;
- still others by *moving* or *doing*—being actively involved or making things;
- some process information globally—by seeing "the big picture";
- others are analytic thinkers and want all the details.

Remember these things when preparing to teach. Try a variety of the teaching methods and options suggested in the text, even if they do not all appeal to you. They will help you incorporate variety in methods and visuals, and capsulize important points in "sound bytes" the children can see and hear over and over. You will soon know which are most effective with your class members.

Many of today's children come from stable homes where parents are working hard to prepare them for the future. Many others come from broken families or from homes where parents have no time to spend with them or listen to them. Most of them...
- are exposed by the media to too much too early.
- are being conditioned to accept materialism, deteriorating moral standards, and a secular world view as the norm. Unless they are taught the eternal Word of God, how are they to know otherwise?
- are assaulted by violence in the media; some, in their homes and neighborhoods.
- feel a deep need for someone to love them, to care about them, to give them a reason to hope.

What a privilege—and what a sobering responsibility—to take to them the wonderful news that God loves them, that He has provided salvation for them, and that He has a plan for their lives! There is hope in Him!

For *GOD never changes!* His truth is timeless! By faith Shadrach, Meshach, and Abednego stood firm in their resolve to obey God and came through the fiery furnace unscathed. By faith today's children can resist the intimidation of peer pressure and the attractiveness of the world to please the Lord and benefit from His guidance. God's eternal Word is a guidebook for living a life that pleases God in any age. Knowing Him and walking in the footsteps of faith and obedience provide security and stability in an uncertain world.

Because we know God and His Word, we can demonstrate God's love to them; we can lead them to that secure place in HIM in the midst of their insecure world. So take time to get to know your students and understand their needs.

Prepare Yourself to Be God's Channel

You, the teacher, are the living link between God's truth and the children in your class. You channel Christ's love to them. You teach them God's Word so that they may understand His truth and receive Christ as Savior, then follow Him in loving obedience. You model how to practice in daily life the truth they are learning. And you are their guide to discovering truth for themselves and attaining their greatest potential for God.

- Submit yourself to God that you may be a Spirit-empowered teacher.
- Expect God to speak to you personally as you study your lesson each week, then to guide you as you prepare to teach.
- Realize that you are a tool in God's hands. As you depend on Him, He will work through you and in the hearts of the children to draw them to Himself.
- Enjoy your class! Be enthusiastic; enter into activities with the children so they see you not only as a teacher but as a friend.
- Encourage the children to bring their Bibles and plan ways for them to use them every week. Teach them how to find passages in Scripture. Frequently have them follow along in their Bibles as you teach the lesson. As you instruct boys and girls to love and respect God's Word, show them how to use it correctly, and inspire them to obey it, you give them an invaluable gift that will go with them throughout life. (If some don't have Bibles, look for a place to get them inexpensively—a Bible society or an organization that distributes free ones.)
- REVIEW, REVIEW, REVIEW! Some studies show that people need to hear new information up to 75 times to learn it.
- Avoid using many questions that can be answered with a simple yes or no.
- Use the open-ended questions suggested in the lesson or others you devise yourself to involve the children in the learning process and find out what they have or have not learned. Then you will have the opportunity to correct faulty understanding and they will learn more because they are thinking and interacting.
- Avoid calling on students who find it difficult or embarrassing to read aloud or answer questions publicly. Find other ways to involve them until they feel safe enough to interact.

Remember that your effectiveness in class often depends upon the relationship that you have established with students both inside and outside of class.

- Find ways to spend time with students, such as attending some of their school or neighborhood activities, and visiting at least some of their homes.
- Learn their names and show a real interest in them.
- Listen when they talk about their families, their friends, and their struggles. Listening shows the child that you care and helps you learn how to apply Scripture effectively.
- Notice individual children's strengths and affirm them regularly.
- Compliment those you see practicing what they're learning.
- Seek to discern the spiritual progress of individual students and help them to grow in Christlikeness.
- Don't be afraid to be explicit when dealing with the issues that surround them. They are exposed to life experiences and life styles far beyond what they should be. They need to know what God has to say and how to live for Him in the midst of their life situations. Ask God to guide you and make you sensitive to their needs and His direction.
- Pray for them.
- Make the brief time they spend with you each week a happy time, a safe place—a refuge.

Prepare Your Lesson

Pray that God will speak to you through the Scripture passage, then guide you as you prepare to teach.

- Study the Scripture passage thoroughly, making notes of points that seem important to you. Look for answers to six important questions: *Who* was involved? *What* was happening? *Where* were they? *When* did it happen? *Why* did it happen? or *Why* did he say that? *How* did it happen?
- Read the printed lesson, thinking it through with your children in mind. Each part of the lesson has a specific purpose.

  The **Aim** is the statement of what you want to accomplish—with God's help—as you present the lesson.

  The **Introduction** is a plan for getting the students' attention and directing their thinking in preparation for the Bible story.

  The **Bible Content** is the Bible story and the Bible truth it illustrates and reinforces.

  The **Conclusion** is a plan for completing the lesson by showing the children how to apply the Bible truth and providing a way for them to respond to it in daily life.

Using a lesson plan keeps you on track. It helps you use your time wisely and accomplish the purpose God lays on your heart for the lesson. Follow the one in the teacher's text or use it as a pattern to write your own.

- Make simple outline notes to use as a guide when teaching. Put them in your Bible so the children will see you teaching from God's Word, not the teacher's manual.
- Sort out the figures you will need and stack them in the order you will use them. Put them in a file folder to carry to class.
- Put the flannel backgrounds on the flannelboard in the order they will be used with the last one on the bottom. Secure them to the top of the board with large binder clips.
- Use sketches in the lesson as guides for placing figures on scenes. Check from the side of the board to see how they appear. Remove them (in the same order you put them there so they're ready to use again) and practice placing them as you stand at the side of the board. Check from the front to see if they are straight and in their proper places.
- Practice telling the story aloud as you put the figures in place until you can do it comfortably and without interruption. This will take some time in the beginning, but—like any skill—it will gradually become easier and less time consuming.
- When you teach, be careful to always work from the side of your board so you don't block students' view. Maintain eye contact with the children and don't turn your back on the class.
- Plan to be at your class location early. Put the room in order, set up your equipment and materials, and pray with your helper before the children arrive. Then you will have a heart free to welcome the boys and girls and listen to their chatter as they come in.
- Arrange seating so every student can see the flannelboard. Try to avoid distractions like having them looking into bright sunlight or facing a door where people come and go during class. Control the room temperature when possible, so that the children are neither too hot nor too cold. Get rid of clutter. A neat and orderly room helps children be orderly. An attractive room contributes to their enjoyment.

Manage Your Class Effectively

A well-managed classroom honors God by creating an atmosphere for learning, providing a secure refuge for students, making learning enjoyable, and preventing many behavior and discipline problems. A well-managed classroom requires three elements.

A prepared teacher
- yielded to God in mind, heart, and spirit
- ready with both lesson and program
- knowing each student's name, characteristics, needs, and interests
- praying for each student
- planning behavioral goals for the children
- arriving early to prepare the room before the children arrive

A prepared environment
- visuals and equipment set up and in working order
- appropriate seating arranged so all can see and hear
- comfortable temperature and adequate lighting
- minimal distractions (e.g., clutter, noise, activities)

Prepared students
- knowing class rules: for example, where to put their coats, where to say their verses, how to answer or ask questions, enter and leave class, and take bathroom breaks
- aware that you expect them to obey class rules, that you appreciate good behavior and will praise them for it, and that there will be consequences for misbehavior

The ultimate purpose of managing your class well is to create an environment in which God the Holy Spirit is able to work through the Word of God to bring about change in the childrens' lives.

Lead Your Children to Christ

Leading children to receive Jesus Christ as their Savior is a glorious privilege and an awesome responsibility. It is our deep conviction that to adequately carry out this responsibility the teacher must do four things:
- Present salvation truth frequently.
- Give students opportunities to respond to the truth.
- Speak privately with those who respond.
- Follow up on those who make a profession of faith.

In class...
- *Present salvation truth.*
  "God is holy. We are sinners, deserving punishment. We must believe the Lord Jesus Christ died for us and receive Him as Savior."
  Use the salvation ABCs:
  - ADMIT I am a sinner: I've done wrong things, displeased God (Romans 3:23).
  - BELIEVE that Jesus Christ is God, that He died on the cross for me, and that He rose again (Romans 5:8).
  - CHOOSE to receive Christ as Savior and Lord (Romans 10:9).
- *Invite the children to respond.*
  "Perhaps you have never received Christ as your Savior and would like to do that today. If so, I'd like to talk with you after class and show you how."

After class...
- *Speak with those who respond.*
  Talk individually with the children, being careful to have the door open, a helper nearby. To find out if they understand why they came, ask:
  - "Is there a special reason you came to talk to me?"
  - "Have you ever received Christ as your Savior before?"
- *Review basic facts about Christ.*
  - Who Jesus is (both God and man) John 3:16; I John 5:20
  - What Jesus did (died on the cross to take the punishment for our sins; rose again to be our living Savior) 1 Corinthians 15:3, 4
  - Why they need Jesus ("You are a sinner deserving punishment for your sins. Jesus can make you right with God and give you eternal life in heaven.") Romans 3:10; 6:23
- *Review the ABCs of salvation listed above.*
  - Say, "Jesus wants to be your Savior right now. Will you receive Him?"
  - If they say yes, ask them to pray aloud. Let them use their own words, but guide them if necessary ("I admit I am a sinner. I'm sorry for my sins and want to be free from them. I believe You died for me, and I receive You as my living Savior") John 1:12.
  - Be sure they base their salvation on God's Word, not on their feelings! Show them Scriptures (Romans 10:9; John 1:12; 1 John 5:11-13) that indicate salvation is by faith, believing what God says.
- *Follow up.*
  Give them a tract, such as BCM's *A Child of God*, as a reminder of what they have done. Read through it with them. Then use it as a guide for Christian growth in the weeks ahead.

Keep in Touch

Use Mailbox Bible Club correspondence lessons to keep in touch after the series is finished. When the children return their completed lessons (either by mail or in person) to be checked and to receive the next lesson, you have an excellent opportunity to answer questions and provide continuing guided help for their walk with the Lord. (See the Teaching Materials & Supplies list on page 180 for information on ordering materials and obtaining a lesson sample.)

**Do you have suggestions or questions? need help?
want training or a catalog of available teaching materials?
Contact us at:**

BCM INTERNATIONAL, INC.
P.O. Box 249, Akron, PA 17501-0249
Phone: 888-226-4685
E-mail: publications@bcmintl.org

685 Main Street East, Hamilton, ON L8M 1K4 CANADA
Phone: 905-549-9810 FAX 905-549-7664
E-mail: mission@bcmintl.ca

39a Swiss Road, Weston-super-Mare, N. Somerset BS23 3AY, ENGLAND
Phone and FAX: 1934-413484; E-mail: BCMUK@aol.com

Important information
about the teaching materials you will use in this course

Listed below are general visual aids you should have available before you begin teaching the course, along with instructions for preparing some teaching aids that are used in most lessons. Check the "Materials to Gather" section in each lesson for items to collect for that lesson. Choose from the Options those learning activities that are appropriate for the various learning styles in your group.

Flannelgraph figures for *God Guides Us*

Cut out the figures and file them in numerical order in separate file folders labeled 1-10, 11-19, 20-29, etc.

Flannelgraph Review Chart for *God Guides Us*

Flannelgraph backgrounds – your own or those available from BCM Publications

BCM's backgrounds are screen-printed on quality white flannel and include instructions for coloring them.

Visualized memory verses from *Bible Verses Visualized* for *God Guides Us*

A verse packet is available in the King James Version only. File the visuals for each verse in a separate file folder or an envelope labeled with the verse reference.

The *God Guides Us Resource CD-ROM* provides visuals for the King James Version or New International Version. Print the visuals on heavy paper and cut them out.

Memory verse tokens & holders – available on the *God Guides Us Resource CD-ROM*

Use these as an incentive to memorize weekly Bible verses. Print the holders on heavy paper. Cut out the tokens before class. When the children can say a verse correctly, have them paste its token on their token holders. Or, paste all tokens on the token holders; then let those who say the verse correctly put a small sticker on their token. Send the token holders home at the end of the course.

Bible Study Helps – available on the *God Guides Us Resource CD-ROM*

Use these to encourage daily Bible reading by giving out one lesson at a time.

Patterns & Map: Use a copy machine to enlarge and print the patterns and map indicated.

To enlarge a pattern or the map to poster board size, trace the pattern or map onto a transparency, project it onto a poster board you have taped to the wall (taking care to center it on the poster board), and use a marker to trace the outline onto the poster board. Attach these visuals (or any chart you make) to the flannelboard with clips or loops of tape when indicated.

Bookmarks: Use a copy machine to duplicate the bookmarks from page 179, on colored heavy paper if available. Cut apart to use. Keep a supply on hand for new children.

Word strips & Cards: Use your computer to prepare and print word strips and cards specified for each lesson. Cut them apart and glue small pieces of sandpaper, flocked paper, or flannel to the back of the strips so they will adhere to the flannelboard. Or, print the word(s) clearly on construction paper strips. Use sandpaper to roughen the back of the strips so they will adhere to the flannelboard.

Handouts: Use a copy machine to duplicate the pattern specified.

Copyright Owner's Permission: Examine the Response Activity in Lesson 14 to determine what song you want to use so you can get permission if needed.

For information about ordering any of the above teaching materials see pages xi and 180.

Elijah Demonstrates God's Power
Theme: The Righteous Way

Part One: Elijah Tells God's Message to Ahab

Lesson 1

 BEFORE YOU BEGIN...

Living in a world that tends to neglect and abuse its children, today's Bible teacher has both the distinct privilege and solemn responsibility of communicating God's love and care to them. But it is not as easy as it sounds. Children have learned to *not* trust; they have had to put up their own guard for self-preservation. Therefore, your challenge is to model consistently the purity and passion of Christ, so that your students will open their heart's door to accept you and your message.

Elijah bravely chose to go God's way of righteousness, even to the point of confronting a wicked monarch and prophesying God's judgment upon a nation that had forsaken Him. It is thrilling to see how God cared for His obedient prophet during the years of drought that followed.

May you have the joy of seeing your students wanting to go God's way of righteousness, choosing to believe in the saving grace of the Lord Jesus and placing their trust in His loving care through all of life. *"For He made Him who knew no sin to be sin for us, that we might become the righteousness of God in Him" (2 Corinthians 5:21, NKJV).*

AIM:

That the children may

- Know that God takes care of those who have been made righteous through believing in the Lord Jesus Christ for salvation.
- Respond by choosing God's way of salvation and trusting Him to take care of their needs.

SCRIPTURE: 1 Kings 16:29-33; 17:1-16

MEMORY VERSE: Psalm 1:6

For the Lord knoweth the way of the righteous: but the way of the ungodly shall perish. (KJV)
For the Lord watches over the way of the righteous, but the way of the wicked will perish. (NIV)

▲ Option #1

Use simple markers such as arrows and written signs to create a trail inside or outside the classroom. Have the trail lead back to the place where you will teach. Place a surprise treat at a point along the trail. When the children arrive, give them the marker design they are to look for and show them where to begin hiking. Instruct them to follow the trail to the end either as a group or individually. When all have returned to the class, discuss how the signs helped them, noting if they discovered the treat. For the benefit of those who did not follow the signs, discuss why they followed their own way and didn't discover the treat.

Variation: Divide the children into groups and have each group design a set of trail markers. Give them an opportunity to show their markers to the class and to tell what they mean.

📁 MATERIALS TO GATHER

Visual for Psalm 1:6 from *Bible Verses Visualized*

Backgrounds: Review Chart, Plain Background, Old Testament Map II, Palace, General Outdoor, Brook Overlay, City Wall, Plain Interior

Figures: R1, R15, R16, 1, 2, 3, 4, 5, 6, 7(3 peices), 8, 8A, 13, 15, 43

Token holders & memory verse tokens (see page xii) for Psalm 1:6

Bible Study Helps for Lesson 1, Part 1

Special:
- **For Review Chart:** A road map; word strip GUIDE; BELIEVE & OBEY footprints; pictures of trail markers (paint markings on trees, colored plastic ties around trees, wooden signs) and road signs
- **For Memory Verse:** Word strips RIGHTEOUS, UNGODLY (or WICKED)
- **For Introduction:** "Choice of Two Ways" sign
- **For Bible Content 1:** Word strips GENESIS to 2 CHRONICLES; a list of all the Old Testament books printed on a piece of poster board or a piece of newsprint. Print GENESIS to ECCLESIASTES with a black marker and ISAIAH to MALACHI with a different colored marker. (Use water-basedmarkers; permanent markers may bleed through newsprint and stain your background.)
- **For Bible Content 2:** "God Guides Us" bookmarks
- **For Bible Content 2 & 3:** Map of Divided Kingdom
- **For Summary:** "Righteous/Ungodly/God's Care" chart, marker; "Choice of Two Ways" sign
- **For Application:** Word strips YOU, ADMIT, BELIEVE, CHOOSE
- **For Response Activity:** "Choice of Two Ways" handouts, pencils
- **For Options:** Additional materials for any options you choose to use
- **Note:** *To prepare the "Righteous/Ungodly/God's Care" chart,* draw two vertical lines to make three columns on a sheet of newsprint. Print these titles: "Righteous" in the first column, "Ungodly" (or "Wicked") in the second column, and "God's Care" in the third column.
  Follow the instructions on page xii to prepare the word strips, the BELIEVE & OBEY footprints (pattern P-2 on page 167), the "Choice of Two Ways" sign (pattern P-3 on page 168), the bookmarks, the Map of Divided Kingdom (pattern P-1 on page 166), the "Choice of Two Ways" handouts (pattern P-11 on page 172), and the Bible Study Helps.

REVIEW CHART

(A road map, word strip GUIDE; pictures of trail markers and road signs)

If you were going to take a trip by car that was far from your home, what would you need to be sure you arrived at the right place? *(Response)* Yes, you would probably need directions and a map. *(Display a road map.)* How would the map help you? *(Response)* Yes, it would show you what roads to take to get there.

A map is like a guide *(show GUIDE)*, helping us find our way to a certain place. Can you think of another time you might need to use a guide or map? *(Response)* Yes, when hiking along a path in the woods. Have you ever been on such a path? *(Response)* ▲#1

As you were hiking along the path, did you notice the markers or signs placed along the way to show you which path to take? *(Show the pictures of trail markers.)* We also need road signs to show us which way to go when we are traveling on the highway. Can you name some of them? *(Show the pictures of road signs.)*

Some markers or road signs help us choose the right way, but others help keep us safe by making us aware of any dangers or changes along the road we are traveling. However, if they are going to be any help to us, we must look at them and then obey what they tell us to do.

Before making a map or road signs, someone had to be the first one to go ahead and see what the road or path was like and then place the appropriate markers or signs in place that would give us clear direction and warn us of any hazards that we might encounter. Then he had to make a map. That person is like a guide. Though he isn't actually here to lead us, his signs and maps provide us with the right directions and help us reach our destination safely.

We are all traveling on the road of life and need something like a map or road signs to guide us through our journey. We need something that has been prepared by someone who has already gone ahead of us, who knows what direction to go, and who warns us about the dangers ahead. Who is it that knows all about us and knows what the future holds? *(Response)* Yes, God is the best guide we could ever have. What has God prepared to guide us in our journey through life? *(Response)* Yes, God has prepared His Word, the Bible. It gives us His instructions and guidance for all the decisions we must make. We can choose to obey or ignore them. The choice we make will determine our destination and what our journey will be like. ▲#2

▲ **Option#2**

Have the children discuss the kinds of road signs they think God would make to warn of danger or give directions. Give paper and markers to the children in groups or individually to illustrate their ideas. Then display their signs for the class to guess what God is telling them.

(Cross gate R15, heaven R16, review token R1; BELIEVE & OBEY footprints)

The path on our "God Guides Us" Review Chart will help us discover how God guides us by what He says to us in His Word *(point to the path)*. It will help us see that we must choose God's Way by believing in the Lord Jesus Christ as our

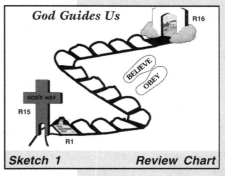

Sketch 1 — Review Chart

⌂ **Note (1)**

If you choose to display the memory verse on the flannelboard, put it on a plain background throughout this course.

▲ **Option#3**

Have those with other versions read the verse so that all can see the differences and how each version helps to understand the verse.

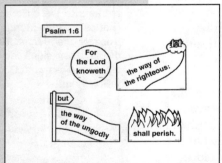

▲ **Option#4**

Definition word card: Righteous = to be without sin.

▲ **Option#5**

Definition word card: Sin = anything we do, say, or think that goes against God's Word.

Savior *(add R15)* if we are to reach heaven *(add R16)* at the end of our life. We will also learn that God's Way is a journey of faith and that we must walk in footsteps of faith, *(add footprints),* believing and obeying what God has told us in His Word, our road map for life.

Each week we will meet people from the Bible who either chose to follow God's Way or chose to go their own way. Some of them were kings, some were prophets, and some were ordinary people like you and me. Those men and women who followed God's Way walked in footsteps of faith, believing and obeying God even when it was difficult. They experienced God's guidance throughout their lives and reached their destination safely. By sad contrast, those who chose to go their own way, refusing to believe and obey God, had a sad end to their lives. We will learn how to travel God's Way as we learn from their example, whether it was good or bad. The lessons they learned are like road signs for us to follow. We, like them, must choose which way we will follow—God's Way or our own way.

What is God's Way like? We will answer that question as we look into God's Word each week. Today we will learn that God's Way is *The Righteous Way (place R1 on the first space on the Chart).* What does that mean? We'll find out as we learn today's verse.

♥ **MEMORY VERSE** ⌂(1)

Use the visual to teach Psalm 1:6 and the word strips RIGHTEOUS and UNGODLY (or WICKED) when indicated.

Our memory verse is in the book of Psalms. *(Display the reference and have someone read it.)* This book is in the Old Testament and almost in the middle of the whole Bible. *(Have the children locate the verse in their Bibles. Display the verse.)* ▲#3

Our verse describes two kinds of people. Who are they? *(Response)* Yes, the *righteous* and the *ungodly (wicked).* These words describe people who are opposite. Let's see why this is true.

What smaller word do you see in the word *righteous?* *(Place RIGHTEOUS on the board.) (Response)* Yes, it is the word *right.* What does *right* mean? *(Response)* Yes, it means correct or good. That helps us to know what *righteous* means. In the Old Testament *righteous* people were correct because they worshiped the true and living God; they loved Him and obeyed Him. In the New Testament the word *righteous* took on an additional meaning: *to be without sin.* ▲#4 Sin means anything we do, say, or think, that goes against God's Word. ▲#5 Those who are righteous are right with God or free from sin. However, there is a problem because no one but Jesus was ever born righteous or sinless. All of us have sinned (Romans 3:23) and deserve to be punished for our sins (Romans 6:23).

How can we become righteous or right with God? God had a wonderful plan to take care of our sin problem. He sent his own Son, the Lord Jesus Christ, to earth to take the punishment for our sins

(Romans 5:19). Jesus is righteous, completely free from sin, and the only one who could take our punishment for us. When we believe that Jesus died and rose again for us, God forgives our sins and makes us right with Him. Then He sees us as righteous because Jesus is our Savior. He gives us eternal life, so that we can live for Him now and with Him in heaven someday. It doesn't mean that we will never sin again. But when we have Jesus as our Savior, He helps us to say no to sin and helps us to begin to do, say, and think what is right. We will begin to live God's Way, which is *The Righteous Way*.

The opposite of *righteous* in our memory verse is the word *ungodly (wicked)*. (Add UNGODLY or WICKED.) ▲#6 In the Old Testament they were people who worshiped false gods and lived wicked lives. In the New Testament they were people who hated Jesus and would not believe in Him; they chose to go their own sinful way.

Today there are still these two kinds of people on the earth—the righteous and the ungodly or wicked. All are following the way of the ungodly or wicked until they have trusted the Lord Jesus Christ as their Savior. Some people refuse to trust Him and choose to continue living in their own ungodly or wicked way.

According to our verse, what will happen to the ungodly or wicked? *(Response)* Yes, they will perish. They will be separated from God forever and be punished for their sins. This is also true today for those who have not believed in the Lord Jesus as their personal Savior (John 3:16). How sad that they will perish, when God has provided a way for them to be forgiven and to live with Him in heaven someday.

What does our verse say about God? *(Response)* Yes, He knows or watches over the way of the righteous. He takes care of us who have chosen to follow God's Way through Jesus. *(Work on memorizing the verse.)* ▲#7

▲ Option#6

Definition word cards: Ungodly = not like God, sinful or wicked. Wicked = very bad, sinful, evil.

If using the KJV, you may want to point out that the prefix *un* in the word *ungodly* changes the word *godly* to an opposite meaning. Give examples of the prefix *un* changing the meaning of other words they know, such as *unlock* and *unpack*. So if people are *ungodly* they are not like God; they are sinful or wicked.

▲ Option#7

Memorizing the verse: Have a child remove one of the visual pieces and ask the class to say the verse without seeing the missing piece. Choosing a different child each time, continue this process until all the visual pieces have been removed. Repeat several times by asking particular groups, such as those wearing different colored clothes, to stand and say the verse without seeing the visual. Then choose one child to put all the visuals in correct order.

📖 BIBLE LESSON OUTLINE

Elijah Tells God's Message to Ahab

■ **Introduction**

Choosing between two ways

■ **Bible Content**

1. Israel turns away from God.
2. Elijah appears before King Ahab.
3. God protects and cares for Elijah.
   a. In a ravine.
   b. In a widow's home.

■ Conclusion

Summary

Application
Deciding whose way we are following

Response Activity
Choosing God's Way of salvation and trusting Him to take care of a specific need

📖 BIBLE LESSON

■ Introduction

Choosing between two ways

Continue to display the verse visual and hold up the "Choice of Two Ways" sign.

Do you know what this road sign means? *(Response)* Yes, you must make a choice to stay on that road or to turn off onto another road. Does it tell you what either road will be like? No, but it does let you know you must choose which way you will go.

This road sign reminds us of our memory verse today. Let's say it together *(recite the verse)*. This verse tells us that there are two ways in life to choose. What are they? *(Response)* Yes, The Righteous Way *(point to the turn-off road on the sign)* and the ungodly (wicked) way *(point to the straight road)*.

In our lesson today we will meet some people who had to choose between these two ways, even though they lived many years ago. Let's listen to see what choice each of them made.

■ Bible Content

1. **Israel turns away from God.**
   (Deuteronomy 16:21, 22; Exodus 20:3, 4)

(Word strips GENESIS–2 CHRONICLES; a list of Old Testament books; idol 1)

The first five books of the Bible—Genesis through Deuteronomy—*(place GENESIS–DEUTERONOMY on the board)* tell how God's people, the Israelites, came into being and how God freed them from slavery in Egypt and made them into a nation of people. *(Have the children recite the names of the books.)*

The history of the Israelites is continued in the books of Joshua through 2 Chronicles *(add JOSHUA–2 CHRONICLES)*. These books tell how God gave the Israelites victory over their enemies and helped them conquer the land of Canaan.

▲ **Option #8**
Have the children hold up the word strips as you mention the books from Genesis to 2 Chronicles. Have the children say the names of the books in order without looking.

Sketch 2   Old Testament Map II

Later, at their request, God gave the Israelites kings to rule over them. In spite of all that God did for them, they continually turned away from Him and began to worship the false gods *(add 1)* of the people living around them—the Philistines, the Midianites, and the other nations who did not believe in the one true and living God. ▲#8

Because of the Israelites' sin and rebellion, God allowed their nation to be divided into two kingdoms—Israel *(indicate ISRAEL)* in the north and Judah *(indicate JUDAH)* in the south. Each kingdom had its own capital city—Samaria *(indicate SAMARIA)* in the north and Jerusalem *(indicate JERUSALEM)* in the south. Each kingdom also had its own king. The Kingdom of Judah had some good kings who honored and obeyed God, but this didn't keep the people from turning to other gods. The people in the Kingdom of Israel were disobedient. They had kings who did not serve or honor God, but who led the people of Israel in worshiping the idols of the nations surrounding them. They were not obeying the command God had given them to not make or worship other gods (Ex. 20:3, 4). ⌐(2) ▲#9

God was very sad with the Israelites' disobedience. He knew their sin would have to be punished; but because He loved them so much, He gave them many opportunities to turn back to Him. He sent them prophets to warn them of punishment if they did not turn away from their sins and come back to Him. These prophets were men whom God loved and trusted and who trusted in Him. He knew they could be counted on to obey what He asked them to do, no matter how difficult it was. They not only warned the people of God's judgment for sin, but they also told the people of God's love and the hope that waited for them when they came to Him.

God told some of the prophets to write down His messages so they would never be forgotten. We can read them in the Old Testament. They have an important message for us too, for they are part of God's way of guiding us through our lives. *(Display the list of Old Testament books and indicate those written by the prophets.)* ▲#10

2. Elijah appears before King Ahab.
(1 Kings 16:29-33; 17:1; 2 Kings 1:7, 8; Deuteronomy 11:13-19)

("God Guides Us" bookmarks, Map of Divided Kingdom; Ahab 5, men 3, 4, Jezebel 13, Elijah 2)

Our lesson today is found in 1 Kings. Let's find it in our Bibles. *(Give the children the "God Guides Us" bookmarks to place at 1 Kings 17.)* King Ahab was the most evil and disobedient king that Israel ever had *(place 5, 3, 4 on the board)* and he sinned against God in many ways. Ahab married Jezebel *(add 13)*, who was from Phoenicia *(indicate on the map)*, a country just north of Israel. She was a strong worshiper of the false god Baal and influenced King Ahab to build a temple and a huge statue to Baal in Samaria. Many hundreds of people became priests of Baal and led the people in worshiping this false god.

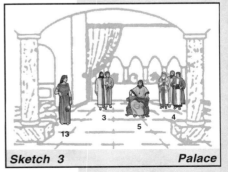

Sketch 3 — **Palace**

⌐ **Note (2)**

For more background information, read 1 Kings 11:29–12:17, 21-24.

▲ **Option#9**

Make a large floor OT world map of newsprint or strips of shelf paper taped together. Enlarge (see page xii) the map on page 000 or use a marker to draw it freehand. Make four large signs and print one of the following places on each sign: Israel, Judah, Samaria, and Jerusalem. Give the signs to four children to hold, and instruct them to stand in the proper spots on the floor map as you mention each place.

▲ **Option#10**

Help the children locate the title page for each prophetic book in their Bibles. Explain that the name of each book is the name of the prophet who wrote it. Have them observe that some books are large with many chapters and others have only one or two chapters.

▲ **Option #11**

Elijah does a lot of speaking in this lesson. Ahead of time give cue cards with Elijah's "lines" to an older child or helper to read at the appropriate points in the story as you narrate it.

▲ **Option #12**

Display name signs around the room for the places Elijah goes to: the palace, Cherith Ravine, Zarephath. Have a child dress as Elijah and move him place to place as the story unfolds. After telling the part of the story that is connected to each place, ask, "How did God take care of Elijah in _____?"

What was happening to God's people? Had the people totally forgotten God? Yes, but God did not give up on them. He loved them, even though He was deeply saddened by their sinful ways and would have to punish their sin if they did not turn to Him. So God chose a special prophet to speak to King Ahab. Who was he? Look in 1 Kings 17:1. *(Response)* Yes, it was Elijah. He was a strong, rugged, outdoors-type of man who dressed in leather and animal skin; but more importantly, he was a man who trusted and obeyed God. ▲#11
God gave Elijah a message for King Ahab. ▲#12 *(Remove 13.)* We are not told how Elijah felt about taking it to the king, but one day Elijah *(add 2)* burst into the palace. He stood before Ahab and announced a very shocking message. *(Have a child read Elijah's words aloud from 1 Kings 17:1.)* What would happen to the land if there was no rain or dew for a long time? *(Response)* Yes, the land would dry up and there would be a drought, which would lead to a famine or having *no* food. The king knew what Elijah meant, for God had warned He would do just such a thing if His people turned away from Him to worship other gods. Then Elijah left the palace.

3. **God protects and cares for Elijah.**
(1 Kings 17:2-16; 18:10)

a. **In a ravine.**

Sketch 4 Gen. Outdoor & Brook Ov.

(Map of Divided Kingdom; Elijah 6, ravens 7[3])
King Ahab was furious. Instead of obeying God he became angry with Elijah and sent soldiers throughout the land to hunt for Elijah. He even sent his troops to nations nearby to look for him. But God protected Elijah because Elijah had chosen to obey God and go His way.
After Elijah left Ahab's palace God said to him, "Leave this place and go to the Cherith Ravine, east of the Jordan River *(indicate on the map)* and hide there. ▢**(3)** Elijah obeyed, and God kept His promise to care for him. *(Place 6 on the board.)* There were no houses or towns near the ravine—it was well hidden. But every day Elijah had water to drink from the brook and food to eat. Let's look at verse 6 of chapter 17 to see how God fed him. *(Have someone read the verse aloud.)* ▢**(4)** Can you imagine how Elijah felt to have ravens *(add 7[3])* bring bread and meat to him every morning? *(Response)* How wonderful of God to take care of him, making sure he had food to eat and water to drink, when the rest of the country was drying up and people were starving. Only God could do such a miracle!

b. **In a widow's home.**

Sketch 5   City Wall

(Map of Divided Kingdom; Elijah 2, woman 8, wood 8A)
The Bible does not tell us how long Elijah stayed in the ravine, but after a time even the brook dried up because

there had been no rain in the land. But God was right there with Elijah.

God spoke to Elijah again, "Go to the town of Zarephath and stay there. I have commanded a widow to provide food for you." Zarephath was along the coast in the country of Phoenicia, which is north of Israel *(indicate on the map)*. If you remember, Queen Jezebel came to Samaria from this country. The people in Phoenicia worshiped Baal and were suffering from the drought as well. If you had been Elijah, how would you have felt about going there? *(Response)* He may have been fearful that the king's men were still looking for him. He would have to be very careful. Elijah may have had all kinds of questions and doubts, but this did not keep him from trusting and obeying God.

As Elijah walked along *(place 2 on the left side of the board and move it toward the center of the board as you speak)* he probably noticed how the land had dried up. When he came to the town gate of Zarephath, he saw a widow gathering some sticks *(add 8, 8A)*. He called to her and asked, "Would you bring me a little jar of water to drink?" Elijah was testing her. When he saw that she was going to get the water for him, Elijah called, "And please bring me a piece of bread."

The widow immediately recognized Elijah as an Israelite and said, "As surely as the Lord your God lives, I don't have any bread; I only have a handful of flour in a jar and a little oil in a jug." Let's read verse 12 to see why the widow was gathering sticks. *(Do so.)* How sad she must have felt that she and her son had only enough food for one more meal and then they would die.

(Elijah 2, widow 8, son 15)
Elijah said to her, "Don't be afraid. Go home and make bread for you and your son. But first make a small loaf for me." The widow may have felt afraid to obey this stranger; but then Elijah continued, "This is what the Lord, the God of Israel, says: 'The jar of flour and the jug of oil will not run out until the day the Lord gives rain on the land.'" What a promise! What would you have done? *(Response)* What would it take for the poor widow to obey this man? *(Response)* Yes, it would take faith in Elijah and his God.

Sketch 6   Plain Interior

Who can tell us what faith is? *(Response)* Yes, faith is believing what God says and trusting Him to do what He promised. ▲#13 The Bible tells us that the widow did exactly what Elijah told her. *(Place 8, 15 on the board.)* Did she show faith in God? *(Response)* Yes, she did. Here in the midst of Baal worshipers was one who believed in the true and living God. Verses 15 and 16 tell us what God did. *(Have someone read the verses.)* Did God keep His promise to care for her? *(Response)* Yes, He did. There was food for Elijah *(add 2)* and the widow and her son every day throughout all the years of the famine. During all that time the oil and the flour never ran out. Who else showed faith in God? *(Response)* Yes, Elijah. Did God keep His promise to him? *(Response)* Yes, God took care of Elijah's needs and protected him. Elijah stayed at the widow's home for many months in his own private room. God had kept His promise to Elijah once again. ▲#14

◰ Note (3)

The KJV "Brook Cherith" and the NIV "Kerith Ravine" are possible translations of the two Hebrew words used in 1 Kings 17:3-7. The word for brook/ravine can refer either to the ravine itself or to the water that runs through it. The brook was a wadi or wash that was dry except during the rainy season. Further, the NIV uses the Hebrew spelling *Kerith*, while the KJV uses the Greek spelling *Cherith* from the Septuagint Version (the ancient Greek translation of the Old Testament). Whichever version you choose to use, be prepared to explain the reason for the different wording in the two versions to anyone who inquires.

◰ Note (4)

Ravens and crows neglect their own young. They do not give food away naturally. They are scavengers, taking food for themselves.

▲ Option #13

Word definition card: Faith = believing what God says and trusting Him to do what He promised.

L1-1

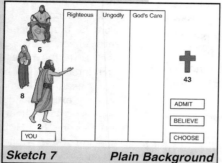

Sketch 7 — Plain Background

▲ **Option #14**

Print FAITH on a word strip or flashcard and show it here. Give paper and markers or pencils to the children to draw a picture illustrating a situation or write about one that requires them to have faith in something, such as sitting in a chair. Then have them do the same thing to illustrate a situation that requires faith in God.

■ **Conclusion**

Summary

("Righteous/Ungodly/God's Care" chart, marker; "Choice of Two Ways" sign; Ahab 5, widow 8, Elijah 2)

Attach the chart to the center of the flannelboard. Place 5, 8, and 2 on the left side of the board as each one is mentioned. Put a check mark under "Righteous" or "Ungodly"("Wicked") opposite each figure as the children respond.

In Psalm 1:6 what are the two ways in life to choose? *(Allow for response throughout.)* Yes, the way of the righteous, which is God's Way, and the way of the ungodly (wicked), which is our own way. *(Display the "Choice of Two Ways" sign.)*

Let's think about the choices the people in our lesson made. First, we have Ahab. Whose way did he choose? Yes, the way of the ungodly (wicked). What about the widow in Zarepath? Yes, she chose God's Way, *The Righteous Way*. She was not an Israelite, but she believed in the living God and trusted His promises given through Elijah.

What about Elijah? Yes, Elijah also chose *The Righteous Way*; he trusted and obeyed God even when it was difficult to do so. What did God ask him to do that was difficult and dangerous? Yes, he had to tell wicked King Ahab of God's judgment of no rain. How did God take care of Elijah in this difficult situation? *(Write the children's responses under "God's Care" on the chart. The responses should include the following: He protected him by hiding him in the Cherith Ravine where there was water to drink; He sent ravens twice a day with meat and bread; He used a widow to provide food and a place to live.)* Elijah and the widow chose *The Righteous Way* and God took good care of them. God's care for Elijah and the widow is a good example of what our memory verse teaches. Let's say our verse again to remind us of what God tells us. *(Recite the verse.)*

Application

(Word strips YOU, ADMIT, BELIEVE, CHOOSE; cross 43)

What about you *(add YOU)*? If I were to put a check mark on the chart for you, under which column would I put it—*The Righteous Way* or the ungodly (wicked) way? Whether you realize it or not, you are already on the ungodly (wicked) way if you have never believed in the Lord Jesus Christ as your Savior. But God has provided an opportunity for you to choose His way. In order to go God's Way and be made righteous, you must believe in the Lord Jesus Christ as your Savior. Believing in Jesus as your Savior means that you trust in Jesus alone to save you from being punished by God for your sins. You do this by admitting *(add ADMIT)* you are a sinner and cannot go to heaven to be with God because of your sinfulness; by believing *(add*

BELIEVE) that Jesus is God and He died on the cross *(add 43)* to take your punishment and will give you eternal life because He is alive; and by choosing *(add CHOOSE)* to receive Him as your personal Savior. When you do this, you will become part of God's family and begin learning to live God's Way. Then when God looks at you, He sees what Jesus did for you and does not look at you as a sinner. He sees you as righteous. ▲#15 As God's child you have the right to ask Him for His help. He will take care of you even when things get difficult, just as He took care of Elijah and the widow.

Let's think of some ways that He cares for you when you follow God's Way. *(Write the responses on the chart under "God's Care." Suggest some ideas to prompt their thinking: helps you with a tough subject or test in school, provides new shoes when your dad or mom is out of work, and protects you when traveling to school.)* Do you believe God can do all these things? *(Response)* Yes, He has the power to do anything.

Does God *always* give us everything we ask for? Does this mean we will *never* get hurt or be in danger? *(Response)* No, but God knows what is best for us, and He will help us. If you are following God's Way, you can trust Him to take care of you and provide all that you need to live each day.

Response Activity

Distribute the **"Choice of Two Ways" handouts** *(see Materials to Gather)* and pencils. Tell the children to write their name under the choice they have made today or at a previous time—either to stay on the ungodly (wicked) "My Way" or to go "God's Way" through receiving Jesus as their Savior. Invite those who want to receive Him to stay and talk with you.

Encourage those who have already trusted Jesus as Savior to think about one need they will trust Him to take care of this week and write it on the line under the sign. Have them silently ask the Lord to help them to keep trusting Him.

✍ TAKE-HOME ITEMS

Distribute **memory verse tokens for Psalm 1:6** and **Bible Study Helps for Lesson 1, Part 1**. Challenge the children to review the verse so that they can say it next week. Encourage them to take ten minutes each day to read the assigned Scripture verses in the Bible Study Helps, answer the questions, and pray, asking God to help them remember and obey what they have read. Explain that it is more effective to do the reading one day at a time than to do it all at once. Next week ask if they did it and if they have any questions about it. ⌂(5)

▲ Option #15

To help the children visualize the point being made here, prepare a simple drawing of a stick figure representing the children and you on a piece of poster board. Print the word SINNER across the center of the stick figure with a black marker. Make a red paper cross, large enough to cover the word SINNER, and place it over the word SINNER.

⌂ Note (5)

Because regular Bible reading is so necessary for the spiritual health and growth of believers, we urge you to give the Bible Study Helps to your children and encourage them week by week to develop this important habit. As an incentive, tell them to bring their completed sheet back next week to receive a sticker.

To obtain inexpensive Bibles, contact:
American Bible Society
http://americanbible.org
International Bible Society
WebMail@usa.ibs.org

Elijah Demonstrates God's Power
Theme: The Righteous Way

Lesson 1

Part Two: Elijah Challenges the Prophets of Baal

❋ **BEFORE YOU BEGIN...**

Doing what is right can be a very lonely experience. When Elijah dared to stand against the 450 prophets of Baal at Mt. Carmel, he stood alone. But Elijah knew that the God who had sustained him during the drought was well able to vindicate His prophet through displaying His mighty power, to the chagrin of the false prophets.

For your children to follow *The Righteous Way* in an unrighteous world leads inevitably to a confrontation when they will have to take a stand for what they believe and what Jesus means to them. It will be unpopular in the eyes of their peers and intolerant in the eyes of their secular educators and leaders.

This lesson will enable you to show how God used the bold stand of Elijah to impact a crowd of people who had forsaken Jehovah for the more politically-correct worship of Baal. Can your children stand alone and impact their generation? They can by the grace of the God of Elijah. Instruct them, challenge them, encourage them; the stakes are significant. *"That you may become blameless and harmless...in the midst of a crooked and perverse generation, among whom you shine as lights in the world"* (Philippians 2:15, NKJV).

☞ **AIM:**

That the children may

- Know that those who have received Jesus as their Savior can trust Him to help them do what is right.
- Respond by asking the Lord Jesus to help them do what is right.

📖 **SCRIPTURE:** 1 Kings 18

♥ **MEMORY VERSE:** Psalm 1:6

For the Lord knoweth the way of the righteous: but the way of the ungodly shall perish. (KJV)

For the Lord watches over the way of the righteous, but the way of the wicked will perish. (NIV)

MATERIALS TO GATHER

Visual for Psalm 1:6 from *Bible Verses Visualized*
Backgrounds: Review Chart, Plain Background, Plain with Tree, Hilltop
Figures: R1, R15, R16, 1A, 1B, 1C(2), 2, 6, 9, 10, 11, 11A, 11B, 12, 14, 27, 89(GOD)
Token holders & memory verse tokens for Psalm 1:6 for any who did not receive them last week
Bible Study Helps for Lesson 1, Part 2
Special:
- ***For Bible Content 1, 3, & Conclusion:*** BELIEVE & OBEY footprints
- ***For Bible Content 1:*** Map of Divided Kingdom
- ***For Summary:*** Word strip TRUST
- ***For Application:*** "Choice of Two Ways" sign from Lesson 1, Part One
- ***For Response Activity:*** "Daily Prayer Reminder" handouts
- ***For Options:*** Additional materials for any options you choose to use
- ***Note:*** *Follow the instructions on page xii to prepare the "Daily Prayer Reminder" handouts (pattern P-12 on page 172).*

 REVIEW CHART

Display the Review Chart with R15 and R16 in place. Ask a child to place R1 on the Chart and read the words on it that describe what God's Way is like. Review the meaning of the theme and then review the memory verse and its meaning. Encourage the children to share how they experienced God's care for them during the past week as they followed The Righteous Way. Use the following questions to review Lesson 1, Part One.

1. How did God take care of Elijah after he gave God's message to Ahab? *(God gave him food and water and protected him from Ahab.)*
2. What difficult thing did Elijah tell the widow to do? *(He told her to first make a little loaf of bread for him.)*
3. What did God do for the widow and her son when she obeyed Elijah? *(He kept the flour and oil from being used up.)*
4. Give an example of one ungodly (wicked) person from last week's lesson and tell why that person was ungodly (wicked). *(King Ahab or Jezebel; they worshiped Baal rather than the true and living God, and they turned the people of Israel against God.)*
5. According to Psalm 1:6, what will happen to the ungodly (wicked) people? *(They will perish—be separated from God forever and be punished for their sins.)*

6. Give an example of one righteous person in last week's lesson and tell why that person was righteous. *(Elijah or the widow; they chose to follow God's Way and trusted Him to take care of them.)*

♥ MEMORY VERSE

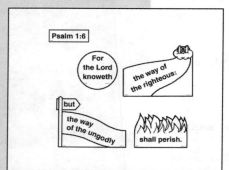

Use the visual to review Psalm 1:6. Display the reference only.

Who can say Psalm 1:6? *(Let one or more children say the verse from memory; then display the verse.)* Who are the righteous today? *(Response)* Yes, people who have followed God's Way by believing in the Lord Jesus Christ to save them from their sin.

Not only does God make us right with Him by forgiving our sin when we believe in the Lord Jesus Christ as Savior, but He also helps us to do what is right. He helps us to do things His way, to do what He wants. It isn't always easy to do what is right. In fact, it can be very difficult. Why is that? Well, sometimes the very thing God asks us to do takes a lot of courage, and sometimes we would rather do things our own way. Sometimes we may be the only one who is doing what is right when everyone else is doing what is wrong. We may be afraid of what others will say if we are the only one who is doing what is right.

Our verse says that He knows or watches over those who follow His way. When we choose to follow God's righteous way, He promises to be with us and to help us (Joshua 1:9). God, the Holy Spirit, comes to live in us when we believe in the Lord Jesus Christ for our salvation. The Holy Spirit gives us His power to do what God wants, to do what is right. ⌐(1) Whenever we are having a hard time choosing to do what is right, we can ask God to help us and He will. We can trust God to do what seems impossible. *(Review the verse.)* ▲#1

⌐ Note (1)

Briefly explain who the Holy Spirit is if your class needs such teaching at this point.

📖 BIBLE LESSON OUTLINE

Elijah Challenges the Prophets of Baal

■ **Introduction**

Matt's difficult situation

■ **Bible Content**

1. The challenge is given.
   a. King Ahab searches for food.
   b. Elijah faces King Ahab again.

2. The contest begins.
   a. The prophets of Baal pray.
   b. Elijah prays to God.
3. The rain comes.

■ Conclusion

Summary

Application
Trusting God to help them do what is right

Response Activity
Asking God for His help and power to do what is right

📖 BIBLE LESSON

■ Introduction

Matt's difficult situation

Matt was in a very difficult situation. At first he had thought his school friends were really fun to be with. They had played ball together. They were his only friends, but none of them were Christians. He had tried to invite some of them to Sunday school, but none of them ever wanted to come. But he figured he could still be friends with them and maybe one day they would come to know Jesus.

Then one day one of his friends said to him, "Come on, Matt. We are going over to Mr. Johnson's after school. We are going to have some fun with him!" Matt went along, not understanding what "some fun" meant. Mr. Johnson was an old man who lived in an old rundown house in their neighborhood. He was always angry and yelling at the kids to get off his property when they tried to get their ball. Most of the kids were afraid of him. When Matt saw the boys laughing and collecting rocks, he felt sick inside. He realized what they were up to as he walked up onto the porch.

"Come on, Matt, grab a rock," one of them yelled at him. Oh how Matt wanted to belong to the gang, but he also knew that what they were doing was wrong. As a Christian he did not belong there; it was disobeying God. He knew what he should do, but it was so difficult. He had learned he could ask God for help and strength when he had a hard time making a right choice, but he had never done it before. And what would his friends think of him?

He began to pray silently for God to help him do the right thing. Then as he began to back down the steps, he heard shouting and laughing and a crash. Then one of the guys yelled, "Hey! Come back Matt. What are you—some kind of wimp? We don't let wimps hang out with us." Would Matt do the right thing and stand up for God, allowing God to give him His power to walk away? We will discover what happens a little later.

▲ Option #1

Reviewing the verse: Before class print the verse on a large piece of newsprint or poster board with a dark marker. Cut the paper into puzzle pieces. Scramble the puzzle pieces and place them on a table or on the floor. Have the children take turns putting the puzzle together. Have them say the verse together each time the puzzle is completed.

Variations: Make two puzzles. Divide the class into two groups and see who can put a puzzle together first. Have each group recite the verse together when their puzzle is completed. Or, distribute paper, crayons or markers, and scissors and let each child make a puzzle. Have the children exchange their puzzles and put them together. When the children have completed the puzzles, let each child say the verse to you and then return the puzzle to its owner. Provide envelopes for the children to put their puzzle pieces in to take home. Encourage the children to have someone at home try to put the puzzle together.

Listen carefully to our lesson today to find out what happened when Elijah had to trust God to help him do what was right. How would he get through it? What would be the result? Open your Bibles to 1 Kings 18:1. *(Have the children find the reference and put their bookmarks in place.)*

Sketch 8 — Plain with Tree

■ **Bible Content**

1. **The challenge is given.**
   (1 Kings 18:1-21)

   a. **King Ahab searches for food.**

(Map of Divided Kingdom, BELIEVE & OBEY footprints; Elijah 2, Obadiah 27, king 14)

God's Word through the prophet Elijah came true; there was no rain in the land of Israel *(indicate on the map)* for almost three years. As a result, there was a great famine (no food) and drought (no water) throughout the land. Many people and animals were dying because of the famine and drought, but God did take care of Elijah and the widow and her son during this time.

In the last year of the famine God spoke to Elijah *(place 2 on the board)* and said, "Go speak to King Ahab and tell him I am going to send rain soon." How do you think this made Elijah feel? What might you have done if you were Elijah? *(Response)* We don't know if he felt afraid, knowing that the king probably still blamed him for what was happening, but we know he believed and obeyed God *(add footprints)*. Immediately he headed for Samaria *(indicate on the map)*.

In Samaria, where the king's palace was located, the famine was very, very bad. People and animals were starving and dying. There was no grass for the cattle and horses to eat and no water to drink. In desperation King Ahab called for his servant Obadiah, who was in charge of the palace. The Bible tells us that Obadiah had faithfully served God. He had risked his own life to hide a hundred prophets when Jezebel, Ahab's wife, was having all of God's prophets killed.

Ahab said to Obadiah, "We need to find grass for the horses and mules to eat. I do not want them to die. We will divide the land between us and look for grass in each area, especially in the valleys and along the streams." He cared more for his animals than for his people.

As Obadiah *(add 27)* was searching out his part of the land he met Elijah, whom he recognized immediately. He told Elijah that Ahab had been searching for him in every surrounding nation and kingdom. Ahab blamed Elijah for the famine.

Elijah said, "Go tell King Ahab that I am here." At first, Obadiah was very afraid when he heard this command. Why do you think he felt this way? *(Response)* Yes, his life was in danger. Obadiah was afraid that God might take Elijah away and he wouldn't be there when Ahab came back to meet with him. But when Obadiah expressed his fear, Elijah promised he would stay there.

b. Elijah faces King Ahab again.

Obadiah showed his faith in God and went to tell Ahab the message. Ahab believed Obadiah and went to meet Elijah *(add 14)*. When King Ahab saw Elijah, he asked, "Is that really you?" Then he added accusingly, "You are the biggest troublemaker in Israel!"

Elijah replied very firmly, "I am not the one who has made trouble. It is you and your relatives who have done this by turning away from the true and living God. Your choice to disobey His commands and worship other gods has brought this trouble on you. Now, call all the people together, along with all the prophets of Baal and Asherah, and meet me at Mt. Carmel *(indicate on the map)*." So King Ahab sent a message throughout the land, calling for all the people and the prophets of Baal and Asherah to meet at Mt. Carmel.

2. The contest begins. ▲#2
(1 Kings 18:22-40)

a. The prophets of Baal pray.

(King 14, people 9, 10, Elijah 2, altar 1A, sacrifice 1B, prophets of Baal 1C[2])

On the day of the meeting, King Ahab *(place 14 on the board)*, the people *(add 9, 10)*, and all the prophets gathered on Mt. Carmel. There were many followers of Baal compared to Elijah, the one lone prophet of God. But Elijah *(add 2)* boldly stood before all the people and challenged them, "How long is it going to take you to decide? If the Lord is really the true and living God, then follow Him; but if you believe Baal is God, then follow him." Perhaps his words made some of the people feel ashamed because they had turned away from the living God. But no one said anything. No Israelite came and stood beside Elijah. There was just silence.

Sketch 9 — Hilltop

But Elijah knew God was with him and would give him all the strength and help he needed. He trusted God completely. He continued speaking, "I am the only one of God's prophets here, but there are 450 of Baal's prophets. ⌧(2) Today we will decide who is the only true and living God. We will get two bulls, one for each side, to offer as a sacrifice. Each of us will prepare our bull by cutting it into pieces and placing it on the wood of our altar. But we will not use any fire. Then each of us will call on the name of our god, and the god who answers by fire to burn up the sacrifice will be the one true God!" When the people heard the challenge, they all said, "Yes, this is a good idea. We agree. Let's do it!"

The prophets of Baal *(add 1A, 1B, 1C[2])* made their sacrifice first. They prepared the bull, the altar, and the wood just as Elijah had instructed. Then they began to call on the name of Baal, shouting, "Oh Baal, answer us!" One of Baal's titles was "fire god," so his prophets must have been confident he would answer. All morning

---

▲ Option#2

Print on three large cue cards these responses of the Israelites to Elijah's challenges and the miracles God performed: (1) "There was just silence." (2) "Yes, this is a good idea. We agree. Let's do it!" (3) "The Lord is God! The Lord is God!" Invite the children to participate in this part of the story, as though they were in the crowd with Elijah, by saying what is on the card you hold up at the appropriate time. You may want to lead them to include these actions with their verbal responses: (1) putting their finger across their lips; (2) clapping their hands; (3) kneeling down and bowing low.

⌧ Note (2)

Elijah did not mean he was the only prophet that Jezebel hadn't killed (see 1 Kings 18:4); he meant he was the only one there for the contest, in contrast to the 450 prophets of Baal.

▲ Option #3

Show a list of the names of the tribes of Israel as a reminder.

Sketch 10   Hilltop

🏠 Note (3)

The children might wonder where all the water came from during the drought. Writers of Bible commentaries are not certain where the water came from. The most reasonable explanation seems to be that Elijah arranged for men to bring water from the Mediterranean Sea throughout the day while the prophets of Baal were trying to get Baal to send fire to burn up the sacrifice.

▲ Option #4

Use a large pan, soil, stones, wood pieces, a toy animal, and containers of water to illustrate how Elijah prepared the sacrifice. Have the children help you as you prepare it. Demonstrate trying to light it with a match, showing how impossible it is for you to do it and would have been for Elijah too.

Variation: Pretending they have the props, have several children act out the above scene in preparing the altar.

---

long they cried out, and then they began to dance and leap around the altar. But nothing happened. The sacrifice was still on the altar.

Elijah began to tease them, saying, "Shout louder! Maybe your god is on a trip or too busy. Maybe he is sleeping and you must wake him up." And so the prophets shouted even louder and cut their arms so that they bled, hoping Baal would answer. But by evening there was no answer—no fire came to burn up the sacrifice. Why didn't Baal answer? *(Response)* That is right. He was not the real god; he was only a statue with no ears to hear. *(Remove 1C[2]. Leave the other figures on the board.)*

b. Elijah prays to God.

(Altar 11, fire 11B, water 11A)

When it was Elijah's turn, he told the people to come and stand close to him *(move 9, 10, 14 closer to 2)*. They watched as he repaired God's altar, which had been lying in ruins. Elijah took 12 stones, one for each of the 12 tribes of Israel, and rebuilt the altar *(add 11)*. ▲#3 Then Elijah did something very unusual. He dug a large ditch around the altar. After Elijah arranged the wood on the altar, he cut the bull into pieces and laid them on top of the wood.

Then Elijah gave the strangest order of all! "Fill four large jars (the size of barrels) with water 🏠(3) and pour it over the altar!"

What were the people thinking? "Pour water over the altar? That is crazy! Doesn't Elijah know that wet wood doesn't burn? He will lose the contest for sure!" Yes, it was a very strange and unusual thing to do! The sacrifice was soaked; it wouldn't burn now unless the true God performed a miracle.

As the people watched, Elijah gave instructions to do something that seemed even more ridiculous! Verse 34 tells us what that was. *(Have one child read the verse aloud and have another tell what Elijah's instructions were.)* Yes, they were to pour the water over the altar two more times! How many barrels of water was that? *(Count them together.)* Yes, they poured twelve of them over the sacrifice. The water ran down the sides of the altar and over the stones, filling the ditch, which held about five gallons *(add 11A)*. Can you imagine why Elijah would do such a thing? *(Response)* That's right! Elijah wanted to make it so hard that only God could do it. God wanted the king and all the people and false prophets to know that the living God could do the impossible. His power was so great that He could burn a water-soaked sacrifice! ▲#4

Then Elijah prayed to the living God. *(Have someone read the prayer in verses 36 and 37 aloud or say it in your own words.)* "Lord, You are the God of Abraham, Isaac, and Jacob. Show everyone today that You are the God of Israel. Show them that I am Your servant and have done what You commanded me to do. Answer my prayer and show these people that You are God and that You are bringing them back to Yourself." Elijah prayed this prayer just once. He didn't spend hours begging God to answer, nor did he beat himself as the prophets of Baal had done.

Immediately God sent fire *(add 11B)* from heaven and burned up the sacrifice, the wood, the stones, and the soil, and even dried up the water in the ditch! *(Remove 11, 11A, 11B.)* Can you imagine what the people thought as they watched it happen? What would you have been thinking? *(Response)* How exciting it must have been for Elijah to watch God answer his prayer! What a miracle from God! The Israelites, the prophets of Baal, and the king could see for themselves that the true and living God was greater than *any* god, even Baal. God had truly honored Elijah's faith and obedience to Him in this very difficult, dangerous situation. God had used Elijah to show His people the power of the true and living God.

Then something very wonderful happened. *(Read verse 38 aloud or have a child do so and let the children tell what happened.)* Yes, when the people saw what God had done in answer to Elijah's prayer, they fell on their faces to the ground and cried out, "The Lord is God! The Lord is God!" What a great day that must have been for Elijah to see God's people turn back to worshiping the only true God—to see them decide to follow God's righteous way.

Elijah then gave a command for the false prophets of Baal to be put to death. That may seem to be too great a punishment, but Elijah did this at the command God gave to Moses many years before (Deut. 13:12-15). Those prophets would no longer be able to influence or deceive the people into worshiping Baal. *(Remove all the figures except 2, 14.)*

3. The rain comes.
(1 Kings 18:41-45)

Sketch 11   Hilltop

(Servant 12, Elijah 6; BELIEVE & OBEY footprints)
Then Elijah said to King Ahab, "Go and get something to eat. Celebrate! It is going to rain." Elijah believed that God was going to keep His promise to send the rain. *(Remove 14.)*

Elijah and his servant *(add 12; move 2, 12 to the top of the mountain; replace 2 with 6)* climbed to the top of Mt. Carmel, where Elijah bowed down with his face between his knees and prayed. The Bible tells us he prayed for the rain to come (James 5:17). Then he sent his servant to look for rain clouds seven times. On the seventh time the servant said, "A tiny cloud the size of a man's hand in the sky is coming from the direction of the sea."

Then Elijah said to his servant, "Go tell Ahab to get his chariot ready and leave now or the rain will keep him from getting home." The servant may have wondered at Elijah's words; but very soon the sky grew dark with clouds, the wind began to blow, and a heavy rain began to fall.

The people of Israel knew that it was the living God who had sent the rain. And Elijah knew that he could completely trust God to help him do whatever God asked him to do. He had followed God's righteous way, believing and obeying *(add footprints)* God even when no one else was doing the right thing.

■ Conclusion

Summary

Sketch 12   **Plain Background**

(Elijah 2, GOD 89, Baal 1, prophets of Baal 1C[2], altar 11, water 11A, fire 11B; BELIEVE & OBEY footprints; word strip TRUST)

What did Elijah *(place 2 on the board)* do to show that he believed and obeyed *(add footprints)* God? *(Encourage response throughout.)* Yes, he delivered God's message to Ahab, and he arranged for the contest between God *(add 89)* and Baal *(add 1)* on Mt. Carmel. What was the test? That's right; Elijah challenged the people to see which god would send fire and burn up the sacrifice. What happened when the prophets of Baal *(add 1C[2])* prayed to Baal? That's correct. Nothing happened. Why? Yes, Baal was only a statue that couldn't hear and answer prayer. What strange thing did Elijah do to the sacrifice to show that he was completely trusting *(add 11, TRUST)* God to answer his prayer? Wow! Imagine his pouring twelve jars of water on the altar *(add 11A)*. What happened when Elijah prayed? Isn't it wonderful how God sent fire *(add 11B)* immediately to burn up the sacrifice, wood, stones, and soil, and to even dry up the water! What did Elijah do to the prophets of Baal? That's right; he had them put to death *(remove 1C[2])*. How did the Israelites respond after they saw the fire burn up the sacrifice? Yes, they fell on their faces and worshiped God. Now they too were following *The Righteous Way* by believing and obeying God.

Application

("Choice of Two Ways" sign, verse visual)

Do you remember the story of Matt that we heard earlier? He had asked God for help to walk away from his friends when they had decided to throw rocks at Mr. Johnson's house. God answered Matt's prayer, and he was able to walk away from them. He felt good about obeying God and doing the right thing, but it was very hard. It was especially hard when his friends ignored him at school and would not let him play ball with them. A few even called him names, but Matt still remained friendly to them.

It was two weeks later when God did something very special for Matt. One of his friends, Jim, met him on the way home from school and asked, "I have been thinking about what happened. I want to know how you were able to walk away from us? Why didn't you go right along with us? I really didn't want to do it, but I was afraid to run away. Oh yes, and how can you act like you are not angry with us?"

Matt was speechless. But once again he sent up a prayer, asking God to give him courage and the right words to say to Jim. He told Jim that Jesus was his Savior and that Jesus had helped him to be strong and to walk away. That next week Jim was in Sunday school with Matt, learning about Jesus for himself.

Can you think of some times when you might have to make such a choice? *(Hold up the "Choice of Two Ways" sign and discuss situations that require them to make right choices, such as refusing to use bad language, to watch an x-rated movie, or to play a video game with bad content.)* ▲#5 Why would it be hard to obey God? *(Response)* Yes, others may react as Matt's friends did and make fun of you or not want to be friends. But if you have believed in the Lord Jesus Christ to save you from your sin, you have God the Holy Spirit living in you to give you the strength and power to do the right things. You can ask Him for strength and help when you need it.

Remember that God knows what is happening to us and wants to help us follow *The Righteous Way*. Our verse reminds us of that. Let's say it together. *(Recite Psalm 1:6 together. Display the verse visual if necessary.)* The next time you are faced with one of these impossible situations, maybe even today, you can trust God and ask Him for His strength and power to help you do what is right—to follow God's righteous way.

Response Activity

Distribute the **"Daily Prayer Reminder" handouts.** *Remind the children that they can trust God to help them and to give them power to do what is right if they are believers in the Lord Jesus Christ.*

Invite any who have not trusted Jesus as Savior to receive Him now. Invite them to talk with you or a helper after class.

Give an opportunity to all who have received the Lord Jesus to pray silently, asking God for His help and power to do what is right. Remind them that they can do this every day, even when it is very difficult. Encourage them to place their handouts where they will see them every day to remind them to ask God for His help in following God's righteous way.

▲ Option#5
As part of the discussion, list the children's responses on newsprint. Provide paper and crayons for the children to illustrate such a situation, including the action they should take in order to obey God. Encourage them to share their drawings with the class.

✎ TAKE-HOME ITEMS

Distribute **Bible Study Helps for Lesson 1, Part 2** *to all and* **memory verse tokens for Psalm 1:6** *to any who did not receive them last week.*

King Ahab Steals from Naboth
Theme: The Narrow Way

Lesson 2

❖ **BEFORE YOU BEGIN...**

What was your reaction when you saw that today's lesson deals with the *narrow* way? Did you let out a sigh or groan within because you have become aware that today's society does not allow for the exclusiveness of Christianity? The twin philosophies of pluralism and tolerance fly in the face of Christ's claim to be the only way to heaven.

Today's lesson presents King Ahab and Queen Jezebel at their worst, showing both their decision to go their own sinful way (the broad way, if you please) and the brutal consequences of their choice.

Your children face the crucial life-choice of which way to go. The choice is complicated by the strong influences of today's culture that pull away from choosing *The Narrow Way*. The broad way looks so attractive and appears to offer so much to young people who want all that life has to offer. They desperately need your clear teaching, consistent influence, and unconditional love. May none of your children miss God's Way just because it is narrow. *"There is a way that seems right to a man, but its end is the way of death"* (Proverbs 14:12, NKJV).

☞ **AIM:**

That the children may

- Know that those who want to be saved from their sins must choose God's narrow way to heaven.
- Respond by choosing God's narrow way to heaven through receiving the Lord Jesus Christ as Savior, or thanking God for saving them if they have already chosen His narrow way.

📖 **SCRIPTURE:** 1 Kings 19:1-3; 1 Kings 20:21; 22:34-39; 2 Kings 9:30-37

♥ **MEMORY VERSE:** Matthew 7:14

Strait is the gate, and narrow is the way, which leadeth unto life, and few there be that find it. (KJV)
But small is the gate and narrow the road that leads to life, and only a few find it. (NIV)

MATERIALS TO GATHER

Visual for Matthew 7:14 from *Bible Verses Visualized*
Backgrounds: Review Chart, Plain Background, Palace, Plain with Tree, Courtyard
Figures: R1-R2, R15, R16, 2, 3, 4, 5, 9, 13, 14, 15, 20(5), 26, 35(2), 43
Token holders & memory verse tokens for Matthew 7:14
Bible Study Helps for Lesson 2
Special:
- *For Review Chart:* Two paper paths
- *For Introduction:* "Road Narrows" sign
- *For Bible Content 1:* Map of Divided Kingdom
- *For Summary:* One 8" x 36" flannel strip, one 4" x 18" flannel strip, word strips CHOICES, CONSEQUENCES
- *For Application:* A 3" x 5" card with your name on it, newsprint & marker or chalkboard & chalk
- *For Response Activity:* "The Narrow Way" handouts, pencils
- *For Options:* Additional materials for any options you choose to use
- *Note: To prepare two paper paths*, cut two 5' lengths of shelf paper (or tape paper strips together to measure 5'), making one path 3" wide and the other one 11" wide.
  Follow the instructions on page xii to prepare the "The Narrow Way" handouts (pattern P-13 on page 173).

REVIEW CHART

Display the Review Chart with R15 and R16 in place. Have the children review the verse and give the theme for Lesson 1 (Parts One and Two) as a volunteer places R1 on the Chart. Have R2 ready for use when indicated. Use the following questions to review Lesson 1, Part One and Lesson 1, Part Two. ▲#1

1. I gave all the food I had left to God's prophet, Elijah. Who am I? *(The widow of Zarephath)*
2. I chose to turn away from God and to lead Israel in worshiping the god Baal. Who am I? *(King Ahab)*
3. God used us to feed Elijah in the wilderness. What are we? *(Ravens)*
4. I influenced my husband to worship the god Baal. Who am I? *(Queen Jezebel)*
5. My life was in danger after I went before King Ahab. Who am I? *(Elijah)*
6. There were 450 of us who served the god Baal. Who are we? *(Prophets of Baal)*
7. God answered my prayer and burned up my sacrifice and altar. Who am I? *(Elijah)*
8. I won the contest with Baal. Who Am I? *(God)*

▲ **Option#1**

Print the names of the people (answers to the review questions) in large letters on 8" x 11" paper (one name on each paper) and place them on a table. As each child volunteers an answer, have him or her choose the paper with the correct answer and hold it up for all to see.

Before class begins, lay each of the prepared paper paths on the floor in different parts of the room.

You may have noticed that there are two different paper paths laid out on the floor of the room. Each of you may take a turn walking on each path, being careful to stay only on the paper. *(Instruct the children how you want them to do this and then give them time to do so.)*

Which path was easier for you to walk along? *(Response)* Of course, it was easier to stay on the wide one. It was wide, and you didn't have to give much thought to where you were going. Some of you were even looking around as you walked on the wide path. What did you have to do to stay on the narrow path? *(Response)* You had to concentrate and be more careful where you were walking so that you would not step off of it.

As we follow God's Way we find that His path is called *The Narrow Way*. *(Place R2 on the Chart.)* Just as you found it hard to walk on the narrow path on the floor, you will find that it is not always easy to walk God's way. Our memory verse will help us to understand why that is true.

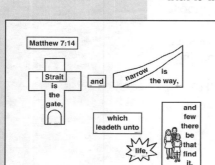

♥ MEMORY VERSE

Use the visual to teach Matthew 7:14 when indicated.
While Jesus was here on earth He talked about two kinds of paths—the wide or broad way and *The Narrow Way*. These two paths give us a picture of the ways people are going through life on this earth.

Matthew 7:13, the verse before our memory verse, tells us about the wide or broad path, which is easier to walk along. All of us start life on this path. Those who want to continue to go their own way in life and not God's Way choose to remain on this path. They choose this because of sin. Who remembers what sin is? *(Response)* Yes, it is anything we do, say, or think that goes against God's Word. Some people think that they do not have to obey anyone; they can make up their own rules to live by. Others think they are good enough to please God, and still others don't want to think about God or heaven at all. Those who think this way are following the wide or broad road. But Jesus said that following this broad way always leads away from God and leads to separation from Him forever.

Our memory verse, Matthew 7:14, tells us three things about the narrow road or way. *(Display all but the last piece of the visual.)* First, the gate to *The Narrow Way* is strait or small. ⌂**(1)** Jesus said it is small, meaning it is difficult to enter. It is difficult for people to give up their own ideas of how to get to heaven and to accept God's one-and-only Way of trusting in Jesus. Second, it is a narrow road or way because it is the only way to heaven. Third, *The Narrow Way* leads to life—eternal life. When we believe in the Lord Jesus Christ as our Savior from sin, God gives us eternal life, His life. His life in us helps us to live for Him now and ensures that we will live with Him in heaven someday.

The last part of our verse *(display the last visual piece)* gives us some bad news about *The Narrow Way*—God's Way. What is it? *(Response)* Correct; not many people find it or choose to walk on it. Why do you think that is true? *(Response)* Yes, it is because we are sinners; we naturally want our *own way* and don't want to be told by anyone else what we must do—not even by God. But there are consequences to this choice. When we refuse to go God's Way, we miss out having God in our lives now; and we will be separated from Him forever and punished for our sins. This does not need to happen, since God has provided a way for us to be forgiven of our sins and to live with Him forever. *(Work on memorizing the verse.)* ▲#2

BIBLE LESSON OUTLINE

King Ahab Steals from Naboth

■ **Introduction**

Narrow road ahead

■ **Bible Content**

1. Jezebel threatens Elijah.
2. King Ahab wants Naboth's vineyard.
3. Jezebel plans to get rid of Naboth.
4. God punishes Ahab and Jezebel.
5. God's Word comes true.

■ **Conclusion**

Summary

Application

Recognizing the need to choose God's narrow way to get to heaven

Response Activity

Choosing God's narrow way by receiving Jesus Christ as Savior, or thanking God for saving them if they have already chosen His narrow way

BIBLE LESSON

■ **Introduction**

Narrow road ahead

("Road Narrows" sign)
What does this sign *(hold up the sign)* tell you when you see it along the road? *(Response)* Yes, the road you are traveling on will

Note (1)

The KJV uses the old English word "strait," meaning restricted or narrow, to describe the gate. Since the word sounds like "straight," it is easy for children to think that it means the gate is not crooked. Be sure to distinguish between the two words if using the KJV. The NIV uses two English words for the one Greek word to describe the gate: "narrow" (v. 13) and "small" (v. 14). The translators probably used "small" in verse 14 to avoid using "narrow" to describe both the gate and the road. It is interesting to note that a different Greek word is used to describe the road (way) from the one used to describe the gate. It is a verb form that literally means "narrowed, made more narrow." God has deliberately made the way to heaven more narrow so that we would know that we can't get to heaven either by our own efforts or by continuing in our sinful ways.

▲ Option#2

Memorizing the verse: Read the verse together. Then display or have a child display the visual pieces in random order. Have the children come, one at a time, and place one of the pieces in the proper order. Have the other children check to see if each move has been done correctly.

▲ Option #3

Prepare a third path in your room to reflect the "Road Narrows" sign, having it begin with a wide path and then narrow into a single lane. Post the "Road Narrows" sign where the path begins to narrow. Have several children, standing shoulder to shoulder, begin walking on the wide path and then continue onto the narrow path, having to change and get into a single line.

Sketch 13 — Palace

▲ Option #4

Before class, print the text of Jezebel's letter to Elijah, found in 1 Kings 19:2, on a paper. In front of the class, sign the letter, roll it up, and seal it with a sticker. Ask a child to deliver it to a helper, who will unseal it and read it aloud.

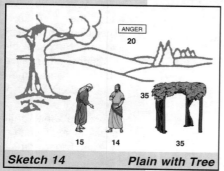

Sketch 14 — Plain with Tree

---

soon narrow from several lanes of traffic to one lane. The cars will need to go one at a time rather than speeding past each other on two or more lanes. ▲#3

Why is this road sign so important to drivers? *(Response)* An accident can occur if they do not know that they have to merge into one single lane or if they see the sign but choose to ignore it.

Do you know that King Ahab was like those drivers who ignore road signs? God wanted Ahab to turn from his sinful ways and follow God's Way, but Ahab continually ignored God's warnings and kept on making wrong choices. Listen to see what happened to Ahab and his family as a result. *(Have the children place their bookmarks at 1 Kings 19.)*

■ **Bible Content**

1. **Jezebel threatens Elijah.**
   (1 Kings 19:1-3)

(Ahab 5, men 3, 4, Jezebel 13, IDOL 20; Map of Divided Kingdom)

God had done a miracle in Israel! He had answered Elijah's prayer and showed His power to all the people by burning up the water-soaked sacrifice. Then He sent rain, just as He had said He would, in answer to Elijah's prayer and the obedience of Israel. Do you remember what all the people did after the sacrifice burned up? *(Response)* Yes, they turned back to the true and living God and worshiped Him. Elijah remained true to God and His way, even when all the people had turned against Him, and God honored Elijah. Elijah was truly walking God's narrow way.

But King Ahab *(place 5, 3, 4 on the board)* continued to walk on the wide road, doing what he wanted to do when he returned to the palace in Samaria *(indicate on the map)*. When he told Queen Jezebel *(add 13)* all that had happened and how Elijah had the prophets of Baal put to death, she was furious! Jezebel had not turned to God. She was still worshiping her idols *(add IDOL 20)*. She immediately sent a message to Elijah, saying, "By this time tomorrow you will be dead because of what you have done to the prophets. And if I am not successful, then may all the gods punish me severely." ▲#4 When Elijah received this message, he was filled with fear; and he ran out of the country to hide from Jezebel.

2. **King Ahab wants Naboth's vineyard.** ▲#5
   (1 Kings 21:1-4)

(Vineyard 35[2], king 14, Naboth 15, ANGER 20)

One day while King Ahab was looking out his window, he noticed a beautiful vineyard *(place 35[2] on the board)* just next door to the palace. The vineyard belonged to a man named Naboth, who had inherited it from his father. Naboth's family had owned the land and grown grapes on it for many generations. But now the king decided he needed to have that piece of land. He spoke to Naboth *(add 14, 15)*, saying, "Let me have your vineyard. It is so close to my palace; I want to make it into a vegetable garden. I will trade you for a better vineyard, or I can pay you whatever your land is worth." It sounded like a fair and good deal. Right?

But Naboth answered, "No, I cannot sell it. God's law forbids me to sell the land I inherited from my family." (Lev. 25:23-28; Num. 36:7) Naboth chose to obey God's Word instead of doing what the king wanted. It was a very brave thing to do.

Ahab left and went to the palace. Let's see how he responded to Naboth's answer. *(Read verse 4 aloud.)* Does this sound familiar? Do you ever respond this way when you don't get your way? Here was a grown man, the king of Israel, a leader of the people, being angry *(add ANGER 20)* and sulking in his room. He even refused to eat. Why? Because he didn't get his own way.

3. Jezebel plans to get rid of Naboth. (1 Kings 21:5-16)

(Jezebel 13, Ahab 14)
When Jezebel found her husband sulking *(place 13, 14 on the board)*, she asked him, "What is the matter with you? Why are you acting so miserably? Why won't you eat?"

King Ahab answered her, "Because I tried to make a deal with Naboth for his vineyard. I offered him a better vineyard or money for his land, but he refused."

Jezebel was amazed at the king's behavior. "Is this any way for the king of Israel to act?" she asked. "Get up and eat something! Cheer up and don't worry! I will get you Naboth's vineyard!" ▲#6

Then Jezebel wrote letters to some of the important men in the city and signed King Ahab's name on them. The letters told the men to plan a celebration and invite Naboth, giving him a special seat of honor at the banquet. Then she told them to get two men who would tell lies about Naboth in front of everyone. They were to say he had spoken against God and the king. The Jewish law said that anyone who spoke against or cursed God should be stoned to death (Lev. 24:15,16). It also stated that two witnesses were needed to condemn the guilty person. Misusing God's Word to carry out her evil plan, Queen Jezebel made up lies about Naboth.

(People 4, 9, 26, Naboth 15, MURDER 20, STEALING 20)
The men *(place 4, 9, 26 on the board)* obeyed the instructions in the letters completely without question. They planned a celebration and invited Naboth *(add 15)* just as they had been instructed. Poor Naboth had no idea what was coming; he was completely innocent. After the two

▲ **Option#5**

Have the children show the appropriate facial expression to "act out" Ahab's feelings at key points in the story you teach from Bible Content 2 – 4: happily planning his garden, getting angry, sulking, being happy to have the garden, surprised and shocked to see Elijah, and sorry to hear God's message from Elijah.

Sketch 15   Palace

▲ **Option#6**

Have the children act out the story, taking the parts of the characters and reading the dialogue from the Scripture passages or acting the parts out silently as someone else reads the dialogue.

Sketch 16   Courtyard

witnesses lied about him, he was taken outside the city and put to death by stoning (Deut. 17:6, 7). What a wicked and sinful thing Jezebel planned against Naboth, but her wicked scheme was also against God!

King Ahab had no idea that Jezebel had planned the murder *(add MURDER 20)* of Naboth; but when she told him that Naboth was dead and encouraged him to act, he went right out and took *(add STEALING 20)* Naboth's vineyard for his own. ◪(2)

4. God punishes Ahab and Jezebel. (1 Kings 21:17-29)

(Vineyard 35[2], Elijah 2, Ahab 14)

No one but Jezebel, Ahab, and the leaders knew what really happened. But is that true? *(Response)* Who else knew? *(Response)* Yes, God did. How do you think God felt about their actions? *(Response)* Yes, their sin made God angry, but it also made God very sad that His own people were acting in such sinful ways.

Because God is holy He had to punish Ahab's sin. God immediately said to Elijah, "Go and speak to Ahab. He has gone to take Naboth's vineyard *(place 35[2] on the board)* as his own." How would you feel if you were Elijah? *(Response)* When he had hid from Jezebel, God reminded him that He was in control of everything. If Elijah *(add 2)* was afraid of Ahab and Jezebel now, it didn't keep him from obeying God. He was so different from Ahab, who thought only of himself!

Can you imagine Ahab's *(add 14)* surprise when he saw Elijah standing there in the vineyard, probably looking very serious? Ahab said to Elijah, "So, you have found me, my enemy!"

"Yes," replied Elijah, "I have found you. You have always chosen to do what God says is wrong, and now God is going to punish you. You are going to die along with all your family. No one will be left to carry on your family name. Dogs are going to lick the blood from your body, and Jezebel will die and be eaten by dogs in the city of Jezreel. This is going to happen because you have made God angry; you have led Israel to sin and to follow other gods." This sounds so horrible, but God was showing Ahab that just as he had dishonored God in his life through his sinful ways, God was going to dishonor him and his family after their deaths. ◪(3) (4)

When Ahab heard these terrible words, he tore his clothes and put on clothing made of rough cloth—something like burlap—which people wore when they were extremely sad. He also stopped eating. The Bible calls this fasting. These were signs that Ahab was truly sorry for his sinful ways. When God saw that Ahab had changed his mind and behavior, He showed love and mercy to Ahab. God spoke to Elijah and said, "Because Ahab has humbled himself before Me and is sorry for his sin, I will not bring these terrible things on him while he is alive. I will wait until his son is king." *(Remove figure 2 only.)*

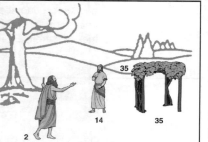

Sketch 17 — Plain with Tree

◪ Note (2)

Your children may question why God allowed such a godly man as Naboth to be killed by such a wicked person as Jezebel. It seems as though it didn't pay Naboth to do what was right, and Jezebel got ahead for doing wrong. While it may look as though Naboth lost and the queen won, in the end quite the opposite took place. Naboth won God's eternal blessing in heaven and Jezebel received God's judgment with a terrible death and eternal punishment in hell. Doing what's right in God's sight is *always* the best policy, even if you suffer for doing so.

5. **God's Word comes true.**
   (1 Kings 22:34-38; 2 Kings 9:30-37)

(DEATH 20, Jezebel 13)
King Ahab was killed *(add DEATH 20)* in battle a few years later. When some men took his chariot to a pool to clean it after his death, the dogs of the city came and licked up his blood, just as God had said. An even more interesting fact is that it happened at the very place where Naboth had died. Jezebel *(add 13)* also died a terrible death just as God had said she would. Ahab's son, Ahaziah, became the next king; but after a number of years all of Ahab's sons were killed, leaving no family to carry on his name. ▱**(5)**

■ Conclusion
Summary

(Word strips CHOICES, CONSEQUENCES; two flannel strips; cross gate R15, Ahab 14, Jezebel 13, IDOL, ANGER, MURDER, STEALING, DEATH 20[5])
Place the 8" x 36" flannel strip across the middle of the board and the 4" x 18" strip in a diagonal position. Tuck the bottom edge of the diagonal strip under the top edge of the horizontal strip. Then place R15 on the board where the two flannel strips connect.

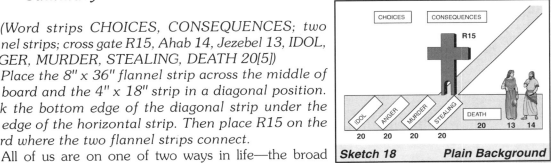

Sketch 18   **Plain Background**

All of us are on one of two ways in life—the broad (wide) way, which is our own sinful way, or *The Narrow Way*, which is God's Way. We start out on the broad (wide) way, but we can choose to stay there or go onto *The Narrow Way (add CHOICES)*. Which way did Ahab and Jezebel choose? *(Encourage response throughout.)* Yes, the wide road *(add 14, 13)*. What did they do that shows they had chosen to follow their own sinful way? That's right, they turned away from God and led the people of Israel in worshiping false gods or idols *(add IDOL 20)*. When Ahab didn't get Naboth's vineyard, he got very angry *(add ANGER 20)*. In order to get the vineyard, Jezebel committed murder *(add MURDER 20)* and this led to stealing *(add STEALING 20)* Naboth's vineyard. What were the consequences *(add CONSEQUENCES)* of their sin? Yes, their sinful way resulted in death *(add DEATH 20)*. Ahab was sorry after he got caught and realized God was going to punish him. How sad that it had come to this, when he had been given so many opportunities to turn from his sinful ways and choose God's Way. *(Remove all the figures and word strips.)*

▱ **Note (3)**

Included in this dishonor to Ahab was the assasination of every male, so that there would be no heir to the throne—a most humiliating situation for a king. God would carry out Elijah's prophecy by Ahab's first reigning son, Ahaziah, dying without a son to succeed him and by Ahab's second reigning son, Joram, along with 70 males of Ahab's progeny, being massacred by Jehu.

▱ **Note (4)**

According to God's law, the Israelites were not to defile a dead body. God was being very graphic in showing Ahab how He felt about him and the terrible way in which he had led the people to sin against God.

▱ **Note (5)**

It is not necessary to dwell on the gruesome details of their deaths, but only share enough to allow the children to see that God kept His Word *exactly* as He had told Ahab and to show that God will punish sin.

Application

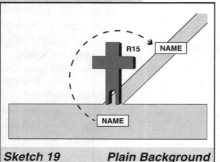

Sketch 19   **Plain Background**

(Card with your name on it, newsprint & marker or chalkboard & chalk)

Unless we choose God's Way, we too will be punished for our sin *(place your name card on the wide horizontal flannel strip)*, for sin separates us from God now and forever when we die. But God has given each one of us the opportunity to have our sins forgiven and to follow His narrow way *(indicate diagonal flannel strip)*. He has made this possible through the death of the Lord Jesus Christ, who took the punishment for our sin when He died on the cross *(indicate cross gate R15)*.

Do you want to choose God's narrow way and receive Jesus today? Here is how you do it: tell him that you admit you are a sinner and deserve to be punished in hell. But you now accept the death of Jesus Christ as the punishment you deserve and you thank Him for dying on the cross for you. Then God will remove your punishment, forgive your sin, give you everlasting life, and place you on *The Narrow Way* to heaven.

Response Activity

Distribute the **"The Narrow Way" handouts** and pencils. Invite any children who have never chosen to be on The Narrow Way by receiving the Lord Jesus Christ as their Savior to do so. Give them an opportunity to stay after class and talk with you.

Those who know they have previously made a decision to be on The Narrow Way should write their name on The Narrow Way (diagonal path) on the handout. Give them an opportunity to silently thank God for saving them and for the privilege of being on God's narrow way to heaven.

📣 TAKE-HOME ITEMS

Distribute **memory verse tokens for Matthew 7:14** and **Bible Study Helps for Lesson 2**.

Naaman Is Healed

Theme: The Jesus Way

Lesson 3

❄ BEFORE YOU BEGIN...

One of the basic needs implanted within the human soul is hope. It is a priceless treasure that comes from a personal relationship with the God of hope through faith in Jesus Christ. Sometimes the only thing that gets us through the nagging problems of this life is the certain hope of eternity in heaven with Jesus.

For Commander Naaman, stricken with terminal leprosy, there was no basis for hope. There was no cure, and he didn't know the God of Israel. Naaman's condition was hopeless, and he would have died an ignominious death at the city dump if he hadn't come in contact with Elisha and obeyed his divine directive.

So many kids today have hung the sign NO HOPE HERE on the door of their life. War, catastrophes, killings, and diseases are bad enough. But then add to these the disintegration of the family unit, and you have children in jeopardy of gigantic proportions. What an opportunity this lesson affords you to bring real hope to your children by sharing the way of salvation from the leprosy of sin! *"Happy is he who has the God of Jacob for his help, whose hope is in the Lord his God" (Psalm 146:5, NKJV).*

☞ AIM:

That the children may

- Know that Jesus is the only one who can give us eternal life and take us to heaven.
- Respond by receiving the Lord Jesus as Savior; by planning to tell someone about Jesus.

📖 SCRIPTURE: 2 Kings 5:1-19

♥ MEMORY VERSE: John 14:6

I am the way, the truth, and the life: no man cometh unto the Father, but by me. (KJV)

I am the way and the truth and the life. No one comes to the Father except through me. (NIV)

📁 MATERIALS TO GATHER

Visual for John 14:6 from *Bible Verses Visualized*
Backgrounds: Review Chart, Plain Background, Council Room, Palace, Road and House, River, River Overlay
Figures: R1-R3, R15, R16, 8, 16, 21, 22, 23, 24, 25, 25A, 26, 27, 28A, 28B, 29, 42, 43, 44, 84, 89(GOD)
Token holders & memory verse tokens for John 14:6
Bible Study Helps for Lesson 3
Special:
- *For Introduction:* Pictures from magazines or the Internet of a church, children showing kindness or being helpful, a child obeying a parent or teacher, money, and a statue or an idol, such as Buddha
- *For Bible Content 1:* Map of Divided Kingdom, newsprint & marker or chalkboard & chalk
- *For Bible Content 4:* Map of Divided Kingdom
- *For Summary:* A large number seven cut from heavy paper or cardboard
- *For Application:* Newsprint & marker or chalkboard & chalk; loops of tape
- *For Response Activity:* "Cross" handouts, pencils
- *For Options:* Additional materials for any options you choose to use
- *Note:* Follow the instructions on page xii to prepare the "Cross" handouts (pattern P-14 on page 173).

REVIEW CHART

Display the Review Chart with R15 and R16 in place. Have the children review the verses and themes as they place R1 and R2 on the Chart. Have R3 ready to use when indicated. Use the following questions to review Lesson 2.

1. Why was Elijah afraid of Queen Jezebel? *(She was trying to kill him.)*
2. What did King Ahab want for himself? *(Naboth's vineyard)*
3. Why wouldn't Naboth sell his vineyard to King Ahab? *(God's laws did not permit him to sell it to anyone outside the family.)*
4. How did Ahab get the vineyard? *(Jezebel had Naboth killed, and Ahab stole it.)*
5. What sad message did Elijah have to give Ahab? *(Ahab and his family were going to die. Ahab and Jezebel were going to die horrible deaths and the dogs would lick up their blood from the ground.)*
6. Why is it often difficult to choose God's Way in life? *(Because of sin, we want to choose our own way.)*

After Jesus returned to heaven, His disciples and other believers were often called "followers of the Way" because they believed Jesus was the only way to God. In some countries people describe those who believe in Jesus as those who "walk the Jesus Way." This means they have chosen to believe in Jesus as the only way to come to God. Today we will learn that God's Way is *The Jesus Way*. *(Have a child place R3 on the Chart.)*

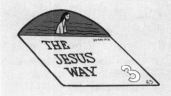

♥ MEMORY VERSE

Display the first three pieces of the visual for John 14:6 (excluding reference) and read the words aloud with the class.

Jesus said these words to His disciples right before He went to die on the cross. He said three important things about Himself. What are they? *(Response)* Yes; first, Jesus said He is *the way*—the only way anyone can get to heaven someday. Second, He called Himself *the truth*. He always tells the absolute truth since He is God. That means we can believe what He says no matter what other people say. Third, He called Himself *the life*. He is the only one who can give us eternal life, God's very own life, which we need in order to live with Him in heaven.

(Display the last visual piece and the reference.) What does Jesus say about Himself in the last part of the verse? *(Response)* Yes, it is only through Jesus that we can go to be with the Father. Who is the Father? *(Response)* Yes, He is God the Father who lives in heaven—the Creator of the universe—the one who sent Jesus into the world to take the punishment for our sins and raised Him from the dead. When we believe that Jesus took the punishment for us and receive Him as our Savior, God will forgive our sins and give us eternal life so that we can live with Him in heaven. *(Work on memorizing the verse.)* ▲#1

📖 BIBLE LESSON OUTLINE

Naaman is Healed

■ **Introduction**

Ways people think they can get to heaven

■ **Bible Content**

1. Naaman has leprosy.
2. A servant girl offers help.
3. The king sends Naaman to Elisha.

▲ **Option #1**

Memorizing the verse: Have the children repeat the verse together once. Then remove the visual pieces one at a time, having the group say the entire verse together each time a piece is removed. Place all the visual pieces in a large paper bag or basket. Have the children take turns drawing a piece from the basket and reciting the words on the visual piece along with the remainder of the verse. Then have another child place that visual piece on the board in the correct place. When all the pieces have been placed back on the board, repeat the verse together once more.

L3   33

▲ **Option#2**

To illustrate the Introduction, prepare the sketch shown below on a large poster board. Make word strips of different lengths. On each strip print one way people think they can get to heaven *(see suggestions in Materials to Gather)*. Attach the word strips in the gap so that they do not reach "GOD." In the Application use this illustration again and place a large cross over the gap, showing that Jesus' death on the cross for our sins is the only way for us to get to God for salvation.

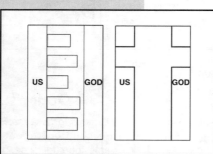

▲ *Option#2*

Sketch 20   Council Room

4. Elisha gives instructions.
5. Naaman is healed.
6. Naaman believes in the true God.

■ **Conclusion**

Summary

Application
Believing that Jesus is the only way to get to heaven

Response Activity
Receiving Jesus as Savior and planning to tell someone about Him

📖 **BIBLE LESSON**

■ **Introduction** ▲#2

Ways people think they can get to heaven

(Pictures showing ways people think they can get to heaven)
Hold the pictures up one at a time or have different children hold them, or attach them to the flannelboard.
Can you think what these pictures might stand for? (Response) They remind us of different ways people think they can get to heaven someday. Let's think about them for a minute. (Discuss the meaning of the pictures. Note that some people try to be good enough for God by going to church, being kind and helpful to others, obeying parents or teachers, or giving money to God.) ▲#3

There are those who think they are going to heaven because they are trying really hard to do things to please God. There is nothing wrong with wanting to please God, but doing good things doesn't make us good enough in God's eyes. When we try to do good things or be good, we can never really be sure we have done enough or have been good enough to get to heaven. There is nothing we can do to take care of our sin problem in our own way.

In our lesson today we will hear about someone who thought he could take care of his problem in his own way. Listen carefully to find out what happened.

■ **Bible Content**

1. **Naaman has leprosy.**
   (2 Kings 5:1)

(Map of Divided Kingdom; newsprint & marker or chalkboard & chalk; Naaman 21, wife 22, woman 8, men 26)

Joram, one of Ahab's sons, became king of Israel. He was just like his father; he did not obey God, and he worshiped false gods. Israel and Syria were finally at peace with one another. *(Indicate places on the map.)* It was during this time that Elijah was taken to heaven by God (2 Kings 2:11, 12), and Elisha was chosen by God to take his place. He lived in Samaria *(indicate on the map)*, the capital of Israel in the northern kingdom. ▲#4

Ben-hadad, the king of Syria, had put Naaman *(place 21 on the board)* in charge of his army. We read about him in 2 Kings 5:1. *(Instruct the children to open their Bibles to 2 Kings 5 and place their bookmarks there. Then have them read verse 1 aloud or silently to find what is said about Naaman.)* What are some things we learn about Naaman as a soldier? *(Write the responses on newsprint if time permits: the commander of the king's entire army, very brave, had won many victories, liked by the king, and honored as a great soldier.)* Though it doesn't say, it is possible that many others in Syria admired him and celebrated his victories in battle, too.

This verse does tell us one other thing about Naaman. What is it? *(Response)* Yes, he had leprosy. Has anyone ever heard of this disease? *(Response)* It is a disease that affects the skin. It starts with a small white spot and then spreads to other parts of the body. Soon the spots become painful oozing sores over the whole body. It is a terrible disease that leaves people helpless, not able to care for themselves, and often ends in death.

Today, there are medicines and treatments to cure leprosy, but in Naaman's day it was hopeless. Anyone who had leprosy was sure to die from this disease; there was no cure. God had given his people specific laws regarding leprosy. When an Israelite had leprosy, he could not live with his family or others because the disease was very contagious; he was considered unclean. Naaman and his family *(add 8, 22, 26)* must have been unhappy, knowing he had no hope of being healed or even living. They did not know the true and living God who could help them. *(Remove 21, 26; leave 22, 8 on the board.)*

2. A servant girl offers help. (2 Kings 5:2-3)

(Servant girl 23)
But there was someone in Naaman's home who did know and trust God! Verse 2 tells us who this was. *(Have a child read verse 2 aloud and have someone else tell who it was.)* Yes, it was a young slave girl from Israel *(add 23)* who served Naaman's wife. The Syrian army had captured her during one of their battles with Israel. We do not know her name, her age, or how long she had been living in Syria. But we do know that she believed in the true and living God. She knew that Elisha was God's prophet and had done wonderful miracles by God's power.

Even though it must have been very difficult for her to be a slave far away from her home, she expressed great concern for her master

▲ **Option#3**

Have the children illustrate ways in which they think people try to be good enough to get to heaven. Let the children show their pictures and talk about them.

For older children: As an extra part of your overall program, discuss some information on specific religions along with showing pictures from the Internet. Do not criticize any religion (you may have some children who come from homes/backgrounds of other religions), but just show the ways many people in the world try to work to be good enough and make themselves right before God or a god so they can live in heaven when they die.

▲ **Option#4**

Use maps to help the children see the relationships and distances between countries where the story takes place. Make an enlarged map of the land of Israel and Old Testament world for use on the floor or a wall. Have the children write the names of towns, rivers, and countries in their proper places as you study them. If using it on the floor, cover the map with contact paper to preserve it.

when she heard about his illness. She said to his wife, "I wish my master would go and see the prophet who lives in Samaria. He will heal him of this leprosy." Maybe she even told her of the miracles Elisha had done.

3. The king sends Naaman to Elisha. (2 Kings 5:4-7)

Sketch 21   Palace

(Naaman 21, king 84)

Naaman and his wife must have had great respect for this young servant girl. When Naaman heard the news, he went right to the king *(place 21, 84 on the board)* and told him what the servant girl had said. How amazing that this high army commander took the word of a servant girl! But God does incredible things through His power. Imagine, God placed this young Israelite girl right in Naaman's house to tell him of the true and living God!

Ben-hadad said to Naaman, "Go at once! I will send a letter with you to give to the king of Israel." So Naaman left for Israel, taking many horses, chariots, and servants with him. He also took many gifts: 750 lbs of silver, 150 lbs of gold, and 10 changes of beautiful clothes.

When he arrived at the palace, he gave the letter to King Joram. It said, "I have sent this letter with my servant Naaman. I want you to cure him of his leprosy." If you had been the king of Israel, what would you have thought? *(Response)* Maybe you would have felt afraid or very nervous by this request because you knew there was no way you could *ever* obey it.

The king tore his clothes; he was very upset. "I am not God," he said. "Why did he send someone with leprosy to me to heal? He is trying to pick a fight with me." If Naaman went back unhealed, maybe the Syrians would attack Israel. What should he do? The king had turned from the true God and didn't even think to ask Him for His help now.

4. Elisha gives instructions. (2 Kings 5:8-12)

Sketch 22   Road and House

(Namaan 21, chariot 25, soldiers 16, 25A, men 26, servant 27; Map of Divided Kingdom)

Word of Naaman's visit to the king soon spread throughout the land. When Elisha heard of King Joram's problem, he sent a message to him. "Why have you torn your clothes? Send the man to me; he will know there is a prophet of God in Israel." Elisha believed God could heal Naaman.

Naaman *(place 21 on the board)* hurried to Elisha's house with his chariots, horses, and servants *(add 25, 16, 25A, 26)*. When he arrived at Elisha's home, Elisha did not go out to meet him. Instead, he sent his servant *(add 27)* out to greet Naaman with these instructions: " Go and wash in the Jordan River seven times and your body will be healed of the disease." *(Indicate the Jordan River on the map.)*

What would you have thought if you were Naaman? *(Response)* Let's see what Naaman said in verses 11 and 12. *(Have one or two children read the verses. Encourage them to read with expression as Naaman might have said it.)* Naaman was furious. Why? *(Response)* Yes, first of all, he was an important man; he thought Elisha would come right out to meet him and perform an official healing ceremony. Then, he was offended because he was asked to wash in the Jordan River, which was very muddy compared to the rivers in Syria. Not only that, the Jordan River was about twenty-five miles away. He would have to travel a long time in his chariot to get there. In a furious rage, he turned to leave. If he couldn't do it his own way, he was going home.

5. Naaman is healed. ▲#5
(2 Kings 5:13-15)

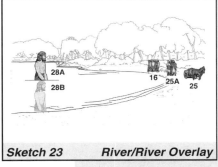

Sketch 23   River/River Overlay

(Soldiers 16, 25A, chariot 25, Naaman 21, 28A, 28B)
Cut a slit in the center of the River Overlay. Place the overlay over the water on the River Background. Slide 28B through the slit so that it is hidden behind the overlay and can be pulled out easily when indicated.

Naaman's servants tried to persuade him to do it. They said, "If the prophet had told you to do some great and difficult thing, wouldn't you have done it? We're sure you would. But this is such a simple thing: wash and be clean. Just try it!" They were right; Naaman had nothing to lose. It was his pride that was keeping him from obeying Elisha's instructions. So Naaman listened to his servants; he knew they cared for him and wanted him to be healed.

Naaman and his servants drove to the Jordan River. Maybe Naaman said to himself as he traveled to the river, "What a silly thing this is! I will look very foolish going into that muddy river. I have washed myself many times, but I have never been healed. This probably won't work." Maybe he even thought, "How foolish to be following orders from an Israelite. Syrians hate Israelites!" But he continued traveling toward the river.

When he reached the river *(place 16, 25A, 25 on the board)*, Naaman got out of his chariot, walked to the river's edge *(add 21)* and took off his outer robe. Then he slowly walked into the muddy river and dipped down under the water. *(Remove 21; move 28A down and up as Naaman dips into the river.)* When he came up, the spots were still there. Perhaps he thought, "It isn't working." But what did Elisha instruct him to do? *(Response)* That's right, he was to dip in the water seven times. So down he went, again and again—five times, six times, probably checking those spots each time. *(Move 28A down and up in the slit six times as the children count. After the seventh*

▲ Option#5

Have several children dramatize the story in this section as you read the passage aloud. Or, at the point where Naaman dips in the river, have the entire class stand up and "dip down" in their places as they count up to seven with you.

dip leave 28A in the slit under the overlay and bring 28B up to the top of the slit opening.) But when he came up the seventh time, Naaman looked at his skin. He could hardly believe it! A miracle had truly happened to him! All the spots were completely gone. His skin was like that of a young boy. He was healed! Imagine his joy! Not only was Naaman healed, but he also saw the power of the true and living God**.** He was healed because he chose to obey what God's prophet Elisha told him to do instead of insisting on his own way.

6. Naaman believes in the true God. (2 Kings 5:15-19)

Sketch 24   **Road and House**

(Soldiers 16, 25A, chariot 25, men 26, Naaman 24, Elisha 29)

Naaman and his servants did not return to Syria right away but went back to Elisha's home instead. *(Place 16, 25A, 25, 26 on the board.)* Naaman was a different man now. He was healed of leprosy, and he was no longer proud and angry, as he had been earlier. The one true God had changed his life.

When Naaman *(add 24)* arrived at Elisha's home this time, Elisha *(add 29)* came out to meet him. Naaman spoke some wonderful words, "Now I know that there is no God in all the world except in Israel." How do you think Elisha must have felt? *(Response)* He probably was very thankful to God and thrilled to hear these words from one who had been an idol worshiper.

Then Naaman insisted, "Please accept a gift from me." This was a common practice, especially in countries where people worshiped false gods. The false prophets often demanded payment for their services.

Elisha refused, saying, "No I cannot take your gift. I did not heal you; the true and living God, whom I serve did this for you." He wanted Naaman to see that the true God does not ask for payment. He only wants us to have faith in Him.

Then Naaman said, "I will never again offer a sacrifice to any god but the true and living God. I'm asking God to forgive me for this one thing: I must go with my master, the king, to the temple of his god. I must bow in that temple when he leans on my arm, but I am not going to worship his god anymore. I will only worship the true and living God."

Elisha replied, "Go in peace." It was as if he were saying, "God will understand."

Nothing more is said about Naaman or what happened when he arrived home. But can you imagine how happy his wife and family were when they saw him healed? How excited the servant girl must have been when she realized that a miracle had taken place because she was willing to tell Naaman's wife about the true God.

■ Conclusion

Summary

(Naaman 21, 24; a large number seven)
There was only one way for Naaman *(place 21 on the board)* to be healed from his leprosy. What was it? *(Response)* Yes, he had to wash in the Jordan River seven times *(add the number seven)*. What if he had not listened to his servants? *(Response)* That's right, he would not have been healed, and he would have died from the leprosy. At the urging of his servants, Naaman put aside his own ideas about the way he should be healed and did what Elisha told him to do. By faith he stepped into the muddy Jordan River and washed seven times. What was the result? *(Response)* Yes, he was completely healed; and more importantly, he came to believe in the one true God. *(Remove 21; add 24.)* This wonderful miracle happened because one young girl was willing to tell her mistress about God, the only one who could heal Naaman.

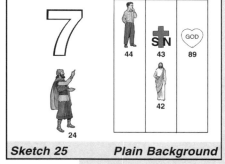

Sketch 25   Plain Background

Application

(Jesus 42, cross 43, boy 44, GOD 89; newsprint & marker or chalkboard & chalk, loops of tape)
Attach a sheet of newsprint to the right side of the board. Use loops of tape to add figures to the newsprint, and use a marker to draw the lines and print SIN when indicated.

Everyone *(attach 44 to the left side of the chart paper)* has been born with something that is far worse than leprosy. It is sin. *(Draw two vertical lines down the center and print the word SIN between the lines.)* Sin separates us from God. *(Attach 89 to the right side of the chart.)* If we do not come to God through Jesus for forgiveness of our sins, we will die and be separated from God forever. There is no other way to have our sin problem taken away. We cannot be good enough or give enough money or do enough good things to be clean from our sins. We must believe that Jesus died on the cross *(attach 43 over the word SIN)* to take the punishment for our sins and then rose again. By faith we must receive Him as our very own Savior for the forgiveness of sins and to receive eternal life. Have you received Jesus as your Savior? If you have, are you helping others to follow *The Jesus Way?*

Because Jesus is the only one who can give us eternal life and take us to heaven, we must tell others about Him so that they too can receive Him as their Savior. We need to be concerned for our family and friends, just as the servant girl was concerned about her master, and tell them how they can have eternal life through Jesus. When we tell others about Jesus, we are giving them the opportunity to follow *The Jesus Way*. Can you think of someone who does not know Jesus as Savior? *(Response)* What are some ways you can let him or her know about Jesus? *(Write the responses on the bottom of the newsprint. To get them started, suggest some ways, such as inviting someone to Bible Club and Sunday school.)*

Response Activity

Invite any who want to receive the Lord Jesus as Savior to stay after class and talk with you.

Distribute the **"Cross" handouts** and pencils. Instruct the children to write on the top line the first name of an individual who needs to receive Jesus as Savior. Then have them choose one of the ways listed on the chart to help that person know about Jesus and write it on the bottom line of the cross. Close in prayer, asking God to help the children to follow through with the decision they have made. Encourage the children to put their cross in a place where it will remind them of their decision and to pray for the person they have written on their cross.

✎ TAKE-HOME ITEMS

Distribute **memory verse tokens for John 14:6** and **Bible Study Helps for Lesson 3.**

Jonah Runs Away from God
Theme: A Prepared Way

Lesson 4

❁ BEFORE YOU BEGIN...

Becoming what God sovereignly ordained you to be in life is not a hit-or-miss game of chance. A question adults playfully ask children is, What are you going to be when you grow up? While some may happen to guess right, most miss it by a mile.

That God has a plan for every child in your class is beyond question. Your task, therefore, is to help the children to recognize that God indeed has a unique plan for each one and to understand that their years of growing up are key to successful preparation for what God wants them to do.

Today's lesson about Jonah graphically brings out the struggle that many times goes on between what *we* want to do and what God wants. For Jonah it was obedience, or else. For your children it is a critical time to realize who is in charge and to choose to cooperate with God for the wisest use of their lives. As William Tyndale said, "The will of God—nothing more, nothing less, nothing else." *"May the God of peace...make you complete in every good work to do His will, working in you what is well pleasing in His sight..." (Hebrews 3:20, 21, NKJV).*

☞ AIM:

That the children may

- Know that God has a plan for their lives and is preparing them now to carry out that plan.

- Respond by choosing to cooperate with God's plan now by obeying His Word.

📖 SCRIPTURE: Jonah 1:1–4:3

♥ MEMORY VERSE: Psalm 86:11

Teach me thy way, O Lord; I will walk in thy truth. (KJV)
Teach my your way, O Lord, and I will walk in your truth. (NIV)

📁 MATERIALS TO GATHER

Visual for Psalm 86:11 from *Bible Verses Visualized*
Backgrounds: Review Chart, Plain Background, Old Testament Map II, Land and Sea, Rough Sea, City Street
Figures: R1-R4, R15, R16, 1, 8, 9, 10, 16, 17, 25, 25A, 25B, 26, 30, 31, 32, 33
Token holders & memory verse tokens for Psalm 86:11
Bible Study Helps for Lesson 4
Special:
- **For Review Chart:** Newsprint with the names of important characters in Lessons 1–3 printed on it
- **For Bible Content 1:** A world map or globe
- **For Bible Content 2:** Map of Divided Kingdom, a world map or globe
- **For Bible Content 3:** Pictures of whales (particularly sperm whales)
- **For Summary:** Word strip PREPARE, BELIEVE & OBEY footprints
- **For Application:** "God's Word Says" chart, marker
- **For Response Activity:** "God's Word Says" handouts, pencils
- **For Options:** Additional materials for any options you choose to use
- **Note:** *To prepare the "God's Word Says" chart, use a marker to print on newsprint the information shown in Sketch 31 on page 49.*

  Follow the instructions on page xii to prepare the "God's Word Says" handouts (pattern P-4 on page 168). Cut out the fish; punch a hole at the top of each one and attach a ribbon or string through the hole for hanging the fish.

 ## REVIEW CHART

Display the Review Chart with R15 and R16 in place. Have individual children say the verses for Lessons 1–3 from memory as they place the corresponding themes R1-R3 on the Chart. Display the newsprint with the names of important characters in Lessons 1–3 printed on it. Ask the children to tell whether those characters followed God's Way or didn't follow it. Have R4 ready to use when indicated. Use the True or False statements below to review Lesson 3. Have the children restate each false statement to make it a true one.

1. Naaman had a disease that could not be cured. *(True)*
2. The young Israelite servant girl hated the Syrians and didn't tell Naaman about Elisha. *(False; she cared about Naaman and told his wife.)*
3. Elisha sent his servant to tell Naaman to go and dip in the Jordan River seven times. *(True)*
4. Only Naaman's arms and hands were healed, and he became angry with Elisha. *(False; he was completely healed.)*

5. Naaman became a believer in the true and living God after he was healed from the leprosy. *(True)*
6. We must receive Jesus as our Savior in order to be cleansed from our sins. *(True)*

(Have a child read the theme on R4 and place it on the Review Chart.)
Our review symbol for today tells us that God's Way is *A Prepared Way*. When something has been prepared, someone has taken the time to get it ready to be used for a specific purpose. For example, when your mom prepares dinner, she has taken the time to get it ready so that you will have a good nutritious meal to eat. When your parents prepare for a family vacation, they work out all the plans for where you are going to go, how long you will be gone, how you are going to get there, and what you will do when you arrive. All the plans and preparations are made for the purpose of having a fun and relaxing time together as a family.

In a similar way, God has prepared a wonderful future for those who are part of His family. He has made a way for us to be forgiven. He has provided everything we need to live for Him here on earth, and He is preparing a place for us to live with Him forever. He has also prepared a special job for you to do—now and in the future—to help accomplish His purpose for His family, and He has provided God's Word to help you accomplish that purpose.

♥ MEMORY VERSE

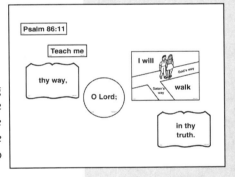

Use the visual for Psalm 86:11 when indicated.
King David wanted to be sure that he was following God's plan and purpose for his life. In one of his prayers he asked God to teach him His way. *(Display the reference and the first four pieces of the visual and have the children read it together.)* This is a good prayer for us to pray too.

God has made His way very clear in His Word, the Bible. We can learn about His way when we read the Bible; but if we can't read it, we can go to Sunday school, Bible Club, or church and learn it from others, just as you are doing right now. We can trust what God says because He tells us that His Word is truth (John 17:17).

God's Word teaches us that Jesus Christ, His Son, is the only way to heaven. If we believe that Jesus died for us and receive Him as our Savior, He will forgive our sins and make us His children. His Word also teaches us how to live as His children by loving, obeying, and serving Him. ▲#1

As David prayed, he made a promise to God. *(Display the rest of the visual and have the children read it together.)* What was it? *(Response)* Yes, David promised that he would walk in God's truth. What do you think that means? *(Response)* Yes, he promised to obey what God says in His Word. David was choosing to obey God's Word step-by-step and day-by-day. Because David learned to walk God's

▲ Option#1

Discuss with the children those things they know God wants them to do and why it might be difficult to obey them. Suggest such things as showing kindness to one who bullies them, telling the truth when it results in punishment, speaking respectfully to someone they don't agree with, obeying a parent when they don't feel like it.

Way, God was able to use him to accomplish His plan for Israel.

When we choose to obey God day by day, we are cooperating with God's plan. Our obedience will help us become the person God wants us to be, and He will be able to use us to accomplish His purpose now and in the future. *(Work on memorizing the verse.)* ▲#2

📖 BIBLE LESSON OUTLINE

Jonah Runs Away from God

■ **Introduction**

Joel's disobedience

■ **Bible Content**

1. God commands Jonah to go to Nineveh.
2. Jonah disobeys God.
3. God punishes Jonah.
   a. God sends a storm.
   b. God sends a fish.
4. Jonah obeys God.

■ **Conclusion**

Summary

Application
   Learning how to obey God

Response Activity
   Choosing to obey God's Word now

📖 BIBLE LESSON

■ **Introduction**

Joel's disobedience

Joel was so excited! It was his dad's birthday and a surprise party was being planned for Friday night. Joel was working with his mom and sisters to get everything ready. It was so much fun, but it was really hard not to give his father any hints. Soon it was Friday morning and his dad had already left for work. "Joel, will you please stop at the bakery after school and pick up the birthday cake?" asked Mom. "They close at 4:30, so you need to go there as soon as school is over to be sure to get the cake."

"Sure, Mom," answered Joel as he ran out the door to go to school. "No problem. I'd love to get Dad's cake." All day Joel thought about how surprised his dad was going to be and all the fun that had

---

▲ **Option#2**

Memorizing the verse: Organize a verse choir by dividing the class into seven groups (or a suitable number for your class) and assigning each group one part of the verse to say. Keep the visual displayed. Have each group stand and say their part with expression as a prayer and promise to God. Then remove the visual and have the class repeat the verse a few times together.

KJV	NIV
Psalm 86:11	Psalm 86:11
Teach me thy way, O Lord; I will walk in thy truth.	Teach me your way, O Lord, and I will walk in your truth.

Variation: Have each group watch for your signal to say their part and give them instructions in how loudly or softly they should speak, or place the groups in random order and have them say the verse in correct word order.

been planned. Some of his dad's friends were coming too.

Before school was over, Joel's friends asked if he would finish the soccer game they had started at lunch. "Sure," said Joel. "That would be great." So the boys set up their game as soon as school was finished. It was a great game with a close score all the way, and Joel was really playing hard.

When the game was over, Joel suddenly realized he had completely lost track of time; and it was five minutes before closing time at the bakery. "Oh wow!" said Joel as he began to run. "I will never make it in time to get Dad's cake." He was right; the bakery had a "CLOSED" sign on the door when he got there. How do you think Joel felt? *(Response)* He wasn't sure what he was going to say to his mother, let alone his father! His mom was going to be very upset as well as greatly disappointed. He tried to think up all kinds of excuses and even some ideas of how to get another cake. But he knew it wasn't going to work. He had spoiled his dad's party and his mother's trust in him.

In our lesson today we are going to hear about a man who did a similar thing when he was asked to do something God had prepared for him to do. Listen carefully to find out what happened.

▲ **Option#3**

Use word strips to review the books of Genesis through Obadiah.

▲ **Option#4**

Conduct a Bible drill using selected Old Testament books that have been learned up to Jonah. Have the children find the first page of each book, ending the drill with Jonah. Be sure everyone has found the book of Jonah before proceeding with the lesson.

■ Bible Content

1. God commands Jonah to go to Nineveh. (Jonah 1:1, 2)

(A world map or globe; soldiers 16, 17, chariot 25, people 25B, 26, idol 1, Jonah 33)

After Elisha died, God chose Jonah to be a prophet to the northern kingdom of Israel *(indicate ISRAEL)*. His story is found in the Old Testament book named after him. Find the first chapter of the book of Jonah and place your bookmark there. ▲#3 ▲#4

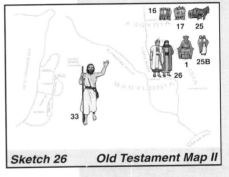

Sketch 26   **Old Testament Map II**

Everyone, including Israel, lived in great fear of the nation of Assyria *(indicate ASSYRIA)*. ⌂(1) Assyria was located to the north and east of Israel and was the strongest nation in the world at that time. The people who lived there were very wicked. Even the king acknowledged that their ways were sinful and violent (Jonah 3:8). The Assyrian army had conquered many cities and nations, killing thousands of people and capturing many prisoners. *(Place 16, 17 on the board.)* The soldiers were known for being very cruel and violent, torturing those they captured.

Nineveh *(indicate NINEVEH)*, the capital city of Assyria, was located about 550 miles from Israel in the present-day country of Iraq *(indicate on the world map or globe)*. ⌂(2) It was a large and beautiful city with over one million people. The city was surrounded with an inner wall and an outer wall, which included many small villages. The inner wall was 100 feet high, protecting the city from its enemies, and wide enough for three chariots *(add 25)* to drive side by side along the top. Since the Assyrians *(add 25B, 26)* were idol worshippers,

⌂ **Note (1)**

Assyria was often called the Assyrian Empire, for it controlled the known world at this time.

⌂ **Note (2)**

Nimrod built the city of Nineveh (Genesis 10:10, 11). Nineveh was located at the site of present-day Mosul, Iraq.

Nineveh was full of gods and temples *(add 1)*. Many people, including the Assyrians, worshiped the god Dagon. 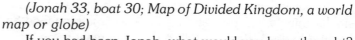 They knew nothing of the true and living God and His love for them and His hatred of sin.

God prepared a way for the people of Nineveh to hear that they needed to stop their evil ways and turn to Him. *(Have a child read Jonah 1:2.)* His plan included the prophet Jonah *(add 33)*. God said to Jonah, "Go and preach to the people in the city of Nineveh. Tell them I have seen all the evil things they are doing and I am going to destroy them." The people of Nineveh deserved to be punished for their sins, but God was willing to save them from being destroyed if they would turn to Him. He wanted to show His mercy to them—not give them what they deserved. ▲#5

▲ Note (3)

Dagon was the chief deity of Nineveh. Unger's Bible Dictionary shows an artist's conception of Dagon as half fish/half man, leading to the conclusion that Dagon was the fish god. However, most findings indicate Dagon was the god of grain and was worshiped by numerous countries including Philistia.

2. Jonah disobeys God.
(Jonah 1:3; 4:1-3)

(Jonah 33, boat 30; Map of Divided Kingdom, a world map or globe)

If you had been Jonah, what would you have thought? How would you have felt? *(Response)* Jonah felt that the people of Nineveh deserved to be punished. He didn't want God to show kindness and mercy to them.

Verse 3 tells us what Jonah did. *(Have a child read verse 3 aloud, or have all the children read it silently and tell you the answer.)* Jonah tried to run away from God. Can anyone do that? *(Response)* Certainly not! Why not? *(Response)* Yes, that is right. God is everywhere and sees us all the time. He lets us make our own choices, just as He did with Jonah. Jonah chose to disobey God and did not want to cooperate with God's Way and His plan for Nineveh.

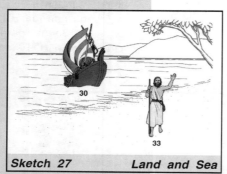

Sketch 27 Land and Sea

▲ Option#5

Definition word card: Mercy = not getting the punishment that is deserved.

Instead of traveling east across the desert to Nineveh, Jonah *(place 33 on the board)* went down to the city of Joppa *(indicate JOPPA)* which is the modern city of Jaffa *(indicate on the world map or globe)*, located by the Mediterranean Sea on the coast of Israel. There he found a ship *(add 30)* that was headed for Tarshish, a city located in southern Spain about 2500 miles from Israel and Nineveh. Jonah paid his fare and boarded the ship. As soon as the ship set sail, Jonah went below deck and fell asleep. Perhaps he was exhausted from trying to figure out how he was going to run away from God.

3. God punishes Jonah.
(Jonah 1:4–2:10)

(Ship 30, Jonah 31, fish 32; pictures of whales)

God did not ignore Jonah's disobedience. He punished Jonah by allowing two difficult things to happen to him to show him that he was wrong and to help Jonah change his mind about obeying God.

Sketch 28 Rough Sea

a. **God sends a storm.** ▲#6

Soon after the ship set sail *(place 30 on the board)*, God sent a violent wind across the sea, which caused a terrible storm. The storm was so powerful that the ship was in danger of breaking apart. *(Move the ship up and down over the waves as you speak.)* The wind roared and the waves tossed the ship around, causing water to come into the ship. The storm was so fierce that the ship's crew were terrified, even though they were experienced sailors. What does verse 5 tell us they did? *(Response)* Yes, each of them began to pray to his own god for help. Then they started throwing some of the cargo overboard to lighten the ship to keep it from sinking. But it didn't do any good; the storm just got worse and worse. Where was Jonah all this time? *(Response)* Yes, he was sleeping below deck. Where do you think God was during the storm? *(Response)* That's right! He was right there—in control of everything!

The ship's captain went below deck and began yelling at Jonah, "How can you sleep in this storm? Get up! Call on your god. Maybe he will notice what is happening and will save us."

Then the frightened sailors said to each other, "Let's cast lots to find out who is responsible for this trouble." ◪(4) When they were finished, the lot pointed to Jonah. As the storm grew stronger and the sea got rougher they questioned Jonah, "Who are you and where do you come from? What is your country and who are your people? What is your job?"

As the storm raged around them Jonah answered, "I am a Hebrew and I worship the Lord, the God of heaven who made the sea and the land."

When they heard this, they were even more terrified. There didn't seem to be any hope of being rescued; they were all going to die at sea. "What have you done?" they asked. They knew he was running away from God because Jonah had told them.

They continued to question Jonah. "What should we do to you to make the sea calm down?"

Jonah replied, "Pick me up and throw me into the sea, and it will calm down. It is my fault that this has happened." Do you think Jonah knew God was behind this? *(Response)* Yes he did!

But the sailors did not want to throw Jonah overboard. Instead they rowed as hard as they could to get to land. When the storm grew even stronger, they realized they must follow Jonah's instructions. But they did not want to be held accountable for taking his life. In desperation they cried out to Jonah's God, "Oh Lord, please do not blame us for doing this. Do not let us die for taking this innocent man's life. We recognize You are in control and are doing what You please." Just think! That terrible storm caused those idol worshipers to call on the living God for help. ▲#7

Then they took Jonah and threw him *(add 31)* into the raging sea. Verse 15 tells us that the storm stopped immediately. The sky became still and the sea grew calm. Can you imagine the sailors' reaction? *(Response)* They must have stood there in shock. Perhaps they ran to

▲ **Option#6**

Instruct the children to help with the following sound effects to create the noises of the storm, and practice them before telling the story: clap for lightning; stamp on floor for thunder; drum fingers on seats for rain; and blow for wind. Make cue cards and print the words on them that the captain, the sailors, and Jonah say. Give the cards to some older children and instruct them to shout out the words above the noise of the storm at the appropriate times in the story. When Jonah is thrown overboard, the noise stops.

◪ **Note (4)**

Casting lots was one of the methods the ancient peoples had of determining the future or what the gods wanted. This was the forerunner of throwing dice. The "lot" could be anything from stones to sticks to pieces of bone. They were thrown, and based on a set of rules, someone interpreted the configuration and what it meant. Today, people sometimes draw straws or pick a slip of paper out of a hat to determine choices.

▲ **Option#7**

Have the children take the parts of the sailors and Jonah by reading Jonah 1:6-14 and/or acting out the scene.

the side of the ship and looked to see if they could find Jonah and rescue him. We don't know. But we do know they were absolutely amazed and knew without a doubt that Jonah's God was more powerful than their gods. Right then and there they offered a sacrifice to God and made promises to praise and worship Him.

b. God sends a fish.

Meanwhile, Jonah *(move 31 down lower into the water)* sank down, down, down into the waves and swirling sea. He knew he had disobeyed God and he deserved to die. But God loved Jonah, and He still wanted to use Jonah to take His message to the people of Nineveh. So God showed mercy to Jonah. He caused a very big fish to swallow Jonah. *(Add 32 and place 31 behind it.)* We do not know what kind of fish it was, but we know there are several whales that are large enough to swallow a person *(display pictures of whales).* **(5)** Jonah must have thought that this was the end. But he didn't die in the fish; he lived in the stomach of that fish for three days and three nights. I'm sure it was a very unpleasant place to be—all smelly and full of gases and digested food.

Look in Jonah 2:1 to find what Jonah did while he was in the fish. *(Have children read silently.)* What did he do? *(Response)* Yes, he prayed. If you had been sitting there, you might have done the very same thing. Jonah knew that God had allowed all this to happen; he knew he could not run from Him. Jonah's prayer is written down for us to read. *(If time permits, read Jonah's prayer [2:2-9] aloud while the children follow along in their Bibles, or have several older children read a few verses each.)* Jonah was thankful to be alive. He said, "I will keep the promises I made to You." Jonah was now willing to obey God.

⌂ Note (5)

The sperm whale is one that can swallow a person quite easily.

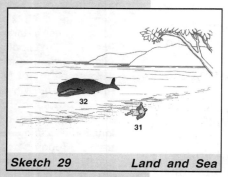

Sketch 29   **Land and Sea**

(Fish 32, Jonah 31, 33)
Because God controls everything He has created, He commanded the fish *(place 32 on the board)* to spit Jonah *(add 31)* out onto dry land. What an unpleasant experience that must have been! Can you imagine what he looked like and how he must have smelled? But, Jonah was glad to be alive! *(Replace 31 with 33.)* He had experienced God's mercy and forgiveness for his sin of disobedience. This was the very thing God wanted to do for the people of Nineveh.

4. Jonah obeys God. (Jonah 3)

(Jonah 33, people 8, 9, 10, 25B, 26)
Now that Jonah was safe on land again, God spoke to him a second time. "Get up!" He said. "Go to the great city of Nineveh and give them My message." What do you think Jonah did this time? *(Response)* He didn't try to run from

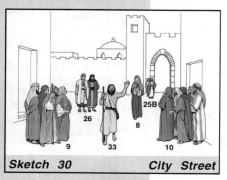

Sketch 30   **City Street**

God. Instead, he immediately obeyed God. He got up and started on his journey to Nineveh. Jonah was now willing to obey and cooperate with God's plan. ⌂(6)

When Jonah arrived in Nineveh *(place 33 on the board)*, he began walking through the city *(add 8, 9, 10, 25B, 26)* shouting, "In forty days Nineveh is going to be destroyed." It took him three days to walk through the entire city and its villages with God's message.

And then an incredible thing happened! When the people heard Jonah's message, they believed God's Word. God had prepared those wicked people to listen to His Word and obey it! To show they were sorry for their sinful actions, they refused to eat for a while, put on rough cloth, and covered themselves with dust. Even the king joined his people when he heard God's message. In fact, he made an announcement to all of his people, "Turn to the true and living God, confess your sins, and give up your evil and violent ways so that He will not destroy us." The people were quick to obey his command.

When God saw that the people were really sorry for their sins, He forgave them and did not destroy their city at that time. He showed them mercy instead; He did not give them what they deserved. What an incredible miracle God had done through Jonah! Because Jonah chose to obey God and cooperate with His plan, God was able to use him to save the entire city of Nineveh from death.

⌂ Note (6)

Remember, this would have been about 550 miles. Jonah probably did most of this trip on foot.

■ Conclusion

Summary

(People 25B, Jonah 33, ship 30, fish 32; word strip PREPARE, BELIEVE & OBEY footprints)

What was God's purpose for the people *(place 25B on the board)* in Nineveh? *(Response)* Yes, He wanted them to turn to Him from their evil ways. How did God prepare *(add PREPARE)* for them to hear His message? *(Response)* Yes, He told Jonah *(add 33)* to go and preach to them. Was Jonah willing to take God's message to them?

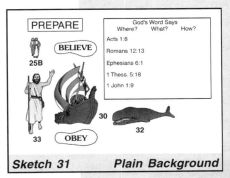

Sketch 31　　　　Plain Background

(Response) No! Why not? *(Response)* That's right. He thought they deserved to be punished for their evil ways. What did Jonah do instead? *(Response)* Yes, he ran away *(add 30)*. What did God use to change his mind? *(Response)* Yes, God used a terrible storm and a large fish *(add 32)* that swallowed Jonah. How did the people of Nineveh respond when Jonah finally obeyed *(add OBEY)* God and preached His message to them? *(Response)* Yes, they believed *(add BELIEVE)* God's message and turned from their evil ways.

Application

("God's Word Says" chart, marker)

To accomplish His purpose God wants to use you in bringing other people to Him and helping them to love and obey Him. He is preparing you right now to do that. He has given you His Word to help you. It is important that *you* learn what it says and obey it. That is what our memory verse tells us to do. Let's say it together. *(Do so. Then attach the "God's Word Says" chart to the flannelboard.)*

Now, let's look at some examples of things God tells us to do in His Word. *(Have the children look up the verses on the chart and read them one at a time. Write their responses in the "What?" column on the chart.)* Whenever we read God's Word, we should look to see if there is anything God wants us to obey. Then we have a choice to make. We can obey God or we can refuse to obey Him as Jonah did at first. If you learn to obey God now, He will begin to show you how He wants to use you to accomplish His purpose now and in the future. ▲#8

Now, let's answer the question "How?" by thinking of some ways that we can obey what God has told us to do. *(Have children suggest ways they can obey what God says in the verses listed on the chart. Write their suggestions in the "How?" column. If the children cannot think of any, give them an example, such as witnessing by telling a friend about Jesus or giving someone a tract.)*

Response Activity

Distribute the **"God's Word Says" handouts** and pencils. Instruct the children to look at the list that was made today and see if there is something there that they need to begin obeying today. Have them choose two verses and print the references in the "Where?" column on their handout, and then print the commands in the "What?" column. Then have them write in the "How?" column what they will do to obey what God tells them to do in each verse.

Give the children time to complete the assignment. Be ready to give them suggestions or help them to write their answers. Then have them think about the promise written on the handout and sign their name only if they are willing to obey God's Word. Close in prayer, asking God to help them obey His Word this week. Encourage the children to place their handout in a place where it will remind them to keep their promise to God.

📖 TAKE-HOME ITEMS

Distribute **memory verse tokens for Psalm 86:11** and **Bible Study Helps for Lesson 4.**

▲ **Option #8**

Distribute paper and crayons or markers and have the children illustrate the items under the "What?" column, writing the verse reference under each picture. Or, have them make a mural, drawing their illustrations on a long sheet of paper. Hang the pictures or mural in a prominent place. As you discuss "How?" ask the children to choose a picture and suggest ways they can obey the verse, or have them illustrate "How?" next to the pictures already drawn.

Variation: Have small groups of children act out the "How?" for each verse and have the rest of the class guess which verse is being dramatized.

Isaiah Prophesies to a Sinful Nation

Theme: A Holy Way

Lesson 5

❋ BEFORE YOU BEGIN...

The issue of right and wrong challenges every generation. What makes the determination? Government? School? Family? For the Christian, God is the determiner; He is holy and His holiness sets the standard for right and wrong, absolutely and eternally.

In stark contrast, the world's fluctuating standard makes everything right in one's own eyes. And each one's opinion cannot be forced on anyone else. There is no absolute truth, no unchanging standard. All laws and rights are to be reevaluated and reinterpreted.

In this kind of environment children are quite vulnerable. Confused by inconsistency and disillusioned by duplicity, today's children too often come off with an "anything goes" attitude that results in the worst of behaviors.

Two men encountered God's holiness. King Uzziah trivialized God's holiness and ended his reign in disgrace. The prophet Isaiah humbled himself before God's holiness and was significantly used in a lifetime of ministry.

Don't miss the opportunity to establish both God's holy standard revealed in His Word and the sinfulness of the human heart to help your children depend on Him to reflect His holiness. *"He chose us in Him before the foundation of the world, that we should be holy and without blame before Him in love" (Ephesians 1:4, NKJV).*

☞ AIM:

That the children may

- Know that God is holy and wants His children to be holy in the way they live.
- Respond by receiving the Lord Jesus as Savior and by trusting God to help them be holy in the way they think, act, and talk.

📖 SCRIPTURE:
Exodus 19:5, 6; Leviticus 20:26; Deuteronomy 28:9, 10; 2 Chronicles 26:1-23; Isaiah 6:1-8; 7:14; 9:6, 7; 53:3-6; 61:1

♥ MEMORY VERSE: 1 Peter 1:15

But as he which hath called you is holy, so be ye holy in all manner of conversation. (KJV)

But just as he who called you is holy, so be holy in all you do. (NIV)

▲ **Option #1**

Definition word card: Holy = pure or clean—without any sin.

⌂ **Note (1)**

The word *conversation* in the KJV is an Old English word meaning *behavior*. It includes everything people do, not just what they say.

▲ **Option #2**

Memorizing the verse: Distribute the pieces of the verse visual to individual children and have them arrange themselves in order, holding up the visual pieces for the class to see. Have the whole group repeat the verse together. Then have one of the children sit down and let a volunteer say the verse without seeing the missing piece. Repeat the procedure until all the pieces of the visual have been removed. Next have all the children who are holding the visual pieces stand and face the class in scrambled order. Let volunteers come up one at a time to move the visual pieces until the words of the verse are in the correct order. Have the children repeat the verse together each time a change is made and then check to see if each change is correct. If time permits, have one of the children give the meaning of the verse each time all the visual pieces have been put in correct order.

52 L5

📁 **MATERIALS TO GATHER**

Visual for 1 Peter 1:15 from *Bible Verses Visualized*
Backgrounds: Review Chart, Plain Background, Old Testament Map II, Palace, Temple
Figures: R1-R5, R15, R16, 1, 2, 4, 18(2), 26, 29, 36, 36A, 37, 38, 39, 40, 41, 42, 43, 45(2), 52, 59, 84
Token holders & memory verse tokens for 1 Peter 1:15
Bible Study Helps for Lesson 5
Special:
- **For Memory Verse:** Word strips THOUGHTS, ACTIONS, WORDS
- **For Introduction:** A 3" x 5" card with HOLY printed on one side and SINFUL printed on the other side for each child
- **For Bible Content 1:** Word strip ISAIAH
- **For Bible Content 2:** Word strips PRIDE, SIN
- **For Bible Content 3 & Summary:** Word strip SIN
- **For Bible Content 4:** "Prophecies about Jesus" chart, marker
- **For Application:** Word strips from Memory Verse above; underlined statements from Introduction listed on newsprint, marker
- **For Response Activity:** "God's Holy Way" handouts, small adhesive-backed magnets
- **For Options:** Additional materials for any options you choose to use
- **Note:** To prepare the "Prophecies about Jesus" chart, print Isaiah 7:14; Isaiah 9:6b, 61:1; Isaiah 53:3-6; and Isaiah 9:7 on newsprint or chalkboard. Leave space to write the prophesies after each passage.
  Follow the instructions on page xii to prepare the word strips and the "God's Holy Way" handouts (pattern P-15 on page 174).

 REVIEW CHART

Display the Review Chart with R1-R3, R15, and R16 in place. Have the children give the theme and recite the verse for Lesson 4 as a child places R4 on the Chart. Have R5 ready to use when indicated. Use the following questions to review Lesson 4.

1. What was God's purpose for the people in Nineveh? *(He wanted them to turn to Him from their evil ways.)*
2. How did God plan for the people in Nineveh to hear His message? *(He told Jonah to go and preach to them.)*
3. Why was Jonah not willing to take God's message to the people in Nineveh? *(He thought they deserved to be punished for their evil ways.)*
4. What did Jonah do instead? *(He tried to run away from God and got on a ship headed for Tarshish.)*

5. What did God use to change Jonah's mind? *(He used a terrible storm and a large fish to swallow Jonah.)*
6. How did the people of Nineveh respond when Jonah finally obeyed God and preached His message? *(They believed God's message and turned from their evil ways.)*

Today we are going to see that God's Way is *A Holy Way*. *(Have a child place R5 on the Chart.)* Holy is a word that describes God and all that He does. It means to be pure or clean—without any sin. ▲#1 Sometimes you see the word *holy* written on the cover of the Bible—*The Holy Bible* (hold up *your* Bible). It reminds us that the words in this book are from God, who is holy. It also tells us how *we* can become holy and how to follow God's holy way.

♥ MEMORY VERSE

Use the visual for 1 Peter 1:15 and word strips THOUGHTS, ACTIONS, WORDS when indicated.

Is it possible for us to be holy and follow God's holy way? Yes, we can with God's help. But we can never be as holy as God is while we are living here on earth. This is because we were all born with a sin nature that we inherited from our parents, who inherited it from their parents, going all the way back to our first parents, Adam and Eve. Our sinful nature causes us to disobey God and to go our own way. Before we receive the Lord Jesus as our Savior, we find it easy to sin; we give in easily to the evil desire of our sinful nature. When we receive Jesus as our Savior, God takes away the punishment we deserve for sinning and makes us part of His family forever. But our sinful nature is not taken away; instead, God gives us a new nature that wants to please Him. Now there is a struggle between the two natures inside us. But God also gives us the Holy Spirit to work in our new nature to help us act like a member of His family. Our memory verse teaches us to do that. *(Display the visual and read it with the children.)*

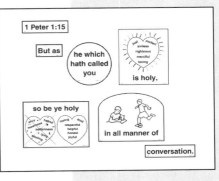

Since God is holy, He wants us to be holy in everything we do—in the way we think *(add THOUGHTS)*, in the way we act *(add ACTIONS)*, and in the way we talk *(add WORDS)*. He has given us the Bible, to tell us how to do this. That is why it is so important for us to read it and obey what it says. When we do, we will become more like the Lord Jesus. Living the holy way is doing things the way Jesus would do them. ◁(1)

It isn't always easy to obey God's Word, but the Holy Spirit who lives in us helps us to say no to sin and yes to God. When we do sin, we still belong to God's family, and the Holy Spirit reminds us that we have sinned until we confess it and receive God's forgiveness. The Holy Spirit also helps us to understand what God's Word means and reminds us of what it says when we are tempted to sin. We must trust Him to help us. When we do, we will be able to be holy, saying no to the sin and yes to God. *(Work on memorizing the verse).* ▲#2

📖 BIBLE LESSON OUTLINE

Isaiah Prophesies to a Sinful Nation

■ **Introduction**

Distinguishing between holy and sinful

■ **Bible Content**

1. God has a purpose for His people.
2. King Uzziah's pride changes his life.
   a. King Uzziah obeys God.
   b. King Uzziah disobeys God.
3. Isaiah's vision changes his life.
4. Isaiah prophesies about Jesus Christ.

■ **Conclusion**

Summary

Application
   Acknowledging that God wants us to be holy

Response Activity
   Receiving Jesus as Savior and trusting God for help in holy living

📖 BIBLE LESSON

■ **Introduction**

Distinguishing between holy and sinful

Give each child a 3" x 5" card with the word HOLY printed on one side and SINFUL on the other side.

I am going to read a list of statements. I want you to respond to each one by using the card I have given to you. If you think the statement describes *A Holy Way* of living, hold up the side of the card that shows the word HOLY. If you think the statement does not describe *A Holy Way* of living, show the word SINFUL. (Read the following statements.)

1. <u>You control your words when someone is annoying you.</u>
2. <u>You do your chores without complaining.</u>
3. You think about ways to get even with those who have hurt you.
4. <u>You refuse to go along with those who gang up on someone.</u>
5. <u>You always tell the truth.</u>
6. You cheat when playing games with your friends.
7. <u>You obey your parents without getting upset about it.</u>

8. <u>You are kind to others even if they are mean to you.</u>
9. You take money from your mother's purse when she isn't looking.
10. You get angry when you don't get your own way.

In some instances you held up the word SINFUL. Why? *(Response)* Yes, those statements describe sinful actions. Sin keeps us from holy living. Our lesson today helps us to understand how much God hates sin and why He wants us to live in *A Holy Way*.

■ Bible Content

1. God has a purpose for His people. (Exodus 19:5, 6; Leviticus 20:26; Deuteronomy 28:9, 10)

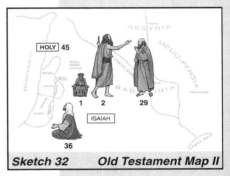

Sketch 32 Old Testament Map II

(HOLY 45, idol 1, Elijah 2, Elisha 29, Isaiah 36; word strip ISAIAH)

God chose the Israelites to be His special people. He wanted them to be different from all the idol-worshiping nations that surrounded them. Since He is a holy God, He wanted the Israelites to be holy *(place HOLY 45 on the board)* and show His holiness in the way they lived and worshiped Him. He gave them His written laws and commandments so that they would know how to do this. He set them apart in this way so that the other nations would see that He is the only true and living God and would come to know Him.

But instead of following God's holy way, the Israelites ignored God and His Word and began to worship idols *(add 1)* like all the nations around them. After the nation was divided, Israel *(indicate ISRAEL)* turned completely away from God, worshiping and serving other gods. Judah *(indicate JUDAH)* soon followed in their footsteps. God hated their sin of disobedience, but He loved His people very much and wanted their love in return. He sent prophets to warn them to turn away from idol worship and turn back to worshiping Him. We have already learned about two of the prophets who were sent to warn Israel. Do you remember who they were? *(Response)* Yes, Elijah and Elisha *(add 2, 29)*.

Today we are going to meet a man who is considered one of the greatest of God's prophets. He served as God's prophet during King Uzziah's reign over Judah. He began preaching when he was fifteen years old and continued to serve God until he died at the age of eighty-five. His message to the people of Judah is written in the book of the Bible that bears his name. It is called the book of Isaiah *(add 36, ISAIAH)*. *(Have the children find the book of Isaiah in their Bibles.)*
▲#3 ▲#4

▲ Option#3

Use word strips to review the Old Testament books Genesis through Isaiah, or have the children say the books from memory if they have already been learning them.

▲ Option#4

Conduct a Bible drill by having the children find the first page in any ten books you randomly choose from Genesis through Isaiah.

2. King Uzziah's pride changes his life.
(2 Chronicles 26:1-23)

a. King Uzziah obeys God.

Sketch 33 — Palace

(Uzziah 84, priest 38, people 3, HOLY 45)
Something happened to King Uzziah that left a great impression on Isaiah while he was still young. Turn to 2 Chronicles 26 to find Uzziah's story. *(Have the children do so and put their bookmarks in place.)*

Uzziah became king when he was sixteen years old and reigned over Judah for fifty-two years. *(Place 84, 3 on the board.)* While Uzziah was still young, Zechariah the priest *(add 38)* taught him to obey God's Word and to trust God for His help. Uzziah learned how to live God's holy way *(add 45)*. As a result, Uzziah led the people in following God's Way, doing what was right and pleasing to God.

(Have a child read the last half of verse 5.) As long as Uzziah put God first and prayed for help, God gave him success in everything he did. He gave him victory over his enemies and ability to train his army and to develop good military strategy. Uzziah built strong defense towers and walls around the city of Jerusalem to protect it against enemy attacks. He was good at growing things. He designed irrigation wells to keep the desert watered to grow crops and to provide water for herds of animals. The last part of verse 8 tells us two other things God gave Uzziah. *(Have the children read it aloud.)* God gave him power over his enemies and made him well known and respected among the nations. While King Uzziah was obeying God and trusting Him for everything, all the nations were able to see God at work in Uzziah and in the people of Judah. ▲#5

b. King Uzziah disobeys God.

(Word strips PRIDE, SIN; altar 39, priest 38, Uzziah 37, UNCLEAN 45, priests 4, 26)
But Uzziah didn't keep his way holy. Verse 16 tells us what caused the change. *(Read the first sentence of the verse and see if the children can discover the cause.)* Uzziah's heart was lifted up—he became proud of his power and what he had accomplished. *(Place PRIDE on the board.)* What is pride? *(Response)* The wrong kind of pride is thinking you are better than other people and do not need any help from anyone, including God. When Uzziah became proud of himself and what he had done, he stopped trusting God for help and wisdom.

In fact, Uzziah's pride led him to disobey God's Word. He totally ignored God's laws for worship in the temple—the very place that represented God's presence among the people. Because God is holy, He had very specific laws about the way worship

---

▲ **Option #5**

Print a list of Uzziah's accomplishments on newsprint and point to each one as it is mentioned. Or, print each of Uzziah's accomplishments on separate pieces of paper. Choose children to display the accomplishments as they are mentioned.

⌂ **Note (2)**

Refer to Bible Content 1 in Lesson 3 on page 56 for information about leprosy.

Sketch 34 — Temple

was to be conducted in the temple, so that the people would remember that He is holy and demanded holiness from them.

One day King Uzziah *(add 37)* pushed his way into the Holy Place of the temple where only the priests were allowed to go. He took a censor filled with incense and started to burn it on the altar *(add 39)*. Azariah the high priest *(add 38)* and 80 other brave priests *(add 4, 26)* tried to stop him, saying, "This is wrong. Only priests who are descendants of Aaron are allowed to do this. You must leave at once! You have been unfaithful to God and He will not honor you for this." Instead of stopping and asking for God's forgiveness for acting in such an unholy way, Uzziah became very angry and began yelling at the priests. He must have thought he had the right to do this since he was the king.

King Uzziah didn't have the right to enter the Holy Place. God's holy laws applied to everyone, including the king. He had sinned against God *(add SIN)*. As Uzziah stood there in front of the priests, white spots of leprosy broke out on his forehead. **(2)** The priests hurried him out of the temple *(remove 4, 26, 38, 37)*. Anyone who had a disease or sickness was considered unclean *(add 45)* and not allowed to be in the temple. Do you think Uzziah knew who had given him this disease? *(Response)* Yes he did. Knowing that God had punished him, King Uzziah was eager to leave the temple. Because of his leprosy, he was never allowed to go into the temple again. He had the disease for the rest of his life and had to live alone in a separate house. His son, Jotham, governed the people and then became king when Uzziah died.

It took leprosy to let Uzziah know that God hated his pride and that being king did not give him the right to disobey God. The people needed to be reminded of God's holiness and that God meant what He said. Uzziah's leprosy taught them a lesson they would never forget. *(Remove 45, word strips.)*

3. Isaiah's vision changes his life. ▲#6
(Isaiah 6:1-8)

(Isaiah 36, angel 40; word strip SIN)
One day, during the year that King Uzziah died, Isaiah went into the temple to worship God *(add 36)*. While he was there he had a wonderful vision; he saw God sitting on a very high throne. He saw angelic beings called seraphim *(add 40)* above the throne calling to one another, saying, "Holy, holy, holy is the Lord Almighty. His glory fills the whole earth." *(Have the children pretend they are angels and read verse 3 aloud.)* The sound of their voices caused the door of the temple to shake, and the temple filled with smoke. ▲#7
▲#8

As Isaiah stood there in the presence of God he felt very afraid. As he compared God's holiness—how perfect and righteous God is—to his own sinful words and actions,

▲ Option#6

Act out this scene of Isaiah in the temple. Have cue cards prepared to give to the children to read their lines. Select a child to take the part of Isaiah and one to take the part of the angel who brought the coal to touch Elijah's mouth. Use a crumbled red paper to represent the hot coal. The rest of the children may be the other angels who are praising God together at His throne. As you describe the scene, the children speak their parts at the appropriate times. "Isaiah" could go on to read aloud the four prophecies about Jesus.

▲ Option#7

Have the children read Isaiah 6:1-4 aloud. Then individually or as a group they could make a wall mural by illustrating what they have read.

▲ Option#8

Prepare a banner by printing the seraphim's words in verse 3 on it. Display it as you present the lesson.

Variation: Let the children make the banner at the close of the lesson. Display it in a prominent place as a reminder of the lesson.

Sketch 35   **Temple**

⌂ Note (3)

This graphic symbol of cleansing Isaiah's sin utilizes two ways fire was used in Bible times: (1) medically as a cleansing agent to burn off infection and to seal wounds; and (2) in the refining process to burn off residue in metal works, such as purifying gold.

▲ Option #9

Print each of the prophecies about Jesus on separate pieces of construction paper or cardstock of different colors. Attach them to the chart.

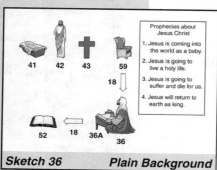

Sketch 36   Plain Background

⌂ Note (4)

Define *virgin* as is appropriate for your class. In Bible times a *virgin* was a girl who had never been married. You may want to define it in today's culture as a girl who has never been sexually active or had sexual relations with a man.

---

he said, "I deserve to die for I have sinned *(add SIN)*. I have unclean lips, and I live among people who are not pure." Isaiah knew he was a sinner and didn't deserve to be in God's presence. Perhaps at this point, he also realized how serious Uzziah's sin was. Uzziah had completely ignored God's holy laws and disobeyed His Word.

Then one of the seraphim took a burning coal from the altar and touched Isaiah's lips with it and said, "Look, this hot coal has touched your lips; your sin is forgiven and you are clean." ⌂**(3)** How happy Isaiah must have been to know that God forgave him and now he was pure and clean in God's sight! *(Remove SIN.)*

(Choose two children to read verse eight aloud; have one read God's questions and the other read Isaiah's answer.) Suddenly Isaiah heard God's voice asking, "Whom shall I send? And who will go for us?"

Without hesitation Isaiah answered, "Here I am. Send me."

Then God said, "Go and give my message to the people, even though they won't listen to you."

4. Isaiah prophesies about Jesus Christ. (Isaiah 7:14; 9:6, 7; 53:3-6; 61:1)

(Isaiah 36, desk 36A, arrows 18[2], baby 41, Jesus 42, cross 43, throne 59, Bible 52; "Prophecies about Jesus" chart, marker

Even though this was a hard assignment, Isaiah obeyed God. He *(place 36 on the board)* faithfully preached God's message, saying, "Turn back to God or you will be punished and taken captive by your enemies." God gave him courage to continue giving this message, even though very few people listened to him. Isaiah not only spoke God's words, but he also wrote them down *(add 36A)*. We can read them in the book of Isaiah *(add 52, 18[1])*, which we found in our Bibles earlier today.

God gave Isaiah prophecies to write, messages about things that were going to happen in the future, including prophecies about the Savior (Jesus), which were written 700 years before He was born. Even though Isaiah did not know that the person he was prophesying about would be named Jesus, he knew there would be someone coming from God who would fulfill these prophecies. Many were fulfilled (completed) when Jesus came to earth the first time, and some are going to be fulfilled when He comes to earth again. Here are four really important things Isaiah prophesied about Jesus.

(Attach the "Prophecies about Jesus" chart to the board. Choose four children to find the verses and read them out loud. As each one is read, have the other children tell what the prophecy is. Write it on the chart beside the reference.) ▲#9

Isaiah 7:14 – *Jesus is coming into the world as a baby.*

First, Jesus is going to come into the world as a baby *(add 41)*. His mother will be a virgin, and His father will be God. ⌂**(4)** He is going to be called Immanuel, which means "God with us." In other words Jesus is God. This prophecy came true when Mary became the mother of Jesus.

Isaiah 9:6b; 61:1 – Jesus is going to live a holy life.

Second, Jesus *(add 42)* is going to be holy (sinless) while living on earth—He is going to be fully God and fully man at the same time. He is going to preach and teach about God and heal and comfort people. Whenever people see Jesus, they will see what God is like.

Isaiah 53:3-6 – Jesus is going to suffer and die for us.

Third, Jesus is going to suffer and die *(add 43)*. Isaiah 53:3 gives a description of His suffering—the terrible way in which He will be treated. Verses 4 and 5 describe Jesus' death for our sins. ▲#10

Isaiah 9:7 – Jesus will return to earth as King.

Fourth, Jesus will come back a second time to reign as King *(add 59, 18[1])* over the whole earth. This has not happened yet; but when it does, there will be peace and the whole earth will be filled with the glory and majesty of God.

Isaiah's prophecies about Jesus showed God's plan for making us holy—pure and clean from sin—through the suffering and death of His Son, the Lord Jesus Christ. They make us realize how holy God is and how terrible sin is—so much so that God sent His Son to take the punishment for our sins. The New Testament part of our Bible tells us exactly how it all came about. God's Word is very clear that we must understand that Jesus' suffering and death was for us and receive Him as our Savior to have eternal life and the forgiveness of sins. When we do this, God makes us holy in His sight. Then His Word tells us how to become holy in all we do. *(Remove all the figures.)*

▲ Option#10

As verse 3 is read have the children listen and then tell what words describe Jesus' suffering, such as *despised*, *rejected*, and *sorrow*. Discuss the meaning of the words as they relate to Jesus' suffering. As verses 4-6 are read have the children identify words that describe our sin, such as *infirmities*, *transgressions*, and *iniquities*.

■ Conclusion

Summary

(HOLY 45, Uzziah 37, Isaiah 36, cross 43; word strip SIN)

God is holy *(place 45 on the board)* and wants His children to be holy in everything they do. Let's say our memory verse together. *(Do so.)*

Today we heard about two men who learned to obey God's Word and live holy lives when they were young. Who were they? *(Encourage response throughout.)* Yes, Uzziah and Isaiah *(add 37, 36)*. Which one chose to sin *(add SIN)* by deliberately ignoring God's holy laws? Yes, Uzziah had stopped trusting God to help him be holy in the way he lived. How did God punish him? Yes, he got leprosy and was never allowed to enter the temple again.

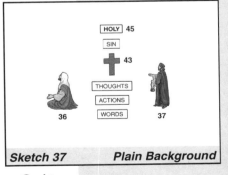

Sketch 37   **Plain Background**

When Isaiah went into the temple to worship God and saw God in a vision, what did he realize about himself? *(Point to the word SIN after a child answers.)* Yes, he was a sinner and deserved to die. Isaiah confessed his sin and received God's forgiveness; he was pure and clean before God. Isaiah continued to obey God and to live in A

Holy Way before the people. God was able to use him in a wonderful way to warn the people about their sinful behavior and of God's judgment if they would not turn to Him. He prophesied about the one who would come in the future and die for their sins *(add 43)*. Who was it? *(Response)* Yes, the Lord Jesus Christ.

Application

(Word strips THOUGHTS, ACTIONS, WORDS, list of underlined statements read in Introduction, marker)

God wants us to be holy in the way we live—in our THOUGHTS, ACTIONS, and WORDS *(add word strips as words are mentioned)*. Do you remember the statements I read to you in the beginning of our lesson? Let's look at the ones that describe holy ways of living. *(Display the list of statements that describe holy ways of living. Encourage the children to think of other ways they can show holy living in their thoughts, words, and actions, and add them to the list.)* ▲#11

▲ **Option #11**

Print the three words on separate cards and have three children hold them as they are discussed. Then divide the class into three groups and have each group take a word and come up with a situation to illustrate or act out for the others in the class to observe. Have the others then tell what the *holy* way would be in each situation. The children may act out or illustrate each situation.

Is holy living easy? *(Response)* No, we can't do it on our own; we need God to help us. We must first recognize that He is the only one who can make us holy. He does this when we understand that Jesus *(point to 43)* suffered and died for our sins and receive Him as our Savior. He forgives our sins and gives us eternal life so that we can live with Him forever.

Then we must understand that He has given us the Holy Spirit to help us be holy in the way we live. The Holy Spirit helps us to obey God's Word so that we will be different from others in our thoughts, words, and actions.

As you looked at our list today, did you see something there that reminded you that you are having a hard time being holy in the way you think, act, or talk? Remember you can trust God to help you.

Response Activity

Invite any who have never received the Lord Jesus as Savior to take that step now. Give them opportunity to speak with you or a helper during this time or after class.

Give the children an opportunity to pray silently, telling God they are going to trust Him to help them be holy in their thoughts, actions, and words. Then distribute the **"God's Holy Way" handouts** *and the small adhesive-backed magnets to attach to the back of them. Encourage the children to place them where they will be reminded of their decision to trust God to help them.*

🖐 TAKE-HOME ITEMS

Distribute **memory verse tokens for 1 Peter 1:15** *and* **Bible Study Helps for Lesson 5.**

Josiah Repairs the Temple
Theme: The Bible Way

Lesson 6

❁ BEFORE YOU BEGIN...

Respect is a lost commodity in our society. Young children call their elders by their first names. Leaders are cartooned. Property is littered and defaced by graffiti. Even God is blasphemed and defamed without giving it a thought. Obedience and respect go together. If parents, police, and teachers are not respected, they most likely will not be obeyed. When this spills over to God and His Word, we are in deep trouble indeed.

In a period of national decline King Josiah was brought the recently found Book of the Law. When he heard its words of judgment, he took them so seriously that he led his kingdom into national mourning, repentance, and revival.

Teacher, how are you modeling one who respects the Word of God? Your children need to see you awed by God's book and fleshing out its life principles. They need to catch your love for God's Word and your enthusiasm to read it daily. Your goal? For each child to affirm: "The Bible is God's Book. I am privileged to have my own copy. I will treat it respectfully, read it regularly, and obey it well." *"But on this one will I look: on him who is poor and of a contrite spirit, and who trembles at My word"* (Isaiah 66:2, NKJV).

☞ AIM:

That the children may

- Know that those who follow God's Way value the Bible.
- Respond by reading and obeying the Bible and treating it with respect.

📖 SCRIPTURE: 2 Kings 21:1–23:25; 2 Chronicles 34:1–35:19

♥ MEMORY VERSE: Psalm 119:33

Teach me, O Lord, the way of thy statutes; and I shall keep it unto the end. (KJV)

Teach me, O Lord, to follow your decrees; then I will keep them to the end. (NIV)

📁 MATERIALS TO GATHER

Visual for Psalm 119:33 from *Bible Verses Visualized*
Backgrounds: Review Chart, Plain Background, Palace, Council Room, Courtyard
Figures: R1-R6, R15, R16, 1, 3, 4, 9, 25, 26, 27, 27A, 38, 46, 47, 48(3), 48A, 50, 51, 52, 54, 65(4), 89(GOD)
Token holders & memory verse tokens for Psalm 119:33
Bible Study Helps for Lesson 6
Special:
- *For Bible Content 3:* A scroll made from paper or cloth and tied with a ribbon or yarn
- *For Bible Content 4:* A 4" square of black felt
- *For Response Activity:* A gold sticker for each child
- *For Options:* Additional materials for any options you choose to use

REVIEW CHART

Display the Review Chart with R15 and R16 in place. Have R6 available to use when indicated. Distribute R1-R5 to the children to place on the Chart. Have the child who places the review token there tell about one of the characters in the corresponding lesson and have another child give the memory verse for that lesson. Use the following questions to review Lesson 5.

1. Who is the only one who is completely holy and without sin? *(God)*
2. What does it mean to follow God's holy way—to be holy? *(Receive Jesus as our Savior and trust Him to help us obey Him in our thoughts, actions, and words)*
3. What great prophet lived during King Uzziah's reign? *(Isaiah)*
4. When King Uzziah was following God's holy way, how did God give him success? *(Uzziah had a well-trained army, victory over his enemies, strong defenses, and an irrigation system to water the desert farmland and to provide water for herds of animals.)*
5. How did King Uzziah sin against God? *(He became proud and disobeyed God's law by attempting to burn incense on the altar in the temple.)*
6. How did God punish Uzziah? *(He gave him leprosy.)*
7. What caused Isaiah to see how sinful he and the people of Judah were? *(He saw God and His holiness in a vision.)*
8. How did Isaiah show that he was following God's holy way? *(He admitted he was a sinner and received God's forgiveness; he obeyed God by giving His message to the people of Judah, even though they didn't listen to him.)*
9. Who is the only one who can make us holy? *(Jesus Christ)*

10. What did Isaiah prophesy about Jesus? *(He would be born of a virgin, would live a sinless life, would suffer and die for our sins, and would come back to earth again.)*
11. Give some examples of how we can follow God's holy way today.

The Bible, which includes the words Isaiah wrote, is a very special book. It is the only book that God has given to us, and it is unlike any other book that has ever been written. First of all, it is God's very words to us. Second, it gives us guidance in following God's Way. Who will volunteer to read the name on our road sign today? *(Have a child place R6 on the Chart and read it aloud.)* Since God has given us this book to guide us through life, His way is *The Bible Way*.

♥ MEMORY VERSE

Display the visual for Psalm 119:33.

A man who wanted to follow *The Bible Way* wrote the words of our memory verse. It is found in the book of Psalms. It is a prayer that contains a request and a promise. What did the writer of this Psalm ask God to do? *(Response)* Yes, he asked God to teach him His statutes or decrees. What does this word mean? *(Let the children respond. If you are using the KJV, explain that statute is not statue. Lift the flap for the meaning of the word.)* Statutes means *instructions* or *demands*. Where do we find God's instructions? *(Response)* Yes, in His guidebook, the Bible. It also tells us who God is and how to become a member of His family by receiving the Lord Jesus as our Savior for the forgiveness of sins and the gift of eternal life. Then it tells us how to live as His child as we continue our journey through this life. You can see why it is very important for us to know what God's Word says.

How does God teach us what His Word says? *(Response)* We can read it for ourselves and ask God to help us understand what it means and to show us how to put it into practice in our lives. We can also listen when it is read and explained to us by our parents, Bible teachers, or pastor.

What did the person who wrote these words in our memory verse promise to do? *(Response)* Yes, he promised to *(lift the flap over the word "keep")* obey God's instructions until the end of his life. Because he valued (thought it was important) and appreciated God's Word so much, he recognized that he couldn't live God's Way without obeying what it said. This is true for us too. However, if we ignore God's Word and do not do what it says, we are showing that we do not love God or His Word. We are showing that we want to live our own way instead of God's Way. *(Work on memorizing the verse.)* ▲#1

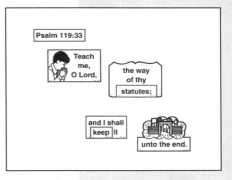

▲ Option #1

Memorizing the verse: Distribute the verse visual pieces to five children. Have the class repeat the words as the children display each piece in the correct order. When the verse is complete, have the class repeat the whole verse. Then distribute the verse pieces to another set of five children. At the signal, have them run to the front of the room and stand in the proper order. Have the rest of the children check to see if the verse visual is in the correct order. Give everyone an opportunity to participate.

📖 BIBLE LESSON OUTLINE

Josiah Repairs the Temple

■ **Introduction**

Bad treatment of a good book

■ **Bible Content**

1. Josiah is crowned king.
2. Josiah chooses God's Way.
3. Josiah hears God's Word.
4. Josiah obeys God's Word.

■ **Conclusion**

Summary

Application
Valuing the Bible

Response Activity
Being challenged to use the Bible Study Helps daily and to respect the Bible

📖 BIBLE LESSON

■ **Introduction**

Bad treatment of a good book

Peter had invited his new friend Johnny to Kid's Klub at church after school. It was to be a special time with games and a special Bible speaker. After Peter stopped at home to pick up his Bible, Johnny started asking questions as they walked to the church.

"What kind of a book is that, Pete?" Johnny asked. "I have never seen it before."

"Oh that is just my Bible. I take it to church all the time," answered Peter.

Johnny was curious, "What is it good for? What do you do with it?"

Peter thought a minute. "Well, it is God's Word, and it tells us all about God and His Son, Jesus, and the things He wants us to do and how to get to heaven."

"Wow," said Johnny, "it must be a special book. I see on its cover that it is even called *Holy*. Do you ever read it?"

"Yes, it is a very special book and we use it at church," answered Peter. "I guess I don't read it much, but I do learn about it in church and at Kids Klub." Johnny wondered why Peter did not bother to read this special book.

Soon they reached the church and joined the other kids. While they were waiting for the leaders to begin the class, some of the boys started tossing their Bibles back and forth to each other. Sometimes they caught the Bibles, but sometimes the Bibles landed on the floor and slid into chairs and the wall. Then right before club began they all tossed their Bibles into a pile on the floor against the wall.

As Johnny sat and watched he thought it was very strange that such a special book was treated like this. He had some books at home that he especially treasured and wouldn't think of throwing around.

Kids Klub was fun and Johnny enjoyed it. When it was time for the story, the leader let several boys help get the Bibles for everyone. Once again Johnny could not understand what he saw. The boys threw the Bibles to the kids, sometimes missing them and allowing the Bibles to crash to the floor. Yet, as the teacher spoke, Johnny heard for the first time some amazing things from that very Bible—how God loved him and sent Jesus to make a way for him to go to heaven someday; how God would forgive his sins because of Jesus. He thought to himself, "Why would anyone treat the Bible so badly when it told such wonderful things about God and made him want to know this God?"

Listen to our story today to find out how the people of Judah treated God's Word. We find this story in 2 Chronicles 34. *(Have the children find the reference and put their bookmarks in place.)*

■ Bible Content

1. Josiah is crowned king.
(2 Kings 21:23-22:2; 2 Chronicles 34:1)

Sketch 38 — Palace

(People 3, 4, 9, 26, Josiah 46)
After King Uzziah died, many kings reigned over Judah. Several of them were evil and did not follow God's Way; they ignored God's Word and chose to worship idols and to lead the people away from the true and living God. One of them even dared to put a statue in the temple.

Amon was one of the evil kings. He was so evil that some of his officials had him killed while he was still a young man *(place 3, 4, 9, 26 on the board)*. His son, Josiah *(add 46)*, was crowned as the next king. Josiah was only eight years old when he began to reign over Judah. How many of you are eight years old? How would you feel if you were crowned a king to rule over a country? *(Response)*

2. Josiah chooses God's Way.
(2 Chronicles 34:2-13)

King Josiah did not follow the evil ways of his father, but instead he chose to follow God's Way. *(Have a child read 2 Chronicles 34:2 aloud.)* The Bible doesn't tell us, but it is possible that Jeremiah the prophet, who lived in Jerusalem at that time, taught him about the true God. We do know that Josiah loved God and began to make

▲ **Option #2**

Use the Map of Divided Kingdom to review the location of the kingdoms and their capital cities. Or make a large map for the floor *(see page xii for methods for enlarging maps)*. Use word strips for JUDAH, JERUSALEM, ISRAEL, and SAMARIA. Add NAPHTALI, located just northwest of The Sea of Galilee, to show the most northern extent of Josiah's reforms. As the children hold the word strips, have them stand at the locations on the map. Have them leave the word strips at the map locations when they return to their seats.

Sketch 39   Council Room

📖 **Note (1)**

The Bible Knowledge Commentary, Old Testament, (Scripture Press Publications, 1985), page 581.

some important decisions about following Him when he was sixteen years old. *(Remove all the figures.)*

(Josiah 47, people 4, Hilkiah 38)
By the time he was twenty years old *(place 47 on the board)*, King Josiah began to lead the people in following God's Way too. He knew they must stop worshiping false gods, and he began to destroy their idols. He enlisted the help of some other men to do this. They destroyed all the idols throughout Judah, starting with Jerusalem, and did the same in parts of Israel as well. They smashed the idols into small pieces and ground them into powder. ▲#2

But King Josiah knew there was another important thing that must be done if the people were going to follow God. The temple had to be repaired so that the people could worship God there. It had not been taken care of for more than fifty years; the people had been too busy worshiping other gods. They forgot about the true God.

Josiah sent his trusted advisers *(remove 47; add 4, 38)* to talk to Hilkiah, the high priest, about overseeing the repair of the temple. They gave him the money that had been collected from the people and brought to the temple for the repairs that were needed. With that money Hilkiah hired carpenters and builders to begin the work. All of the men worked faithfully on the temple until the job was done.

3. Josiah hears God's Word.
 (2 Kings 22:8-20; 2 Chronicles 34:14-28)

(Hilkiah 38, Scroll 27A, Shaphan 27; scroll)
One day Hilkiah *(place 38 on the board)* went into the temple to get the money to pay the workers. While he was there he made an incredible discovery; he found the Book of the Law! *(Place 27A in the hands of 38; show the scroll.)* The words in this book were God's words—the very words God had commanded Moses to write down 800 years earlier for the people of Israel to obey. The Book of the Law is the same as the first five books of the Old Testament in our Bibles—the books of Genesis through Deuteronomy. *(Have the children find these books in their Bibles.)*

The priests had been commanded by God to read the Book of the Law to the people once every seven years. But as the people turned to the worship of idols, they did not want to hear it. They did not want to hear about God's righteous and holy way. It is believed that Josiah's father, Amon, or his grandfather, Manasseh, destroyed many copies of God's Word, as they were seeking to stop the worship of the true and living God. 📖**(1)** To preserve God's Word, the priests hid a copy of it in the temple where it would be safe. But eventually even this copy of God's Word was lost and forgotten for over sixty years.

Hilkiah said to Shaphan *(add 27)*, the king's secretary, "I have found the Book of the Law in the temple of the Lord." Then he gave it to Shaphan.

(Josiah 47, Shaphan 27, scroll 27A, Hilkiah 38, people 3, 4)

Shaphan went to King Josiah with the book *(place 47, 27, 27A on the board)* and said, "We have finished the work that you have given us to do. The temple has been repaired and the workers have been paid. Hilkiah gave me a book that he found in the temple." Then Shaphan began to read from the Book of the Law.

As the king listened he heard God's words for the very first time, "Do not worship any other gods or make any kind of idol" (Exodus 20:3, 4). "Don't turn away from the commands I have given you. If you do not obey the Lord your God, you will be punished greatly" (Deut. 28:14, 15). *(Have several children read the verses.)* ▲#3

Sketch 40   Palace

When Josiah heard God's words, he became very troubled. He realized that the Almighty God of the universe not only meant what He said, but He also had the right to tell them what to do and to punish them for their disobedience. His people and his family had been disobedient to God, and God was angry with them. Josiah never realized how much God hated sin and how terrible God's punishment for sin was until he heard God's Word. He became so upset that he tore his robes and cried.

Then Josiah spoke to Hilkiah *(move 27 to the right side of the board; add 38, 3, 4)* and the others, saying, "We have not obeyed the commands written in this Book of the Law. God is angry with us and He is going to punish us." Then he sent his advisers to Huldah, a godly woman who gave God's message to the people as Isaiah and Jeremiah did, to see what God had to say about the wrong they had done. She told them, "Tell the king that God is going to punish the people of Judah for their disobedience. Since Josiah is sorry for his sins and the sins of his people and wants to make things right before God, this is not going to happen while he is alive."

4. Josiah obeys God's Word.
(2 Kings 23: 1-25; 2 Chronicles 34:29–35:19)

(Josiah 47, people 3, 4, 9, 26, Hilkiah 38, Shaphan 27, scroll 27A)

After King Josiah *(place 47 on the board)* received Huldah's answer, he called all *(add 3, 4, 9, 26, 38)* the leaders, the priests, and the people—young and old—to gather together in Jerusalem. He wanted them to hear what God said and to obey it. Everyone, including the children, stood as the Book of the Law was read. *(Add 27, 27A; show the children how many pages are in the first 5 books of the Old Testament.)* It must have taken a long time, but the people listened. Imagine the leader of our country calling all the people together to read the Bible to them aloud! Find 2 Chronicles 34:31 and we'll read it to see what Josiah promised God. *(Have a child read it.)* Yes, Josiah promised to obey God with

Sketch 41   Courtyard

▲ Option#3

Ahead of time print the words of Exodus 20:34 and Deuteronomy 28:14, 15 on a paper scroll so that it reads from right to left. Have a child open the scroll at the appropriate time in the story and read one or both passages to the class, or divide the larger passage into smaller portions for more children to participate. Have the class stand as they listen to the verses being read. Explain that this is a special way to show respect for God's Word.

Variation: Hide the scroll in a corner of the room before the class begins. Have a child search for the scroll and then read it to the class.

all his heart and with *all* his soul. ▲#4 Then he made the people promise to do the same.

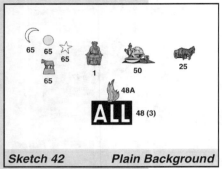

Sketch 42   Plain Background

(Baal 1, sun, moon, stars, calf idol 65[4], dishes 50, ALL 48[3], chariot 25, flame 48A; a 4" square of black felt)

Place the black felt and all the figures, except 48(3), on the board ahead of time. As each item is mentioned, remove it and place it behind the black felt "altar" to indicate that it had been burned up.

It is one thing to make a promise, but it is another thing to keep it. Josiah knew that he could not ignore God's Word. Immediately Josiah took steps to obey God. He ordered the priests to remove everything from the temple that was used in worshiping Baal *(remove 1)* and the sun, moon, and stars *(remove 65[3])*. All the bowls and dishes were removed *(remove 50, 25)* and the chariots were burned up. All the idols *(remove the calf idol 65)* and places of idol worship were completely destroyed throughout the whole country. It was not easy for Josiah to do these things because the people had been worshiping those idols for many years. But God helped Josiah keep his promise. Then Josiah led the people in observing the Passover Feast, which had not been celebrated for many years. ⌂(2) Verse 33 sums up everything Josiah did in obedience to God's Word. *(Read it to the children.)* Josiah completely destroyed *all* the idols from *all (place 48[3] on the felt)* the land, and *all* the people served the Lord. For as long as Josiah lived, the people kept their promise to follow the Lord.

▲ **Option#4**

Using 2 Chronicles 34:29-33, have some children read the parts of the verses where *all* is mentioned, and write them on a piece of newsprint as they are read.

⌂ **Note (2)**

God commanded the Israelites to celebrate the Passover Feast every year at a specific time to commemorate their deliverance from Egypt (Exodus 12:14-20).

■ **Conclusion**

Summary

(Josiah 46, 47, GOD 89, people 4, scroll 54, heart 51, ALL 48[3], idol 1, Bible 52)

Some of the kings of Judah did not value the Word of God. They ignored it and even took measures to destroy it in their desire to stop the worship of God among the people. They did not want to be reminded of God's holy way because they chose to go their own way. They did not want to follow *The Bible Way.*

What king did choose to follow *The Bible Way? (Allow for response throughout.)* Yes, King Josiah. How old was Josiah when he became king? Imagine being a king at eight years old *(place 46 on the board)*! When did he begin making choices about following God's *(add 89)* Way? Sixteen is still young, isn't it *(add 47)*? What was the first thing he did to lead the people *(add 4)* of Judah in following God's Way? Yes, he repaired the temple so they could worship God there. What did Hilkiah find in

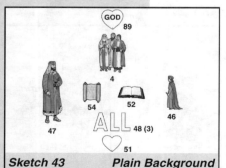

Sketch 43   Plain Background

the temple that had been lost for many years? That's right, he found the Book of the Law *(add 54)*. Why was this book so important? Yes, it was God's Word. What did Josiah promise to do after he heard God's Word read? Yes, he promised to obey it with *all* his heart and *all* his soul *(add 51, 48[3])*. What did Josiah do to show that he was keeping his promise? Yes, and it took courage to remove and to destroy all the idols *(add 1)* throughout the land, along with everything that was used in worshiping them. Josiah valued the Word of God and followed *The Bible Way* the rest of his life. He was a good example of someone who did what our memory verse teaches us to do. Let's say it together. *(Do so.)*

Application

God wants us to value the Bible *(add 52)* too. It is the most important book that has ever been written because it is God's very own words written to us. Since it tells us the absolute truth about God and how we can know Him through receiving His Son as our Savior, we can trust it completely. If we read the Bible and obey what it says, we will become the person God wants us to be—one who follows His way, *The Bible Way*.

Sometimes we don't value the Bible. Oh, we probably wouldn't destroy it as some of the kings of Judah did. But many of us have ignored the Bible by not reading it or listening to what it says, and by not obeying it. And some of us have mistreated the Bible as Peter and his friends did—tossing it around and throwing it on the floor.

If we really value the Bible we will treat it with respect and take good care of it. We will refuse to join in with those who are mistreating it. In fact, we should be willing to speak up and help them see its value. But more importantly, we should value the Bible by reading it and obeying what it says. Are you willing to promise God you will value God's Word by reading it every day?

Response Activity

Distribute copies of the **Bible Study Helps for Lesson 6**. *Review how to use this Bible reading program—reading the assigned passage of Scripture each day and answering the questions. Encourage the children to pray the words of today's memory verse before reading the Bible each day and then obey what God tells them to do. Give each child a gold sticker. Instruct the children to place the sticker inside the front cover of their Bible if they treat God's Word with respect throughout the week.* ▲#5

✍ TAKE-HOME ITEMS

Distribute **memory verse tokens for Psalm 119:33**.

▲ Option #5

Give each child a rectangular-shaped piece of colored construction paper and a marker to make a Bible bookmark. Instruct the children to print their name and the memory verse on their bookmark and to draw an open Bible on it and print the verse reference on the open Bible. Tell them to keep the bookmark in their Bible to remind them to treat God's Word with respect, to read it, and to obey what God tells them to do.

Jeremiah Delivers God's Warning
Theme: A Witnessing Way

Lesson 7

❋ BEFORE YOU BEGIN...

Ever since the risen Christ declared, "You shall be My witnesses," His followers have been called to leave their comfort zone and venture into the dangerous arena of sharing the gospel with others. For many, leaving their comfort zone means being fearful about what to say and how they will be received, which at worst means being laughed at or rejected. But for many more it has meant suffering persecution to the point of death.

Even 600 years before Christ, the prophet Jeremiah struggled with having to leave his comfort zone to deliver God's message to an obstinate people, who accused him of treason and sought to kill him.

Teaching this lesson could have a negative effect on your children: "If that's what happened to Jeremiah, I'm certainly not going to risk *my* life for the gospel; let someone else do it." On the other hand, God can impress them with the benefits of obeying His command to witness. Bathe all your children in prayer as you prepare them to unashamedly let their family, peers, and neighbors know about their wonderful Lord Jesus, by lip and by life. *"Do not fear, nor be afraid; have I not told you...? You are My witnesses..."* (Isaiah 44:8, NKJV).

☞ AIM:

That the children may

- Know that God wants His children to witness about the Lord Jesus Christ and will help them do it.

- Respond by planning a way to witness to someone this week and trusting God to help them.

📖 SCRIPTURE: Jeremiah 1:1-10; 5:15-19; 7:1-3; 20:1-11; 22:1-5; 25:10-12; 33:14-16; 36:1-32; 37:11-21; 38:1-13; 39:15-18

♥ MEMORY VERSE: Proverbs 3:6

In all thy ways acknowledge him, and he shall direct thy paths. (KJV)
In all your ways acknowledge him, and he will make your paths straight. (NIV)

MATERIALS TO GATHER

Visual for Proverbs 3:6 from *Bible Verses Visualized*
Backgrounds: Review Chart, Plain Background, Plain Interior, City Street
Figures: R1-R7, R15, R16, 4, 5, 8, 9, 10, 12, 14, 15, 26, 36, 36A, 53, 54, 55, 56, 57, 87
Token holders & memory verse tokens for Proverbs 3:6
Bible Study Helps for Lesson 7
Special:
- *For Bible Content 1:* Map of Divided Kingdom
- *For Bible Content 2 & Summary:* Jeremiah 1:7, 8 visual
- *For Application:* Newsprint & marker or chalkboard & chalk
- *For Response Activity:* 4" x 6" cards, pencils, response list from the Application, *Child of God* tracts, invitations to your class or to an upcoming event
- *For Options:* Additional materials for any options you choose to use
- *Note: To prepare the Jeremiah 1:7, 8 visual,* use a marker to print the verses on a large sheet of newsprint or chart paper.

 REVIEW CHART

Display the Review Chart with R15 and R16 in place. Place R1-R6 in mixed-up order on the open side of the Chart. Have the children work in pairs, one child choosing a review token and placing it on the Chart and the other child saying the corresponding verse.

Review the highlights of Lessons 1-6 by playing the game below. Encourage the children to make up some "I'm thinking of ..." descriptions and call on someone to answer. Have R7 ready to use when indicated.

I'm thinking of
1. someone who gave God's message to King Ahab. *(Elijah)*
2. someone who was healed from leprosy because he obeyed what Elisha told him to do. *(Naaman)*
3. what God used to save Jonah from death. *(Big fish)*
4. the people who tried to get their god to burn up their sacrifice. *(Prophets of Baal)*
5. someone who caused Isaiah to feel sinful when he went into the temple. *(God)*
6. something the high priest found when the workmen were repairing the temple. *(Book of the Law)*
7. what God used to feed Elijah in the desert. *(Ravens)*
8. the verse that tells the only way we can come to God. *(John 14:6)*

Today we are going to see that God's Way is *A Witnessing Way*. *(Place R7 on the Chart.)* That simply means that we have the

responsibility to tell others about God and what He has done for us. Our memory verse today instructs us to do this.

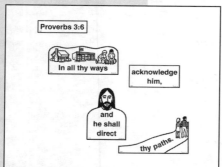

♥ MEMORY VERSE

Use the visual to teach Proverbs 3:6. Display the reference and first two visual pieces of the verse and read the words together.

What does God tell us to do? *(Response)* Yes, we are to acknowledge Him. Acknowledge means to *own up to* or *give recognition to*. There are two ways to do this. First, we are to own up to the fact that He is our God—the one who has saved us from being punished for our sins, because we have believed on the Lord Jesus Christ as our Savior. Second, we are to recognize His right to guide our lives every day. We can trust Him to show us what He wants us to do and to help us live for Him. As we see how God helped us, we can *acknowledge* Him by telling others what He has done. That is what witnessing is all about—telling others about our God and His Son, Jesus Christ, and what He has done for us.

When are we to acknowledge God? *(Response)* Yes, in all our ways or in everything we do. Sometimes it is difficult to acknowledge God to others. They may ignore what we say, make fun of us, get angry, or even choose to stop being our friends.

When we acknowledge God by witnessing about Him, He promises to help us. *(Display the rest of the verse and read it.)* He promises to direct our paths or make them straight. That means that He will help us overcome some of the obstacles that make it hard for us to acknowledge Him. He is the one who will give us the right words to say. He will give us the courage to speak up for Him when we are afraid. He will help us show kindness to those who get angry with us when we try to talk with them about Jesus. Even the difficulties we may experience give us an opportunity to acknowledge God by demonstrating His love to others in the way we respond to them. *(Work on memorizing the verse.)* ▲#1

▲ Option#1

Memorizing the verse: Have the children do the following actions for each phrase of the verse as they recite it. Begin reciting it with the verse visual displayed. Next, remove the visual and repeat the verse. Then do only the actions. Finally, repeat the verse with the actions. (The NIV words are in parentheses.)

Proverbs 3:6
In all
  Spread arms wide open.
thy ways (your ways)
  Point to yourself and then downward and out as if pointing to a path.
acknowledge him
  Salute and point upward.
and he
  Point upward again.
shall direct thy paths (will make your paths straight)
  Point downward toward feet and walk forward.

Variation: Divide the children into pairs; have each pair create actions for the verse and then present their actions as they say the verse to the class.

📖 BIBLE LESSON OUTLINE

Jeremiah Delivers God's Warning

■ **Introduction**

  Rebekah's invitation

■ **Bible Content**

  1. Jeremiah is chosen to be God's prophet.
  2. Jeremiah gives God's message to the people.

3. Jeremiah is punished for giving God's message.
   a. In the stocks.
   b. In the prison.
   c. In the cistern.
4. Jeremiah writes God's Word on a scroll.

■ Conclusion

Summary

Application
Being willing to trust God to help us witness to others

Response Activity
Planning a way to witness to someone this week

📖 BIBLE LESSON

■ Introduction

Rebekah's invitation

Rebekah was nervous. Today was *the* day! She was going to ask two of her friends, Naomi and Abigail, to go to church with her. She had been praying for a long time that they would come to know Jesus as their Savior. Then one day her mom gave her a good idea. "Why not invite the girls to go with you to the kids' meetings at church during spring break?" asked her Mom.

"That is a great idea!" said Rebekah. She wanted to talk to them about Jesus, but she felt scared. This seemed easier, and it would be fun to have them go with her. So she made a special invitation for each of them. As they walked home from school Rebekah prayed silently for help and courage, and then she asked, "Would you like to come with me to some special kids' meetings during our break from school? It is coming up in two weeks; I thought it would be fun for us to go." Then she held her breath, waiting to see what they would say. Were they going to laugh or get angry or agree to come?

"Is it at your church?" Abigail asked.

"Yes it is. Here are the details," she said as she handed each of them an invitation and waited while they read it.

All of a sudden Abigail started to laugh as she said, "What a silly idea for us to spend our time off from school going to church." When they arrived at her house, she gave the invitation back to Rebekah.

Naomi didn't say anything. She did put the invitation in her pocket and kept walking. Before going into the house, she said, "Maybe I will go, but I have to ask my mom first. I will let you know tomorrow."

"Sure thing!" replied Rebekah. She kept on walking toward home, feeling very discouraged. She really thought the girls would be excited about having something fun to do that week.

In our lesson today we are going to meet a man who experienced the same kind of discouragement that Rebekah felt. Even though people became angry with him and hurt him when he spoke to them about God, Jeremiah was faithful in being a witness for Him. *(Have the children find the first chapter of Jeremiah and place their bookmarks there.)*

■ Bible Content

1. Jeremiah is chosen to be God's prophet. (Jeremiah 1:1-10) ◻(1) ▲#2

Sketch 44 — Plain Interior

◻ **Note (1)**

Because the book of Jeremiah is not arranged chronologically, the lesson follows a thematic format rather than a strictly chronological one.

▲ **Option#2**

Using Jeremiah 1:1-10, give God's and Jeremiah's parts to two children and have another child read the narration. Instruct them to read their parts with expression, the way the words might have been spoken. Instruct the other children to follow in their Bibles, or print out the verses as a script for all to follow.

(Map of Divided Kingdom; man 14, woman 8, Jeremiah 12, 15)

Just three miles east of Jerusalem in the little town of Anathoth (An'-a-thoth; *indicate on the map*) lived one of the temple priests and his wife *(place 14, 8 on the board)*. Into their home was born a son whom they named Jeremiah. Jeremiah *(add 12)* grew up during the reign of King Josiah and lived during the reigns of the last four kings of Judah. *(Remove 8, 12, 14; add 15.)*

Jeremiah was just a teenager when God told him he was to be one of His prophets. A prophet is a person chosen by God to give His message to the people. God said to him, "Jeremiah, I knew all about you before you were born, and I have planned a special job for you to do for Me. You are to be a prophet to the nations."

How would you feel if God said this to you? *(Response)* Perhaps you would be amazed and afraid that you couldn't be a good messenger for God. That is exactly how Jeremiah felt. He answered, "O God, I am only a child and I do not know how to speak. I don't know what to say."

God said to him, "Don't say, 'I am just a child.' You are going to go everywhere I send you and say everything I tell you to say. Don't be afraid. I am with you and will help you and take care of you." Then God touched Jeremiah's mouth and said, "See, I have put My words in your mouth, and you will give My message to nations and kingdoms."

2. Jeremiah gives God's message to the people. (Jeremiah 5:15-19; 7:1-3; 22:1-5)

Sketch 45 — City Street

(Jeremiah 1:7, 8 visual; Jeremiah 53, people 4, 8, 9, 10, 26)

After King Josiah died, the last four kings to rule in Judah led the people to return to worshiping idols. They refused to listen to God's Word and obey it. Their sins became so great that God could no longer keep from punishing them.

But first God sent Jeremiah to give them another warning. God told him to say, "You have sinned against the Lord. You have turned away from His love and followed after false gods. If you turn back to God now, He will care for you and forgive you. But if you refuse to listen and do what God says, a very strong nation from the north is going to come against you. They will take your land and take you as prisoners back to their country."

God told Jeremiah to go to Jerusalem and stand by the temple gate *(place 53 on the board)* and give His message to all the people *(add 4, 8, 9, 10, 26)* who passed by. Then God told him to go to the palace and speak directly to the king.

None of the people wanted to hear about their sins or of God's judgment. So they became very angry with Jeremiah and threatened to kill him if he didn't stop preaching to them. ▲#3

But Jeremiah did not stop; he faithfully gave God's message to the people. He had God's promise. Do you remember what it was? *(Hold up the Jeremiah 1:7, 8 visual and have the children read it together.)* Yes, God told Jeremiah He would be with him and help him.

3. Jeremiah is punished for giving God's message. (Jeremiah 20:1-11; 37:11-21, 38:1-13; 39:15-18)

(Jeremiah 55, 53, 56, captain 87)

a. In the stocks.

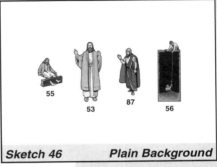

Sketch 46   Plain Background

Jeremiah continued to warn the people of God's punishment, but they ignored the warning and continued to worship their idols. They also began to make Jeremiah's life difficult. They did not like what he said to them.

One day when the temple priest heard Jeremiah's message, he had Jeremiah beaten and put in the stocks *(place 55 on the board)* near the gate at the temple. Because his feet were locked in place in a wooden frame, he couldn't move his legs or stand up. He was forced to sit there until someone came and freed him. As the people passed by him they laughed and made fun of him and called him a traitor.

The next day the priest set Jeremiah free, thinking Jeremiah would probably be afraid of him now and wouldn't talk to the people anymore. But Jeremiah *(add 53)* stood up boldly and said to him, "The Lord says that this entire city is going to be captured by the king of Babylon, and the people are going to be taken to Babylon as captives. You and all your family are going there too. You are going to die there because you have been telling lies to the people." The priest had been telling the people that Jeremiah was not telling the truth.

Jeremiah became so discouraged that he wanted to stop giving God's message to the people. He felt as though God had let him down. But Jeremiah could not stop obeying God. He complained, "When I decided to stop speaking, God's Word was like a fire burning in my heart. I could not stop speaking His words." So Jeremiah kept going, trusting God was with him and would protect him.

b. In the prison.

Sometime later the Babylonian army came and camped right outside the city walls. One day when Jeremiah was trying to leave the

▲ Option#3

To reinforce the theme that Jeremiah was committed to speaking God's message even when it was hard, ask the children each time Jeremiah is faced with a challenge (threatened, beaten and put into stocks, beaten and put into prison, and put into a cistern), "Did Jeremiah stop sharing God's message?" Then have the children respond, "I must keep sharing the message."

city to take care of some family business, the captain of the guard *(add 87)* in Jerusalem stopped him and said, "You are deserting to the Babylonians."

"No, I am not," replied Jeremiah, trying to defend himself.

The captain of the guard would not listen to him. Instead, he arrested Jeremiah and brought him before the officials. They were very angry with Jeremiah and had him beaten and thrown into a dark, cold underground prison. What a terrible place for Jeremiah to be! But God was with Jeremiah even in that terrible place.

Then the king sent for Jeremiah so that he could speak to him privately. Jeremiah told him that he was going to be captured by the Babylonians. Then he pleaded with the king, "Don't send me back to the dungeon or I will die there." The king gave orders for Jeremiah to be placed in the courtyard of the guard and given bread to eat every day.

c. In the cistern.

But even while Jeremiah was locked in the courtyard, he continued to speak God's message to the people and the king. He said, "Don't fight against the Babylonians; God is allowing this as a punishment. If you surrender without fighting, it will go well for you."

Some of the officials said to the king, "This man is a traitor; he should be put to death. He is discouraging the soldiers and the people by what he is saying. He does not want good things to happen to them; he wants to ruin them."

The king answered, "I am not able to do anything to stop you. Do whatever you want with him." They took Jeremiah *(add 56)* and lowered him by ropes into a cistern in the courtyard. A cistern was like a well with no water in it—just deep thick mud. Jeremiah sank down into it when he reached the bottom. Then they left him alone to die of thirst and hunger.

But Jeremiah was not alone. God had not forgotten or left him. He already had someone ready to rescue him. His name was Ebed-Melech, an Ethiopian official who was working in the palace. When Ebed heard what had been done to Jeremiah, he went right to the king and said, "My master and king, your officials have treated Jeremiah the prophet badly. They have thrown him into a cistern where he will starve to death."

Immediately the king gave Ebed permission to take thirty men with him to get Jeremiah out of the cistern. Can you imagine Jeremiah's relief and joy when he heard Ebed say he had come to rescue him? Ebed tied some ropes to a bunch of old clothes and rags and lowered them down to Jeremiah. "Put these rags under your arms," he said, "so that the ropes won't hurt you as the men pull you out." Jeremiah did as he said, and the men pulled him out. After that, Jeremiah was kept under guard in the courtyard of the prison and given freshly baked bread every day. ▲#4

God was with Jeremiah and took care of him during this difficult time. Later, when the Babylonians entered Jerusalem to capture it,

▲ **Option #4**

Have the children act out the scene of Ebed-Melech and the men helping Jeremiah out of the cistern. Provide a rope and some rags for them to use.

God saved Ebed's life because he had helped Jeremiah. *(Remove 55, 56, 87; leave 53 on the board.)*

4. Jeremiah writes God's Word on a scroll. ▲#5
(Jeremiah 36:1-32; 25:10-12; 33:14-16)

(Scribe 36, desk 36A, king 5, fire 57, scroll 54)
One day God said to Jeremiah *(move 53 to the left side of the board)*, "Jeremiah, take a scroll and write down all the words I have told you concerning Israel, Judah, and all the surrounding nations from the reign of King Josiah until now. When the people hear how I am going to punish them for their evil ways, maybe they will turn from their sin to Me. Then I will forgive them."

With the help of Baruch (Ba-rōōk'), the scribe, *(add 36, 36A)* Jeremiah obeyed God's instructions. Jeremiah spoke the words aloud that God had given to him, and Baruch wrote them down on the scroll. It must have taken a long time to write it all by hand. When they had finished, Jeremiah sent Baruch to read the words to the people at the gate of the temple.

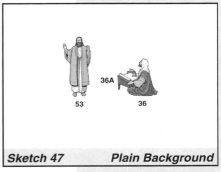

Sketch 47   Plain Background

Then Baruch was invited to read the scroll to the king's officials in the royal palace. When they heard about the punishment God was going to bring on the people because of their sins, they were really afraid. They said, "We must tell the king about this!" Then they said to Baruch, "You and Jeremiah must go and hide; don't let anyone know where you are."

Then the men placed the scroll in a nearby room and went to the king and reported what they had heard. *(Remove 53, 36, 36A; add 5.)* The king sent for the scroll *(add 54)* and had one of his assistants read it to him as he sat by a fire *(add 57)* to keep himself warm. As he listened, the king took a knife and cut off the columns of words as they were read and threw them into the fire. He did this to the entire scroll *(remove all the figures)*, even though some of his servants pleaded with him not to do it.

Can you imagine someone cutting up the pages of your Bible? *(Hold up your Bible.)* What would this show about someone who would want to destroy God's Word? *(Response)* Yes, that person would have no love or respect for God and His Word. The king did not seem to care about God or fear Him. He gave an order to some of his men, "Go find Jeremiah and Baruch and arrest them." But no one could find them because God had hidden them.

God spoke to Jeremiah *(add 53)* again, "Take another scroll *(add 36, 36A)* and write down all the words that were in the first scroll. Tell the king that I am going to punish him and his family and officials: no one from his family is going to sit on the throne again."

God gave him the words to write down again—words of warning and words of hope for the future. God said he was going to bring His people back to the land after being taken captive into Babylon. He kept this promise seventy years later. He told them that God's Son

▲ Option#5

As you tell the story have the children act out the following events involving Jeremiah, Baruch, and the king: writing God's message on a scroll, reading the message to the people and then to the king's officials, delivering the scroll to the king, and the king listening to the reading and cutting up the scroll.

was going to come to earth and reign as king. That has not happened yet, but we know God is going to keep this promise, too. His Words are preserved in the book of Jeremiah in our Bibles for us to read today. As we read it we are warned about sin and blessed by God's promise of hope for the future.

Jeremiah was a faithful witness for God throughout his life as a prophet. Even though he faced great difficulties, he never stopped giving God's message to the people, and God never stopped helping Jeremiah to acknowledge Him to others.

■ Conclusion

Summary

(Jeremiah 1:7, 8 visual)
Jeremiah was a great example of one who lived out the truth in Proverbs 3:6. Let's say it together. *(Do so.)* What do we call someone who acknowledges God to others? *(Encourage response throughout.)* Yes, a witness. How did Jeremiah witness for God? Yes, he told the people what he heard God say to him. Was it easy for Jeremiah to give God's message to the people? No, but he was faithful in giving God's message even when he was treated badly. How was he able to be a witness for God when he was being treated so badly? Yes, he trusted God's promise to be with him and to help him to not be afraid. *(Show Jeremiah 1:7, 8 visual as a reminder of God's promise.)* In what ways did God keep His promise to Jeremiah and help him? *(Add to the children's responses any of the following answers they do not give: God gave Jeremiah courage to speak words that no one wanted to hear; He helped him to not be afraid when he was in prison or in the stocks; He sent a man to save him from death in the cistern; He provided Baruch to help him write down God's words; He caused the king's men to warn him to hide from the king.)*

Application

(Newsprint & marker or chalkboard & chalk)
God wants His children to be His witnesses to others. We are to tell others what Jesus did for us—that He forgave our sins and made us part of His family when we received Him as our Savior. We are to tell them how powerful He is and how He helps us day by day as we trust Him.

Being a witness for Jesus can include more than speaking to people about receiving Jesus as their Savior. In the story at the beginning of the lesson, Rebekah used another way to witness. What did she do? *(Response)* Yes, she invited her friends to go to meetings with her where they could hear about Jesus. She wanted them to come to Jesus, but she just wasn't ready to tell them at that time, and perhaps they were not ready to listen.

What are some ways you can be a witness? *(Use a marker to write the children's responses on a sheet of newsprint. Suggest the following if necessary: Talk to your friends about Jesus while you are playing; invite a friend to Sunday school, Bible Club, or a special church event; show by your words and actions that you are letting the Lord control your life; obey your parents and those in charge; give someone a tract that explains how to become a Christian.)* ▲#6

Perhaps, like Rebekah, you have had the experience of having someone make fun of you or get angry because you tried to be a witness for God. It is not always going to be easy. Perhaps Rebekah thought God had not helped her. What do you think? *(Response)* Yes, God did help her. He gave her courage to speak to her friends and give them the invitations. Even though one girl refused and the other did not give her an answer right away, Rebekah did invite them to go to the meetings with her. Now she had to trust God to work in the hearts of her friends to want to go with her.

Can you think of someone who does not believe in Jesus—maybe someone in your family or at school or in your neighborhood? Are you willing to trust God to help you be a witness to that person even if it is hard—even if you are rejected and treated badly, as Jeremiah was?

Response Activity

Remind the children that they cannot be a witness for Jesus if they have never received Him as their Savior. Invite any who want to receive the Lord Jesus as Savior to speak with you after class.

Distribute 4" x 6" cards and pencils. Ask the children to think of someone they can witness to this week and to write the person's name on the card. Display the list of ways to witness you made earlier. Instruct them to decide how they will witness and to write their idea on the card. Ask the children if they are willing to witness even if they are rejected and persecuted. Remind them that God will help them be a witness. Then encourage them to put their card in a place at home where they will be reminded of their decision to witness this week. Emphasize the importance of their praying for the person they have selected and of trusting God to help them. ▲#7

For those who wish to use them, provide "Child of God" tracts and invitations to your next class or to an upcoming event. Close in prayer by giving them an opportunity to pray out loud or silently, asking God for His help in witnessing this week. ◰(2)

Be sure to allow time next week for the children to share their witnessing experiences. Be prepared to deal with both positive and negative responses the children share.

✍ TAKE-HOME ITEMS

*Distribute the **memory verse tokens for Proverbs 3:6** and **Bible Study Helps for Lesson 7.***

▲ **Option#6**

Prepare flashcards from poster board or construction paper by using a broad-tip marker to write a witnessing idea on each card. As each one is mentioned give it to a child to hold in front of the class or display it on a wall or bulletin board. Have several blank cards ready for additional ideas children may have.

▲ **Option#7**

Provide construction paper, stickers, pictures, crayons, markers, scissors, and glue sticks for the children to make invitations to give to special friends as they ask them to come to next week's class.

◰ **Note (2)**

You will greatly encourage your children to witness if you participate in the Response Activity yourself.

God's People Are Taken Captive
Theme: The Way of Life

Lesson

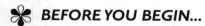

8

❧ BEFORE YOU BEGIN...

Life can be very cruel and exacting when it comes to getting what we deserve. On the other hand, there is a definite trend for people to try to escape responsibility for what they do, especially when they do something wrong. Children have been greatly influenced by this trend and are using it for their own advantage. The result? There is little deterrent to wrongdoing; children know that even if they get caught, they can probably get out of it.

But it's not so in God's economy. In today's lesson God's people finally received the punishment they deserved for failing to return to God. "The soul that sins shall die" (Ezekiel 18:20) and "The wages of sin is death" (Romans 6:23) remind us that God, the righteous judge, makes no mistakes; no guilty person will be exonerated. And were it not for God's marvelous grace in providing salvation, we would all be justly under condemnation.

Your children need to know that there are consequences when they sin, even if they are Christians, and that God has made a way for sinning Christians to be forgiven and restored to fellowship with Him. *"He has not dealt with us according to our sins, nor punished us according to our iniquities" (Psalm 103:10, NKJV).*

☞ AIM:

That the children may

- Know that there are consequences to the wrong choices they make in life, but God has the power to help them make right choices.
- Respond by choosing God's way of life and depending on the Holy Spirit to help them make right choices daily.

📖 SCRIPTURE: Exodus 20:3, 4; 2 Kings 17:1-23; 23:36–25:21; Jeremiah 25:11-13; 29:11-14; 37:8-10; 38:17-21; 39:13, 14

♥ MEMORY VERSE: Proverbs 3:6

Thus saith the Lord, Behold, I set before you the way of life, and the way of death. (KJV)

This is what the Lord says: See, I am setting before you the way of life and the way of death. (NIV)

📁 MATERIALS TO GATHER

Visual for Jeremiah 21:8 from *Bible Verses Visualized*
Backgrounds: Review Chart, Plain Background, Old Testament Map II
Figures: R1-R8, R15, R16, 1, 9, 16, 18(2), 45, 50, 53, 54, 61, 62, 63, 64, 65(4), 66A, 66B, 66C, 71
Token holders & memory verse tokens for Jeremiah 21:8
Bible Study Helps for Lesson 8
Special:
- *For Introduction:* "STOP Sign" visual; word strips CHOICES, CONSEQUENCES
- *For Bible Content 2:* A current world map; word strips CHOICES, CONSEQUENCES
- *For Bible Content 3:* A current world map; word strips DIFFERENT, PRISONERS, 70 YEARS, SIN, CHOICES, CONSEQUENCES, HOPE
- *For Application:* Print the following titles on chart paper: Verse, Obey, Consequences for Disobedience. Print the following verse references under Verse: Ephesians 6:1, 2, Ephesians 4:32, and Ephesians 4:29. *(See Sketch 52 on page 88.)*
- *For Response Activity:* "I Choose" handouts, pencils
- *For Options:* Additional materials for any options you choose to use
- *Note: Follow the instructions on page xii to enlarge the "STOP Sign" visual (pattern P-6 on page 169) on red paper, and to prepare the "I Choose" handouts (pattern P-16 on page 174).*

REVIEW CHART

Display the Review Chart with R15 and R16 in place. Have R8 ready to use when indicated. Distribute R1-R7 to individual children or place the tokens in mixed-up-order on a table for individual children to choose. Allow the children to come one at a time in any order and place their review token in the proper space on the Chart and then tell the meaning of the theme on the token. Use the following questions to review Lesson 7.

1. What does it mean to be a witness for Jesus Christ? *(A witness is someone who tells others about God and what He has done for him or her.)*
2. When Jeremiah was just a young man, what did God tell him he was going to do? *(God told Jeremiah that he was going to be a prophet to nations and kingdoms.)*
3. What made it difficult for Jeremiah to keep on telling God's message? *(The people became angry and tried to kill him.)*

4. How did God rescue Jeremiah from the cistern? *(An Ethiopian official got permission from the king to get him out of the cistern.)*
5. Recite Proverbs 3:6 and tell what it means.
6. How was Jeremiah an example of Proverbs 3:6? *(He gave God's message to the people, even though they did not want to hear it; he did not give up even when he was treated cruelly. God kept His promises to Jeremiah and helped him through the hard times.)*
7. Tell one way you can acknowledge God in your life today.

God has made us with a mind to think and reason and with a will to make choices. Can you think of some choices you made today? *(Let the children respond. As time permits, respond to those choices mentioned.)* You probably chose when to get up this morning, what food to eat for breakfast, and the clothes you wore to school today. All of us make choices many times a day—our friends, the TV programs we watch, computer games we play, and, more importantly, whether or not we will be obedient.

Our memory verse and lesson today remind us that those who choose God's Way choose *The Way of Life*. *(Have a child place R8 on the Chart.)*

♥ MEMORY VERSE

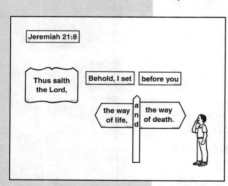

Display the visual for Jeremiah 21:8. Have the children find it in their Bibles.

Jeremiah told the people living in Jerusalem to make a choice. Let's read our verse together to find out what it was. *(Have those with different versions read the verse aloud if time permits.)* What was the choice? *(Response)* Yes, they had to choose between life and death. This was a choice between physical life and death. If they chose to cooperate with God's plan and obey Him, they would live; but if they refused to cooperate, they would die. We will learn more about this choice and its consequences later in our lesson.

There is a more important choice that each one of us must make. It is a choice between spiritual life and death. If we refuse to accept Jesus as Savior and the only way to God, we are choosing the way of spiritual death. This means we will be separated from God forever when our life on earth is finished. But if we choose God's way of life by receiving the Lord Jesus Christ as our Savior from sin, we know we will live forever with Him in heaven someday. When we make this choice, God the Holy Spirit comes to live in us, and then we have His power within us to help us make right choices every day. *(Work on memorizing the verse.)* ▲#1

▲ Option #1

Memorizing the verse: Display the verse visual. Have the children repeat the verse together. Choose a child to remove one visual piece and hand it to another child. Then have another child say the verse without looking at the visual piece

(Continued)

📖 BIBLE LESSON OUTLINE

God's People Are Taken Captive

■ **Introduction**

Obeying the STOP sign

■ **Bible Content**

1. God's people worship other gods.
2. God punishes Israel.
   a. The people reject God and His warnings.
   b. The Assyrians take Israel into captivity.
3. God punishes Judah.
   a. Judah becomes unfaithful to God.
   b. The Babylonians take Judah into captivity.
   c. God gives Judah hope for the future.

■ **Conclusion**

Summary

Application
Recognizing there are consequences to the wrong choices we make in life

Response Activity
Choosing God's way of life and depending on the Holy Spirit to help them make right choices

📖 BIBLE LESSON

■ **Introduction**

Obeying the STOP sign

("STOP Sign" visual; word strips CHOICES, CONSEQUENCES)
When a driver of a car sees this sign *(have a child hold up the "STOP sign" visual)*, what is that driver supposed to do? *(Response)* Yes, the driver is to stop the car where the STOP sign is located. Why do drivers have to obey it? *(Response)* Yes, it is the law for all drivers and it will help protect people from accidents if they obey the sign. Drivers have a choice to make when they see this sign—to obey or not to obey. *(Place CHOICES on the board or have a child hold it up next to the STOP sign.)* ▲#2

What happens when a driver does not obey this sign? *(Response)* There is a consequence *(add CONSEQUENCES)* for not obeying this law. What may that consequence be? *(Response)* Yes, the driver may be stopped by a policeman and made to pay a fine; or a worse consequence, someone may be injured or killed.

---

that was removed. Continue with this procedure until all the visual pieces have been removed. When all the pieces have been removed, have everyone repeat the verse together. Then have the children who are holding the visuals place them in the correct order. Have the rest of the class check to see if the visuals are in the correct order. Remove all the visuals and have the children say the verse together one last time.

Variation: Have each child or a small group of children make up their own verse visual. Distribute paper, crayons or markers, and scissors. Encourage the children to be creative and to check their work, making sure that all parts of the verse are correct. If the children are working alone, let them take their visual home and use it to review the verse.

▲ Option#2

Make CHOICES and CONSEQUENCES signs from card stock or poster board for the children to hold up along with the STOP sign. Make the CHOICES sign an octagonal shape like the STOP sign as a reminder to stop and make the right choice. You may make the CONSEQUENCES sign a starburst or another shape of your choosing. Tape a small dowel or paint stick to each sign for the children to hold.

Consequences are the results of choices we make; they can be good or bad. Do drivers have to obey the law only when they feel like it? No, they must obey the law at all times. Why? *(Response)* Those who are in authority over us have made the law for everyone's good, so everyone must obey it or suffer the consequences.

Listen to our lesson today to learn what happened when God's people chose to break His laws.

■ Bible Content

1. God's people worship other gods. (Exodus 20:3, 4)

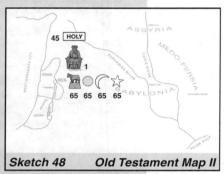

Sketch 48   **Old Testament Map II**

(Scroll 54, HOLY 45)
Many hundreds of years before Jeremiah lived, God gave His people, the Israelites, the land of Canaan to be their own land. *(Indicate ISRAEL and JUDAH.)* He also gave them laws *(place 54 on the board)* to live by—laws that set them apart as His holy people *(add 45)*—laws that demonstrated that Israel worshiped a holy God. These laws helped the Israelites to live godly lives among the wicked people already living in the land. Some of these laws are called The Ten Commandments and are found in the Old Testament book of Exodus. These laws reminded God's people to worship and serve God as the only true God. The first two commandments taught them not to worship any other god or to make an idol in the shape of anything. God gave them many other laws to help them live together successfully and to make right choices. ▲#3

God promised to protect them from their enemies and to make their nation great if they obeyed Him. But if they did not obey Him, there would be consequences for their disobedience. They would experience difficult problems and be captured by their enemies and taken to a foreign land. (Deuteronomy 30:15-20.) While many people obeyed God, most of them chose to disobey God's laws again and again, even though God gave them many warnings about the consequences of their sinful actions. Finally God allowed them to suffer the consequences, and they were divided into two separate nations. Do you remember what they were called? *(Response)* Yes, the northern kingdom of Israel *(indicate ISRAEL),* which was made up of ten tribes (large family groups descended from Jacob's sons) and the southern kingdom of Judah *(indicate JUDAH),* which was made up of two tribes. Both kingdoms continued to make wrong choices, totally disregarding God's laws and worshiping the gods of the nations that surrounded them. Even though God loved His people very much and was patient with them, He finally had to punish them for their sin by allowing them to suffer the consequences of their choices. *(Remove 54.)*

▲ **Option#3**

Purchase and display a poster with The Ten Commandments on it. Or, print the first two commands on newsprint or poster board. Have the children look up Exodus 20:3, 4 and read the laws aloud.

2. **God punishes Israel.**
   (2 Kings 17:1-23)

   a. **The people reject God and his warnings.**

   (Calf, sun, moon, stars 65[4], idol 1)
   Samaria *(indicate SAMARIA)* was the capital city of Israel. From there the kings of Israel ruled that land. There were nineteen of them all together, and every one of them led the people in worshiping other gods. Jeroboam, their first king, made gold calves *(add calf)* for the people to worship. Soon the people began to worship Baal *(add 1)* and to bow down to the sun, the moon, and the stars *(add sun, moon, stars)*. God sent faithful prophets to warn the people: "Turn away from your false gods. God is not pleased, and He will punish you for your sin." But the people ignored God's warnings and refused to stop worshiping their false gods.

   ▲ **Option#4**

   Have the children read each verse silently and then describe the people in their own words.

   b. **The Assyrians take Israel into captivity.**

   (A world map; word strips CONSEQUENCES, CHOICES; arrow 18[1], soldiers 16, people 66A)
   Because the people of Israel chose to follow false gods and worship idols, they could no longer be called holy *(remove 45)*. They were just like the nations around them, and God was very angry with them. Find 2 Kings 17:14, 15 in your Bible and place your bookmark there. In these verses God tells us what the people were like. *(Choose several children to read the verses silently, and have each one read aloud only one of the descriptive phrases in this passage.)* They did not trust God and did the things He told them not to do. ▲#4

   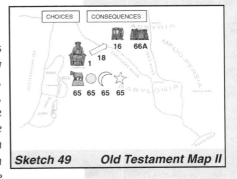

   Sketch 49   **Old Testament Map II**

   Assyria *(indicate ASSYRIA)* was located many miles to the east of Samaria in the northern part of present-day Iraq *(indicate on the world map)*. It wasn't long before God allowed the Assyrian army to invade Israel and take some of the people captive to Assyria, just as Isaiah had prophesied (Isaiah 8:4). Then the kings of Israel were forced to pay a large sum of money to the Assyrian king every year. Eventually King Hoshea (Ho-she'-a), the last king of Israel, refused to pay the tax. When the Assyrian king found out about this, he became very angry and put Hoshea in prison. Then he invaded the entire land of Israel and took the rest of the people captive to Assyria. *(Add 18[1], 16, 66A. Move 16, 66A across the map and place them under ASSYRIA.)* ▲#5

   ▲ **Option#5**

   Have the children become a "human map." Before class begins, lay out the areas of Israel and Assyria on the floor. Print poster board labels of places, people, prophets, and other items in the scene and attach string to them. Hang them from the ceiling to reach just above the heads of the children, and instruct the children to move into place as you recount the information from Bible Contents 1 and 2.

   The Israelites were scattered throughout Assyria and soon lost their identity as Israelites. They became known as the lost ten tribes of Israel. God allowed this to happen because He was angry with the people of Israel due to their sin of disobedience. *(Read 2 Kings 17:18 to the children.)* This punishment was the result of their refusal to love and serve Him as the only true God. Yet He still loved them very much and wanted them to love Him in return. He had given them many opportunities to turn away from their evil practices, but they had refused and were now paying the consequence *(add CONSEQUENCES)* for making their sinful choices *(add CHOICES)*. *(Leave all visuals on the board.)*

3. God punishes Judah.
(2 Kings 23:36–25:21; Jeremiah 25:11-13; 29:11-14; 37:8-10; 38:17-21; 39:13, 14)

a. Judah becomes unfaithful to God.

Sketch 50   Old Testament Map II

(HOLY 45, temple 61, city 63, Jeremiah 53)
Some (8 out of 20) of the kings of Judah *(indicate JUDAH)* were true to God, following His holy way *(add 45)*. They faithfully led the people in worshiping the true and living God as they offered their sacrifices at the temple *(add 61)* in Jerusalem *(add 63)*. But most of the kings were unfaithful to God and turned the people's hearts away from God and His ways. Like Israel, they refused to listen to the prophets that God sent to warn them of punishment for their sinful ways.

King Josiah was one of the kings who remained true to God. In fact, he was the last good king of Judah. ▲#6 After Josiah died, three of his sons and a grandson succeeded him as king, but they did not follow God's Way as Josiah had. Instead, they turned away from God and led the people in worshiping false gods *(move 1, 65[4] to the lower part of the map)*. They refused to listen to God, even though He sent the prophet Jeremiah *(add 53)* to warn them of punishment for their sinful ways. Like Israel, they were no longer living as God's holy people *(remove 45)*. The people of Judah had made their choice *(move CHOICES to the lower part of the map)*; now they were going to suffer the consequence *(move CONSEQUENCES to the lower part of the map)* of their sinful choices.

▲ **Option #6**

Have the children recall some facts about Josiah's life as a young king—what he did to obey God and how God blessed him and Judah.

b. The Babylonians take Judah into captivity.

(A world map; king 71, dishes 50, arrow 18[1], people 66B, soldiers 66C, temple ruins 62, city ruins 64)
It had been a little more than 100 years since Israel was taken captive to Assyria. During that time the Babylonians grew in power and eventually conquered the Assyrians. The capital city of Babylon *(indicate BABYLON)* was located just south of the present-day city of Baghdad *(indicate on the world map)* in Iraq. When Nebuchadnezzar became king of Babylon, he began to conquer all the surrounding nations, advancing westward toward Judah. He was a powerful and cruel king, causing the people of Judah to be terrified of him and his

army. Eventually God allowed Nebuchadnezzar to invade Judah and to make the people his subjects right in their own land.

When the king of Judah rebelled against him, Nebuchadnezzar attacked Jerusalem, bound the king in chains, and took him prisoner to Babylon. Nebuchadnezzar returned to Jerusalem three months later and removed all the treasures from the temple of the Lord *(add 71, 50)* and from the palace of the king. *(Have the children read 2 Kings 24:13-16 silently and tell what Nebuchadnezzar took from Jerusalem.)* He also took prisoners—the king's family, soldiers, princes, carpenters and other skilled workmen *(add 18[1], 66B, 66C)*. Then he made Zedekiah, Josiah's youngest son, king over those who remained in Judah. (1)

Note (1)

This was the first of three deportations from Judah, in which Daniel, Shadrach, Meshach, and Abednego were taken to Babylon (Daniel 1).

At first Zedekiah submitted to King Nebuchadnezzar's authority, but sometime later he gave in to pressure from his officials and rebelled against him. Jeremiah warned him not to do this, but he would not listen. As a result, Nebuchadnezzar returned with his army and camped outside the walls of Jerusalem. Zedekiah closed the gates and tried to keep the Babylonian army out. During that time Jeremiah kept saying to the king and the princes, "Don't try to fight against Nebuchadnezzar; he is going to conquer this city. God is allowing him to do this. If you surrender to him, your lives will be spared. But if you do not, you will be captured and Jerusalem will be burned."

The princes became angry with Jeremiah and said to him, "You are a traitor." But the king refused to listen to God and surrender to the Babylonians. He was an example of what our memory verse tells us. Let's say it together. *(Do so.)* Zedekiah chose the way of death; he chose his own way instead of God's Way.

One year later the Babylonian army broke into the city of Jerusalem and burned it down. They took everything of value, burned the palace and the temple *(replace 61 with 62)*, and broke down the walls around the city of Jerusalem *(replace 63 with 64)*. When Zedekiah tried to escape, he was captured and made to watch as his sons were killed. His eyes were put out, and he was bound with chains and taken to Babylon. The rest of the people, except for the very poorest who were left to farm the land, were taken as slaves to Babylon. The Babylonian commander gave Jeremiah permission to stay in the land of Judah as well.

c. God gives Judah hope for the future.

(Word strips DIFFERENT, PRISONERS, 70 YEARS, SIN, CHOICES, CONSEQUENCES, HOPE; people 9)

How different *(place DIFFERENT on the board)* life became for the people *(add 9)* who were taken to Babylon. They were now prisoners *(add PRISONERS)* in a strange land, living among people with very different customs, language, food, and religion. There was no temple in which to worship the true and living God. How do you think they felt? How would you have felt? *(Allow the children time to express their*

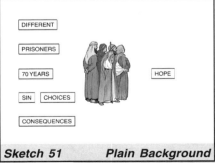

Sketch 51 **Plain Background**

▲ **Option #7**

Have the children tell all the new things the captives would possibly face in Babylon. List them on a chart. Or, provide materials for the children to illustrate these things and tell why each might be a problem for the captives.

feelings.) Probably they felt abandoned and very frightened, and wondered if they were ever going to get used to life there. Jeremiah had told them they would be there for seventy years *(add 70 YEARS)*. That was a long time, and many people were going to live and die in Babylon without ever seeing Judah again. It was a sad time for God's people. None of this would have happened if they had been faithful to the Lord God, who loved them and wanted their loving obedience in return. They deserved this punishment; they had sinned *(add SIN)* against God. Because of their sinful choices *(add CHOICES)*, they were now suffering the consequences *(add CONSEQUENCES)*. ▲#7

However, God did not forget His people or stop loving them. He gave them a promise of hope *(add HOPE)* for the future. He promised to take them back to their own land after the seventy years of captivity were over. He also told them he was going to punish the king of Babylon for his wickedness and cruelty toward them. God did not abandon His people. He was going to take care of them while they were in Babylon.

■ **Conclusion**

Summary

Because both the people of Israel and of Judah refused to turn away from their sin of worshiping false gods, they suffered the consequence of their sinful ways. What was the consequence? *(Response)* Yes, they were taken into captivity by other nations.

When the people in Jerusalem were given the choice of life or death, what did they choose? *(Response)* Yes, they chose death because they refused to submit to the Babylonians. Many were killed when the Babylonians finally broke into the city and destroyed it. Because of their disobedience they suffered the consequences of their wrong choices.

Application

Verse	Obey	Consequences for Disobedience
Ephesians 6:1, 2	Obey parents.	Grounded, disciplined, you get hurt, hurt someone else.
Ephesians 4:32		
Ephesians 4:29		

Sketch 52 — Chart

(Prepared chart, marker)

There are consequences to the choices we make in life. The most important choice we will ever make is a life or death choice. If we receive the Lord Jesus Christ as our Savior from sin, we are choosing the way of spiritual life, which means we will be with Jesus forever in heaven when our body dies. If we do not receive the Lord Jesus Christ as our Savior, we are choosing the way of spiritual death, which is separation from God forever. Which way have you chosen?

If you have chosen *The Way of Life*, God's Holy Spirit lives in you to help you make right choices each day. If you ask Him, He will help you to turn away from sinful thoughts and actions and to live according to God's Word. If you refuse to ask for His help and disobey God's Word, you will be sinning against God and will suffer the consequences of your choices.

Let's look at some verses in the Bible to discover some ways we can obey God. *(Display the prepared chart. Have the children look up the verses on the chart, one at a time. Have individual children read one verse at a time and tell how God wants them to obey. Write their responses on the chart.)* Now let's think about each verse and what the consequence might be if we choose to disobey what God says. *(Discuss with the children what the consequences of disobeying these verses might be, and write their ideas on the chart.)* ▲#8

Sometimes the consequences of our choosing to disobey God can be very hurtful—to us, to others, and to God. And whether we suffer the consequences immediately or later, we must recognize that we have sinned against God and need to confess it to Him. God promises to forgive us, even though we still may have to bear the consequence for our disobedience. It isn't always easy to obey God and make the right choices, but we have the Holy Spirit living in us to help us when we ask Him. We can depend on Him to help us make the right choices.

Response Activity

Invite any who want to receive Christ as Savior to come and talk with you at the end of the class.

Give those who have received Christ as Savior an opportunity to confess any known sin and to ask the Holy Spirit to help them obey God. Remind them that those who choose God's way of life depend on the Holy Spirit to help them make right choices.

*Distribute the **"I Choose" handouts** and pencils. Talk about the meaning of the handout and give the children time to sign it.*

✎ TAKE-HOME ITEMS

*Distribute **memory verse tokens for Jeremiah 21:8** and **Bible Study Helps for Lesson 8**.*

▲ Option#8

Instead of using the chart, make large cards from poster board. Punch two holes in the top of each, and attach string to hang the cards around the necks of the children. Print one verse reference and verse on each card. Leave space at the bottom of each card to write the children's responses. Choose some children or have them volunteer to display the cards at the front of the class. To discuss the verses, follow the same procedure given in the text.

Variation: Divide the children into groups of two or three and instruct each group to take a verse and discuss its meaning and how it would influence the choices they make. Or have them dramatize their responses with real-life situations.

Daniel and His Friends Honor God
Theme: A Protected Way

Lesson 9

Part One: Daniel Interprets the King's Dream

❦ BEFORE YOU BEGIN...

When it comes to honoring people, we feel quite adept. We honor students, military personnel, athletes, and musicians. But what about honoring Almighty God, the creator and sustainer of the universe? We seem to be at a loss to know how to honor *Him*. Maybe it's because we suppose God's greatness precludes His need to be honored. The preponderance of Scripture informs us that God wants to be known and adored by all His creatures. His strategy is for His redeemed family members to make Him known in supernatural ways: by loving those who hate them; by maintaining inner joy during suffering and bereavement; by being faithful and forgiving when persecuted; by being victorious when tempted.

God wants believers of all ages to honor Him, so that includes your children who claim Christ as their Savior. Just as God used Daniel and his three friends to honor Him in Babylon, He will give your children opportunities to honor Him—whether at home, at school, at church, or in their neighborhood. Challenge them to hold God up before others as one who is worth living for, and dying for. *"Those who honor Me I will honor, and those who despise Me shall be lightly esteemed" (1 Samuel 2:30b, NKJV).*

☞ AIM:

That the children may

- Know that God will help His children when they choose to honor Him.
- Respond by choosing to honor God even when they are in difficult situations.

📖 SCRIPTURE: 2 Kings 24:14-16; Daniel 1, 2

♥ MEMORY VERSE: Psalm 91:11

For he shall give his angels charge over thee, to keep thee in all thy ways. (KJV)

For he will command his angels concerning you to guard you in all your ways. (NIV)

MATERIALS TO GATHER

Visual for Psalm 91:11 from *Bible Verses Visualized*
Backgrounds: Review Chart, Plain Background, Plain with Tree, Old Testament Map II, Council Room, Palace
Figures: R1-R9, R15, R16, 1, 4, 18(1), 24, 26, 27, 66B, 66C, 68, 69, 70, 70A, 71, 82
Token holders & memory verse tokens for Psalm 91:11
Bible Study Helps for Lesson 9, Part 1
Special:
- **For Review Chart:** "Crown" visual
- **For Bible Content 1:** Word strips ISAIAH, JEREMIAH, LAMENTATIONS, EZEKIEL, DANIEL; a list of Hebrew and Babylonian names of Daniel and his three friends
- **For Bible Content 3:** "Statue" visual, word strips GOLD, SILVER, BRONZE, IRON, IRON/CLAY; a rock or picture of one
- **For Application:** Newsprint & marker or chalkboard & chalk
- **For Response Activity:** "Crown" handouts, pencils
- **For Options:** Additional materials for any options you choose to use
- **Note:** *Follow the instructions on page xii to prepare the "Crown" visual (pattern P-8 on page 170), the "Statue" visual (pattern P-23 on page 178), and the "Crown" handouts (pattern P-17 on page 175).*

 REVIEW CHART

Display the Review Chart with R15, R16, and R1-R7 in place. Ask the children to give the name of God's Way for Lesson 8, and choose a child to place R8 on the Chart. Have R9 and the "Crown" visual ready to use when indicated. Use the following True or False statements to review Lesson 8. Have the children give the correct statement for each False statement.

1. God's people in Judah always chose to follow His way. *(False; many times they chose their own way.)*
2. God used the Babylonians to bring punishment on the people of Judah. *(True)*
3. The people from the northern kingdom of Israel were taken to Assyria and scattered among the people there. *(True)*
4. King Nebuchadnezzar was the king of Assyria. *(False; he was King of Babylon.)*
5. God gives eternal life to those who believe in His Son. *(True)*
6. Jeremiah was given permission to live in Judah when the others were taken to Babylon. *(True)*
7. God promised to take the people of Judah back to the land of Israel in twenty years. *(False; it was seventy years.)*
8. We don't need anyone to help us make right choices. *(False; we need God.)*

Today we are going to see that God's Way is *A Protected Way*. *(Place R9 on the Review Chart.)* God is sovereign *(place the "Crown" visual on the board).* That means that He reigns over or is in control of everything that happens. Everything is protected or guarded by Him, so that nothing happens without His permission. He uses people and circumstances, whether they are good or bad, to carry out His purpose of making Himself known and receiving the honor He deserves. Our memory verse tells us one way He protects His children as He uses them to accomplish His purpose.

♥ MEMORY VERSE

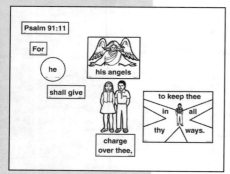

Display the visual for Psalm 91:11 and read it together.
Psalm 91:11 tells us that God uses angels to protect and care for those who belong to Him. Angels are spirit beings created by God to serve Him, and His children on earth (Hebrews 1:7, 14).

The Bible tells us of times when angels helped those who were in trouble or in need (Mark 1:9-12). Because we do not see the angels, we don't know how often they protect us from harm. Can you think of a time when you realized God had protected you in a special way? *(Allow the children to share their experiences.)* Maybe you were protected from an angry animal, from getting hit by a car, from being hurt during a dangerous storm, or from another person who wanted to hurt you.

This verse does not promise that we will always be protected from danger or harm. ▲#1 Sometimes God allows difficult circumstances to happen to us so that our faith in Him will grow stronger as we trust Him to help us. Sometimes He uses our difficult experience to help someone else believe in Him when that person sees how God has taken care of us and helped us. God wants us to trust Him even if we don't understand why bad things are happening. We can be sure that His angels are taking care of us and will not allow anything to happen to us that God has not allowed. *(Work on memorizing the verse.)*
▲#2

▲ Option #1

Discuss more in depth the fact that God does not always protect as we think He should. He often allows Christians to go through very difficult and dangerous situations and even to die. But even when we can't understand the "why," we can trust Him to allow what will show others—and us—His power in the way He helps us. He also wants to bring others to believe in Jesus as a result of our suffering or difficulty. He also may allow the trouble so that we can show we *really* trust Him and not just say we do.

📖 BIBLE LESSON OUTLINE

Daniel Interprets the King's Dream

■ **Introduction**

What do you do in a difficult situation?

■ **Bible Content**

1. The people of Judah are taken to Babylon.
2. Daniel refuses to eat the king's food.

3. Daniel interprets King Nebuchadnezzar's dream.
   a. The king makes an impossible demand.
   b. Daniel asks God to reveal and interpret the dream.
   c. Daniel gives God the credit for interpreting the dream.

■ Conclusion

Summary

Application
Thinking about ways to honor God in difficult situations

Response Activity
Choosing to honor God in a difficult situation this week

📖 BIBLE LESSON

■ Introduction

What do you do in a difficult situation?

Have you ever found yourself in a difficult situation? Perhaps someone in your family has been in an accident or is very ill, or friends have laughed at you when you refused to go along with their wrong actions. *(Allow for response throughout.)* What happened? How did you feel? What did you do? Listen to our story today to find out what some young men did when they found themselves in a very difficult situation.

■ Bible Content

1. The people of Judah are taken to Babylon. (2 Kings 24:14-16; Daniel 1:1-4)

(Word strips ISAIAH, JEREMIAH, LAMENTATIONS, EZEKIEL, DANIEL; Baal 1, arrow 18[1], people 66B, soldiers 66C)

The books of Isaiah and Jeremiah *(place ISAIAH, JEREMIAH on the board)* tell us of God's warning of judgment for Judah's sin of worshiping idols *(add 1)*. Their prophecies came true, and most of the people *(add 18[1], 66B, 66C)* were taken to the land of Babylon *(indicate BABYLON)*. Jeremiah then wrote the book of Lamentations *(add LAMENTATIONS)*, expressing his great sorrow for what happened to the people and the city of Jerusalem. The prophet Ezekiel wrote the book called by his name *(add EZEKIEL)*. He was taken prisoner to Babylon and gave God's message to the Jews in captivity. Daniel *(add DANIEL)* is another prophet who was taken to Babylon while he was just a young man. His book tells us what happened to him and some of God's

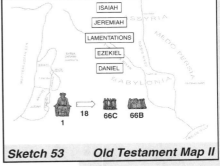

Sketch 53   Old Testament Map II

▲ **Option #2**

Memorizing the verse: Use the popcorn method to memorize the verse. Display the visual and have the children repeat the verse together. Beginning with the first word, point to a child and have them "pop up" and say it. Then point to another child to "pop up" and say the next word. Continue with this procedure until the whole verse has been said. Repeat the method but this time have the children say the next *two* words until the verse is completed.

Variation: Divide the class into two groups and have them sit on opposite sides. Beginning with the reference, have each group "pop up" and say the next word when you point to them. *(Divide the reference into three parts: book name, chapter, and verse.)* Do not let them know which side will begin, and intermittently choose the same side twice in consecutive order. Continue until the verse is completed.

▲ **Option #3**

Display a visual of the Old Testament books, either in poster or word strip form, and add these new ones to the list as you explain their background and authors. Have the children locate each new book in their Bibles and then leave the book of Daniel open to use in the lesson.

Sketch 54   Council Room

◨ **Note (1)**

Names were considered very important because of the significance of their meanings. The Hebrew names of these men all contained a name of God or Yahweh. God's name was removed when their names were changed, and they were given names containing a name of a Babylonian god.

Sketch 55   Council Room

people living in Babylon during that time. Turn to the first chapter of Daniel and place your bookmark there. ▲#3

The captives from Judah marched for many weeks (over 500 miles) through the hot desert to their new home. The journey was very difficult, but it must have been even more difficult when they arrived in Babylon. The language, customs, clothing, and food of the Babylonians were very strange to the people of Judah. The Babylonians worshiped the god Bel instead of the true God. Instead of having the Word of God, the Babylonians had books of magic and astrology. There was nothing in this land to remind the captives of their own customs or of the one true God and His laws. They were continually reminded that they were paying the consequence for their sinful ways.

(Daniel 69, Daniel's friends 68; a list of the Hebrew and Babylonian names of Daniel and his friends)

Some of the very first people taken to Babylon were the young princes from the royal family. King Nebuchadnezzar chose some of them who were intelligent, wise, and very handsome to be educated in the ways of the Babylonians so they could serve in his court. Four of these young men were Daniel, Hananiah, Mishael, and Azariah *(place 68, 69 on the board)*, who were about fifteen or sixteen years old at the time. The king wanted these young men to look and live like Babylonian men. He even changed their names to Babylonian ones. *(Display the list of their Hebrew and Babylonian names.)* Daniel's name was changed to Belteshazzar. His new name began with the name of Bel, the Babylonian god. Perhaps you recognize these three names–Shadrach, Meshach, and Abednego. Yes, these were the names given to Daniel's three friends. *(Leave the figures on the board.)* ◨(1)

2. Daniel refuses to eat the king's food. ▲#4
(Daniel 1:4-21)

(Commander 70, guard 24, table 82, food 70A, Nebuchadnezzar 71)

King Nebuchadnezzar gave an order for Daniel and his friends, along with many others, to be trained for three years to serve the king. During this time they were taught the ways of the Babylonians—their religion, literature, math, science, and Chaldean language.

King Nebuchadnezzar also wanted these men to be strong and healthy, so he ordered them to eat the same kind of food and to drink the same wine that was served to him. However, this created a big problem for Daniel and his friends. As Jewish young men, they had been taught God's laws about the kind of food they could eat. Some foods were considered unhealthy or unclean. They were not to eat any food that had been offered to idols. The king's food and wine had probably been offered as a sacrifice to his god before being served to him. Daniel and his friends knew they would be disobeying God if they ate or drank it. So they determined to honor God by obeying His commands and refusing to eat the king's food. Daniel *(remove 68; add 70)* went to the commander of the officials and asked permission to be excused from eating the king's food. ⌂(2) ▲#5

God caused the commander to be kind to Daniel, but he said to him, "I'm afraid of my master, the king. If he sees you looking worse than the other young men, he will cut off my head." *(Remove 70.)*

Then Daniel went to the guard *(add 24)* who was in charge of him and his three friends and said, "Please test us for ten days. Give us vegetables to eat and water to drink. Then compare us to the other young men and see who looks healthier."

Look in verse 14 to see what the guard did. *(Have a child read the verse aloud.)* Yes, he agreed to test them for ten days. We can be sure God was working in the heart of this Babylonian man. *(Add 82, 70A, 68; remove 24.)*

What was the result of the test? Look at verse 15 to see what happened. After ten days Daniel and his three friends looked healthier than all of the young men who ate the king's food. From then on, the guard allowed them to continue eating and drinking their own food. *(Remove 70A, 82.)*

God gave Daniel and his friends wisdom and the ability to learn. Daniel was given a special ability to understand all kinds of dreams and visions. When the three years of training were complete, all the young men were brought before King Nebuchadnezzar *(add 71)* to be questioned about all the things they had been studying. He discovered that non of the other young men were as smart as Daniel and his friends. In fact, Daniel and his friends were ten times smarter than all the magicians, sorcerers, and wise men in the entire kingdom. The king was so impressed that he made these four young Jewish men his personal servants in the palace.

Daniel and his friends honored God by obeying Him in this very difficult place. God helped them by making them healthier and stronger than all the others and allowing them to be given important positions in Babylon.

3. **Daniel interprets Nebudchadnezzar's dream.**
   (Daniel 2:1-49)

   a. **The king makes an impossible demand.**

(Nebuchadnezzar 71, men 4, 26, 27)
Some time later, Daniel had another opportunity to bring honor to God as he served King Nebuchadnezzar. *(Place 71 on the board.)* One night the king had a dream, which really upset him. He called in his astrologers and

▲ **Option#4**

Before class have each child write "I will honor God" on a 3"x 5"card. During the lesson, each time Daniel is faced with a difficult decision, have the children hold up their cards. Reinforce that when Daniel honored God, God honored him.

⌂ **Note (2)**

The Jews had dietary laws regarding the preparation of their food. Food prepared by Gentiles (non-Jews) was considered "unclean." The king's meat would not have been prepared in accordance with Jewish law. The king's wine would have been served full-strength, while the wine the Jews drank was very diluted with water.

▲ **Option#5**

Bring to class two different kinds of food and drink— one very appealing to the children and the other a simple vegetable and water. Ask the children which they would rather have and why. Explain that Daniel had to make that choice, but it wasn't just a choice of which one he would *like* to eat but which one would honor God.

Sketch 56   Palace

▲ **Option#6**

Draw a three-foot simple illustration of the statue on newsprint or wide white shelf paper. Have the children color the sections that represented the different kingdoms with the appropriate colors as mentioned in the story. Have the children use markers or crayons to label each kingdom. Then have a child draw a large boulder alongside the statue, color it, and label it. Hang it on the wall.

Variation: Punch holes in the top of the paper statue, thread a string through the holes, and hang it from the ceiling away from walls so it can be struck like a piñata.

Sketch 57   **Council Room**

Make a paper-machè rock or form one from rolled-up paper. To simulate the rock crushing the statue (nations), have the children throw the rock at the paper statue hard enough to tear it down.

magicians (*add 4, 26, 27*) and said, "I had a dream that bothers me. I want to know what the dream means."

As the men came and stood before him, they said, "O king, live forever! We are your servants. Please tell us your dream, and we will be glad to tell you what it means."

"No!" said the king. "If you do not tell me both the dream and what it means, you will be killed and your homes will be destroyed. But if you can do this, I will give you rewards and gifts and great honor. So tell me the dream and what it means."

Again they pleaded, "Please tell us the dream and we will tell you what it means."

The king became very angry and said, "You are trying to get more time. You know that I meant what I said. Hoping I will change my mind, you have all agreed to make up your own interpretation. Now tell me the dream!"

The men answered, "There is not a man on earth who can do what the king asks! No king has ever asked his astrologers and magicians to do such a thing. This is too difficult for us to do. Only the gods can tell you the dream, but they do not live with us."

The king was so furious that he gave an order for *all* the wise men of Babylon to be executed immediately. This included Daniel and his friends, for they also served the king as his wise men.

b. Daniel asks God to reveal and interpret the dream.

(Daniel 69, Arioch 24, Daniel's friends 68)

When Arioch, captain of the king's guard came to Daniel *(place 24, 69 on the board)* to carry out the king's order, Daniel spoke very politely to Arioch and asked, "Why did the king order such terrible punishment?" Then the captain told him what happened. Immediately Daniel went to King Nebuchadnezzar and asked for more time so that he could tell him the dream and its meaning. The king agreed.

Then Daniel went home and explained the whole story to his three friends. *(Remove 24; add 68.)* If you had been these men, what would you have done? *(Response)* Verse 18 tells us what they did. *(Read verse 18 aloud or have a child do so.)* Yes, they immediately began to pray and asked God to show them the dream and its meaning. That very night God answered their prayers. He revealed to Daniel the king's dream and its meaning. What did Daniel do then? *(Response)* What would you do? *(Response)* Yes, perhaps you would run right to the king and tell him the dream so that your life would be saved. But Daniel and his friends took time to thank God for answering their prayer. *(If time permits, read aloud Daniel's prayer in verses 20-23).*

c. **Daniel gives God the credit for interpreting the dream.**

(Daniel 69, Arioch 24, Nebuchadnezzar 71; "Statue" visual; word strips GOLD, SILVER, BRONZE, IRON, IRON/CLAY, a large rock or picture of one)

Then Daniel *(place 69, 24 on the board)* went to Arioch and said, "Do not kill the king's wise men! Take me to the king and I will interpret the dream for him."

Arioch took Daniel to the king *(remove 24; add 71)* and said, "I have found a man among the captives of Judah who can tell you what your dream means."

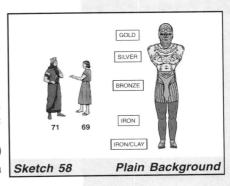

Sketch 58   **Plain Background**

Daniel stood before the king and said, "No one, no matter how wise, is able to tell you your dream, but there is a God in heaven who is able to reveal secrets. He has chosen to show you what will happen in the future. *(Add "Statue" visual. Point to the parts of the statue as you mention them.)* In your dream you saw a huge statue with a head of gold, chest and arms of silver, belly and thighs of bronze, and iron legs with feet of iron and clay. Then you saw a rock, cut from a mountain without human hands, crush the statue and become a mountain filling the whole earth. *(Show the rock or a picture of one. Ask the children to imagine the rock being cut from a mountain without human help and being hurled at the statue so that it is destroyed.)* ▲#6

Then Daniel told King Nebuchadnezzar the meaning of the dream, explaining that each part of the statue stood for a great nation that would gain power and rule the world for a period of time. The head of gold *(add GOLD)* stood for the mighty King Nebuchadnezzar and his kingdom. The second kingdom would be inferior, pictured as chest and arms of silver *(add SILVER)*. The third kingdom, pictured as belly and thighs of bronze *(add BRONZE)*, would rule over the whole earth. The fourth kingdom, pictured as legs of iron *(add IRON)*, would be strong and smash everything in its way. Yet it would become weak and divided, pictured as feet of iron mixed with clay *(add IRON/CLAY)*. The rock that destroyed the statue and became a mountain filling the whole earth *(show the rock)* would be the kingdom God would set up that would never be destroyed. Daniel finished by saying to the king, "The great God has shown you what is going to take place in the future. The dream and its meaning are true, and you can trust them."
▲#7

When Daniel had finished speaking, King Nebuchadnezzar knelt before him and said, "Your God is the greatest of all gods. He is the only one who is able to reveal secrets." Then Nebuchadnezzar gave Daniel many gifts and made him ruler over the entire province of Babylon and its wise men. At Daniel's request, King Nebuchadnezzar promoted Shadrach, Meshach, and Abednego to important positions in the government. Because Daniel and his friends honored Him, God helped them through this very difficult problem.

▲ **Option #7**

Only what Daniel actually told the king is included in the text. You may want to include the following additional data regarding the meaning of the dream. Visualize the data on a chart or word strips.

1st Kingdom: Babylonian – head of gold (605-539 B.C.)

2nd Kingdom: Medo-Persian – chest and arms of silver (539-331 B.C.)

3rd Kingdom: Greek – lower body of bronze (331-190 B.C.)

4th Kingdom: Roman – legs of iron with feet of clay (190 B.C. – A.D. 476)

5th Kingdom: God's – rock that became a mountain that filled the earth (The New Testament identifies this kingdom to be the future millennial reign of Christ on the earth.)

■ Conclusion
Summary

Did Daniel and his friends have an easy time in Babylon? *(Response)* No, they had a difficult time. *(For the next three questions add to the children's responses any of the stated answers they do not give.)* What were some of the difficulties they faced? *(Response)* That's right. They were taken from their families, their homes, and even their country. They became prisoners of a very ungodly king and were forced to learn a language and culture very different from their own. They were expected to eat the king's food, and they faced death when the wise men couldn't interpret the king's dream. How did God protect them? *(Response)* Yes, He caused the guard to be sympathetic to Daniel's request for a diet of vegetables and water, and He caused the four friends to be healthier and smarter than all the others. God answered their prayer by revealing to Daniel what the king's dream and its meaning were. In what ways did Daniel and his friends honor God? *(Response)* That's right. They obeyed God by refusing to eat the king's food. They prayed and asked God to reveal the dream, and Daniel thanked Him for the answer. Daniel gave God the credit for revealing the dream when he told it and its meaning to King Nebuchadnezzar.

Application

(Newsprint & marker or chalkboard & chalk)
God helped Daniel and his friends when they chose to honor Him in a very difficult and dangerous place. God has placed each one of us in a particular place where we can bring honor to Him, too. Can you think of ways you can honor God even when it is difficult to do so? *(Attach the newsprint to the board and record the children's responses. Suggest the following ways if the children do not think of them: refusing to get angry or get even when your family and friends make fun of you; doing your best in school or doing your chores well, even when you do not feel like it; refusing to join your friends in going to places that are not pleasing to God or in seeing and doing things that are sinful; letting your friends and others know that you do or do not do certain things because you love Jesus Christ and want to honor Him.)* ▲#8

Are you willing to honor God, no matter what happens? God is in control of everything in your life, and He will help you when you choose to honor Him.

Response Activity

Distribute the **"Crown" handouts** and pencils. Explain that the crown reminds us that God reigns over all, controlling all that

▲ **Option#8**

Suggest some difficult situations the children might face. Ask the children to hold up their "I will honor God" cards *(see Option #4)* if they have an idea how they would honor God in the situations you describe. Call on those children to share their ideas.

happens—even the difficult things that are happening to us. Have the children write down one way they plan to honor God this week, even though it will be difficult. Lead them in prayer, asking the Lord to help them do what they have written on their crown. Remind them that they need to depend on God to help them when they choose to honor Him.

✎ TAKE-HOME ITEMS

*Distribute **memory verse tokens for Psalm 91:11** and **Bible Study Helps for Lesson 9, Part 1.***

Daniel and His Friends Honor God
Theme: A Protected Way

Lesson 9

Part Two: God Saves Daniel's Friends from Burning

❋ BEFORE YOU BEGIN...

Can God always be trusted? On the one hand, we can readily answer yes. After all, He is the Sovereign Lord who controls all He has made. Further, He is everywhere, sees all, knows all, and can do anything. But God's ways defy our simplistic logic; He transcends our neat little boxes. God always can be trusted to do what is best according to His eternal plan. And that plan goes far beyond the restricted confines of our finiteness.

Case in point: When Shadrach, Meshach, and Abednego stood before the powerful King Nebuchadnezzar, they did not know if God would rescue them from the fiery furnace; they knew He could and that He was completely trustworthy to do what was best. They were equally sure they were not going to disobey God's laws to spare their own lives.

Your children will face situations when they must choose between obeying God's Word and protecting themselves from loosing favor and friends or being ostracized and abused. May they be willing to step out on God's sure promises and obey Him, no matter what happens! *"The Lord knows how to deliver the godly out of temptations and to reserve the unjust under punishment for the day of judgment" (2 Peter 2:9, NKJV).*

☞ AIM:

That the children may

- Know that God is in control of everything and is able to protect them in difficult situations.
- Respond by trusting God to take care of them and help them remain true to Him when they are in a difficult situation.

📖 SCRIPTURE: Daniel 3

♥ MEMORY VERSE: Psalm 91:11

For he shall give his angels charge over thee, to keep thee in all thy ways. (KJV)

For he will command his angels concerning you to guard you in all your ways. (NIV)

MATERIALS TO GATHER

Visual for Psalm 91:11 from *Bible Verses Visualized*
Backgrounds: Review Chart, Plain Background, General Outdoor, Council Room, Wilderness, Furnace Overlay
Figures: R1-R9, R15, R16, 4, 9, 16, 17, 25A, 25B, 26, 27, 68, 69, 70, 71, 72, 73, 74(4), 75, 81
Token holders & memory verse tokens for Psalm 91:11 for any who did not receive them last week
Bible Study Helps for Lesson 9, Part 2
Special:
- *For Application:* Newsprint & marker or chalkboard & chalk
- *For Response Activity:* "Furnace" handouts, pencils
- *For Options:* Additional materials for any options you choose to use
- *Note:* Follow the instructions on page xii to prepare the "Furnace" handouts (pattern P-18 on page 175). Punch a hole at the top of each handout, and attach a piece of yarn for hanging it.

 REVIEW CHART

Display the Review Chart with R1-R8, R15, and R16 in place. Have R9 ready to use when indicated. Arrange figures 70 and 71 on the left side of the Chart and figures 68 and 69 on the right side. Choose four children and have each one choose one of the figures and tell what he or she remembers about the character it represents from the previous lesson. Have one child place R9 on the Chart and say Psalm 91:11. Ask for a volunteer to explain the meaning of the verse. Use the following questions to review Lesson 9, Part One.

1. Why were Daniel and his three friends given an education in Babylon? *(They were trained to serve in the palace.)*
2. What did Daniel decide he would not do? *(He decided he would not eat the king's food or drink his wine.)*
3. How were Daniel and his three friends tested? *(They were given water and vegetables for ten days.)*
4. What was the result of the test? *(They were healthier than all the other young men.)*
5. How did Daniel and his three friends compare to all the other young men at the end of their training? *(They were ten times smarter than all the wise men in the kingdom.)*
6. What did Daniel and his friends do when they heard about the king's order to kill all the wise men? *(They prayed and asked God to reveal the dream and its meaning.)*
7. After God answered their prayer, what did Daniel do first? *(He thanked God for His answer.)*

8. How did Daniel honor God when he interpreted the dream for Nebuchadnezzar? *(He gave God the credit.)*

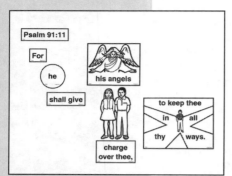

♥ MEMORY VERSE

Display the visual to review Psalm 91:11 and its meaning. ▲#1

📖 BIBLE LESSON OUTLINE

God Saves Daniel's Friends from Burning

■ **Introduction**

Learning to trust

■ **Bible Content**

1. The king builds a large gold statue.
2. The king orders everyone to worship his statue.
3. Daniel's friends disobey the king's order.
4. Daniel's friends are thrown into the furnace.
5. God protects Daniel's friends in the fire.

■ **Conclusion**

Summary

Application
  Being willing to trust God for help to honor Him

Response Activity
  Trusting God to take care of them and help them be true to Him

📖 BIBLE LESSON

■ **Introduction**

Learning to trust

Have you ever had to trust someone? Why did you need to trust that person? *(Let the children respond.)* Let's try a little experiment to see if one of you can trust me. *(Use a "Trust Fall" experiment to help the children understand what it means to trust. Choose someone whose weight you can support and who trusts you. Instruct the child to stand facing away from you and to fall backwards into your arms without looking back or bending the knees when you say, "Go." Assure the child that your hands and arms are right*

▲ **Option#1**

Reviewing the verse: Print the verse reference and each word of the verse on separate plain paper plates. Distribute the paper plates and see how quickly the children can put the words in the correct order by arranging themselves across the front of the room. Repeat several times until all the children have had an opportunity to participate. Repeat the method, timing them to see how long it takes each group to form the verse.

Variation: Scatter the plates on the floor in front of the class. Give several children an opportunity to put the plates in order by themselves. Then divide the class into two groups. Time them to see which group can put the plates in order first.

102

there to catch him [her]. Make sure the whole class can see what is happening.) Was it easy for you to trust me? *(Response)* Why was it difficult to do? *(Response)* That's right. You could not see my hands and arms. You had to trust that I would do what I said. Trust is relying upon or placing confidence in someone or something. Sometimes we must trust even when we don't understand what is happening.

There is only one we can trust all the time—God! Listen to our lesson today to see who had to trust God completely in a very difficult and dangerous situation.

■ Bible Content

1. The king builds a large gold statue. ▲#2 (Daniel 3:1)

(Nebuchadnezzar 81, statue 75)
Even though King Nebuchadnezzar admitted that Daniel's God was great, he still worshiped idols. He thought that God, although very powerful, was just one of many gods. But God used Shadrach, Meschach, and Abednego to show the king and his leaders that He was the *only* living and powerful God, who was in control of everything that would happen.

One day the king decided to build a very large statue *(place 81 on the board)*. The workmen placed it a short distance outside the city of Babylon. We read all about it in Daniel 3:1. Find it in your Bible and place your bookmark there. *(Have a child read it, or have all the children read it silently.)* What was the statue made of? *(Response)* Yes, it was made of pure gold *(add 75)*, which means it must have been very beautiful and very expensive. How tall was it? *(Response)* It was ninety feet tall, about the height of an eight-story building. It was nine feet wide. *(Compare its width to the size of your room or an area the children know.)* What an awesome statue it must have been! Can you imagine how it sparkled and glistened as the sun shown on it? It could be seen from a great distance. *(Leave the figures on the board.)*

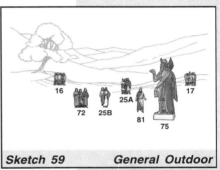

Sketch 59   General Outdoor

2. The king orders everyone to worship his statue. (Daniel 3:2-7) ▲#3

(People 25B, Daniel's friends 72, soldiers 16, 17, 25A)
When the statue was finished, the king requested all his officials and leaders *(add 25B, 72, 16, 17, 25A)* to come to a special ceremony to dedicate it. All his important leaders came—governors and their assistants, military commanders, treasurers who controlled the money, advisers, wise men, judges, and all other leaders throughout the Babylonian Empire. As they gathered together in front of the great statue, the man who made announcements for the king spoke in a loud voice, "Everyone listen! This is what the king commands you to do. When you hear the musical instruments begin to play, you must

▲ Option#2

Reenact the entire chapter or certain parts of it like Daniel 3:16-18, 19-23, or 28, 29 with several children reading aloud while others mime the parts. If time permits use costumes and props.

Variation: Have the children make up what they think the men might have answered the king in verses 19-23 as well as use the dialogue from the Scripture.

▲ Option#3

Have the children act out the scene as you teach it. Choose children to take the parts of Daniel's three friends, the announcer, and the king. Instruct the remainder of the children to be the crowd. Use recorded band music to signal the crowd to drop to the floor, leaving the three men standing.

▲ **Option#4**

Have the children read the names of the instruments listed in verse five. Be prepared to describe the instruments along with their sounds by looking up their descriptions and pictures of them on the Internet.

fall down and worship the gold statue that King Nebuchadnezzar has set up. Anyone who refuses to do this will be immediately thrown into a blazing furnace and burned to death." *(Remove all the figures except 81, 75.)* ▲#4

3. Daniel's friends disobey the king's order. (Daniel 3:8-18)

(People bowing 74[4], men 72)
Because the people were afraid of the king and knew he would keep his word, they all bowed *(add 74[4])* before the statue when they heard the music. By doing this, the people gave their allegiance to the king and his religion. This was like saying, "We worship the same god you worship and obey you as our only leader."

What an incredible sight this must have been—the ninety-foot gold statue shining in the sun, the loud music playing, and hundreds of people bowing down to the statue! But there was one problem! Not everyone bowed down before the statue! Some of the king's wise men saw it first. There in the middle of all the people bowing to the ground before the statue were three men *(add 72)* standing straight and tall! This was unbelievable! Who would dare defy the king? Who would choose to die instead of obeying the king? Can you guess who these men were? *(Response)* That's correct; Shadrach, Meshach, and Abednego—Daniel's three friends. ◳(1)

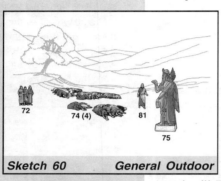
Sketch 60 General Outdoor

◳ **Note (1)**

Daniel is not mentioned, not because he would have bowed to the statue, but because he was either away from the capital on business or for some legitimate reason was unable to be there.

(Nebuchadnezzar 71, man 27, men 4, Daniel's friends 68)
Then some of the wise men went straight to the king with their news *(place 71, 27, 4 on the board)*. "O king, live forever!" they said. "You commanded everyone to bow down to your statue when they heard the music play. Some men of Judah whom you made important officers in Babylon do not worship your gods. Now they have not paid attention to your order and have not bowed down to your statue."

When Nebuchadnezzar heard this he was furious. At once he called for Shadrach, Meshach, and Abednego to appear before him. *(Move 27 to the far right; place 68 beside 71.)* He said to them, "Is it true that you do not serve my gods or worship my gold statue? I will give you one more chance to obey. This time if you do not fall down and worship the gold statue when you hear the music, you will be thrown immediately into the blazing furnace. Then what god will be able to save you?"

Sketch 61 Council Room

How do you think these three young men felt? What would you have done if you had been Shadrach, Meshach, and Abednego? *(Response)* It must have been very frightening for them, but God gave them courage to tell the king, "O Nebuchadnezzar, we do not need to defend ourselves to you. You can throw us into the blazing furnace. The God we serve is able to save us from being burned.

But even if He chooses not to do so, we want you to know, O king, we will not worship the gold statue you have set up." What did their answer to the king show about their trust in God? *(Response)* They knew they could trust God completely. They really loved God and were willing to die for Him. If that happened, they knew they would live forever with God in heaven.

4. Daniel's friends are thrown into the furnace. (Daniel 3:19-23)

(Nebuchadnezzar 71, Daniel's friends 68, 72, people 4, 26, man 73)
How did King Nebuchadnezzar react to their words? The Bible says he was furious and his whole attitude toward them changed. He had respected them and given them high positions of authority. How dare they disobey him! He gave orders for the furnace to be fired up seven times hotter than it usually was. This guaranteed that the men would die instantly in the fire. *(Place 71, 68, 4, 26 on the board.)* How do you think these three young men were feeling now? *(Response)* Probably they were terribly

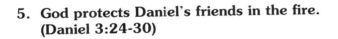
Sketch 62   Wilderness/Furnace Ov.

frightened of what was before them. They remained true to God and trusted Him to take care of them, no matter what happened.

The king, wanting this done quickly, watched as the three young men, wearing all their silk robes and turbans, were tied up and thrown into the blazing fire *(remove 68; place 72, 73 on the Furnace Overlay)*. The fire was so hot that the flames of the fire killed the soldiers as they threw the men into the fire.

5. God protects Daniel's friends in the fire. (Daniel 3:24-30)

Then King Nebuchadnezzar looked with amazement at what he was seeing. Excitedly he asked, "Didn't we tie up three men and throw them into the furnace?"

"Yes, O king," his advisers replied.

Stepping closer, King Nebuchadnezzar exclaimed, "Look! I see four men in there. They are untied and walking around. They don't even look burned. The fourth man looks like a son of the gods." The Bible doesn't tell us who the fourth person was. Some people think it was the Lord Jesus Christ. It may have been an angel. Our memory verse reminds us that God uses angels to protect His children. Let's say it together. *(Do so.)* In either case, God protected Shadrach, Meshach, and Abednego in that blazing furnace. He showed He was in control of everything, even the fire!

The king walked toward the opening of the blazing furnace. *(Move 71 closer to the furnace.)* As he stood there, he called out to the men inside, "Shadrach, Meshach, and Abednego, servants of the Most High God, come out." *(Remove 72, 73.)*

▲ **Option#5**

To drive home the import of this miracle of not even having the smell of smoke on the men, first have the children discuss the smell of smoke from various sources (campfire, burning leaves, etc.) and how the odor gets into everything (clothes, hair, skin, etc.). Before the class begins, burn the end of a cotton rope or piece of cloth and extinguish the fire after a small area has been burned. Then in class, light a candle and blow it out as you are talking. Have the children smell the odor of the candle. Then have them smell the rope/cloth you have previously burned. Discuss how the odor still remains. You can also carefully burn some paper or fine silky cloth over a metal tray to show how quickly it would burn from just a small match. This will dramatically bring out the awesome power God has even over fire and the odor it produces and His ability to protect us when and how He chooses.

▲ **Option#6**

Have the children act out situations that would take courage and trust in God to stay true to Him in their own environments.

The men came walking out *(place 68 beside 71)*, and the king and all his advisers and leaders crowded around them to see the miracle that God did. Let's read about it. *(Have the children read verse 27 aloud.)* The men had no burns or singed hair on them. Their robes weren't burned, and they didn't even smell like smoke! All those standing around had never seen anything like it. ▲#5

King Nebuchadnezzar recognized that God had rescued Shadrach, Meshach, and Abednego. He said, "Praise be to the God of Shadrach, Meshach, and Abednego who sent His angel to rescue His servants. They trusted in Him and refused to obey my command. They were willing to die rather than worship any other god except their own God. So now I am making this law: The people of any nation who say anything against the God of Shadrach, Meshach, and Abednego will be punished with death and their houses will be torn down. No other god is able to save like this."

Then the king promoted Shadrach, Meshach, and Abednego to higher positions in Babylon. But more importantly, by remaining true to God, they honored God before all those who ruled over Babylon and showed them that He is in control of everything. ▲#6

■ **Conclusion**

Summary

What did King Nebuchadnezzar order all the people to do at the dedication of his gold statue? *(Encourage response throughout.)* Yes, they were ordered to bow down and worship his statue when the music played. What was the consequence for those who did not do this? Yes, they were to be thrown into a blazing furnace. Did Shadrach, Meshach, and Abednego bow down before the statue? No, they bravely kept standing. Did they change their mind when given a second chance? No, they were determined to remain true to God. How did they show that they were trusting God? That's right; they told the king that God was able to rescue them, but even if He didn't, they were not going to bow down and worship the statue. How did God protect Shadrach, Meshach, and Abednego? Yes, He sent His angel (or Jesus) to be with them, and He kept them from being burned in the fire. How did God get honor in this situation? Yes, King Nebuchadnezzar recognized that God had rescued Shadrach, Meshach, and Abednego. He even made a law that no one could speak against their God.

Application

(Newsprint & marker or chalkboard & chalk)

There are many Christians in our world today who are facing great difficulties because of their love for the Lord Jesus Christ. They are being killed, put in jail, or treated badly because they will not worship other gods and give up their faith in the Lord Jesus Christ. They know that God is in control and protecting them from anything that is not part of His plan. Even if they die, they know they will go immediately to be with the Lord Jesus Christ in heaven. ◰(2)

You may never be treated this way, but you may experience other difficult situations because you want to remain true to the Lord Jesus. Can you think of some difficult situations you are facing or know that others are experiencing? *(Attach newsprint to the flannelboard and list the children's responses. If necessary, suggest the following to start their thinking: Schoolmates or family may make fun of you because you read your Bible and pray or go to church and Bible Club; you may not be invited to parties because you refuse to listen to certain kinds of music or watch certain kinds of movies; some may laugh at you because you give thanks before eating your lunch; some may push you around because you refuse to smoke or take drugs; some may get angry with you when you try to talk to them about the Lord Jesus; someone may tell lies about you.)* ▲#7

Jesus said that His children can expect such treatment, but He is with us when this happens. The Holy Spirit is living in us to make us strong. He will help us remain true to Him in these difficult situations. We can trust Him to protect us from anything that is not part of His plan for us. Remember that others are watching to see how we respond when we are treated badly. God uses everything that happens to us to make His name known to others and bring honor to Himself. He may use your difficult experience to help your friends see their need of putting their trust in the Lord Jesus Christ as their Savior or to encourage other Christians to remain true to Him. Are you willing to trust God to take care of you and help you be true to Him in the difficult situation you are experiencing?

Response Activity

Distribute the **"Furnace" handouts** and pencils. Remind the children that they will honor God when they trust Him to take care of them and help them remain true to Him in a difficult situation, as Shadrach, Meshach, and Abednego did. If this is a choice they are ready to make, have them write down a difficult situation they are facing. Then have them pray silently, telling God they are going to trust Him to take care of them and help them be true to Him in that situation. Encourage the children to place the handout where it will remind them of their decision to trust God. Be sure to ask the children in the weeks to come how God helped them.

✍ TAKE-HOME ITEMS

Distribute **memory verse tokens for Psalm 91:11** and **Bible Study Helps for Lesson 9, Part 2.**

◰ Note (2)

For more information on the persecuted church around the world, check online for The Voice of the Martyrs' website at www.persecution.com.

▲ Option#7

Provide paper and crayons, and instruct the children to illustrate a time when it was hard for them to remain true to Jesus in their home, in school, or with their friends.

The Persians Conquer Babylon

Theme: *An Obedient Way*

Lesson 10

Part One: Daniel Reads the Writing on the Wall

❦ BEFORE YOU BEGIN...

There are several ways of saying no to God's offer of salvation. Some people ignore it and act indifferently about it. Others put it off and say, "Not now." Still others deny its validity. Then there are those who openly oppose it and spurn its message.

King Belshazzar is a prime example of one who got used to saying no to God. He had ample evidence from his grandfather Nebuchadnezzar of the sovereignty and righteousness of the God of Daniel. Yet he rejected the evidence and recklessly pursued a course of defying God. He paid for it with his life and the overthrow of his empire.

Are there children in your class who are saying no to God's way of salvation? Perhaps some are trying to look like a Christian to avoid saying yes. Then there may be those who have declared they are not interested, that they are not bad enough to go to hell.

Pray that the truth of this lesson will be used by the Holy Spirit to bring those saying no to change to a life-transforming yes. *"He who is often rebuked, and hardens his neck, will suddenly be destroyed, and that without remedy"* (Proverbs 29:1, NKJV).

☞ AIM:

That the children may

- Know that God will judge those who continue to reject Him by ignoring and disobeying His Word.

- Respond in obedience by receiving the Lord Jesus Christ as Savior.

📖 SCRIPTURE: Daniel 5

♥ MEMORY VERSE: Psalm 37:34

Wait on the Lord, and keep his way, and he shall exalt thee to inherit the land. (KJV)

Wait for the Lord and keep his way. He will exalt you to inherit the land. (NIV)

MATERIALS TO GATHER

Visual for Psalm 37:34 from *Bible Verses Visualized*
Backgrounds: Review Chart, Plain Background, Old Testament Map II, Courtyard
Figures: R1-R10, R15, R16, 4, 10, 14, 22, 26, 27, 43, 50, 53, 68, 69, 70, 71, 74, 75, 76, 78(2), 82, 87, 88, 89(GOD)
Token holders & memory verse tokens for Psalm 37:34
Bible Study Helps for Lesson 10, Part 1
Special:
- *For Memory Verse & Summary:* BELIEVE & OBEY footprints
- *For Introduction:* Poster board hands
- *For Bible Content 1:* A current world map
- *For Bible Content 3:* Word strips BABYLON, MEDES/PERSIANS; "Statue" visual
- *For Application:* Word strip YOU
- *For Response Activity:* "Choosing God's Obedient Way" handouts, pencils
- *For Options:* Additional materials for any options you choose to use
- *Note: To prepare the poster board hands,* use markers to print the following words on hands cut from poster board: STOP; CAUTION; SLOW DOWN; WORK AREA AHEAD; SLIPPERY WHEN WET; ROAD CLOSED; BUMP.
  Follow the instructions on page xii to enlarge and reproduce the hands (pattern P-7 on page 170) to be cut from poster board and to prepare the "Choosing God's Obedient Way" handouts (pattern P-19 on page 176).

 REVIEW CHART

Display the Review Chart with R15 and R16 in place. Place R1-R9 on a table or on the lower right corner of the Chart in mixed-up order. Have individual children choose one of the review tokens and place it on the Chart while explaining its meaning and saying the corresponding verse. Have R10 ready to use when indicated. Use the following figures to review the previous lessons: Jeremiah 53, Nebuchadnezzar 71, Arioch 70, Daniel 69, Shadrach, Meshach, and Abednego 68, statue 75, people 74. Call on individual children to choose one of the figures and place it on the board while telling what they know about the character it represents.

Who would like to volunteer to read how our new review token describes God's Way and place it on the Chart for us? *(Have a child place R10 on the Chart and read it aloud.)* Obedience to God is doing what He tells you to do. When we follow God's obedient way, we submit to His authority and do what He tells us to do. That means that we give up our own way to live God's Way. Our memory verse

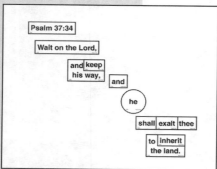

▲ Option #1

Memorizing the verse: Print (large enough to be read from a distance) each of the words of the verse, the book name, the chapter number, and the verse number on separate cards made of poster board or construction paper. Attach yarn or cord to the cards and hang them around the necks of the children. Instruct the children to sit in a circle of chairs with their cards hanging in front of them. (The reference and words should not be in order going around the circle.) Toss a lightweight ball or sponge to the child displaying the book name. Have the child say, "Psalm" and then toss the ball to the child who is displaying *37*. Then that child, after saying "thirty-seven," should toss the ball to the child displaying *34*. Continue this procedure until the entire reference and verse have been said. Repeat the procedure and then instruct the children to exchange cards and change seats as well. Toss the ball again and proceed through the verse. As you collect the cards, lead the class in reciting the verse together.

(Continued)

today tells us what God will do when we choose to obey Him and do things His way.

♥ MEMORY VERSE

Display the visual to teach Psalm 37:34; use the BELIEVE & OBEY footprints when indicated.

God made a wonderful promise to the Israelites. *(Read the verse together.)* What did God say He would do for them? *(Response)* Yes, He said He would exalt them to inherit the land. Exalt means *to lift up (lift the flap to show the meaning of the word)* or *make great*, and inherit means *to receive (lift the flap)*. He wanted them to be a great nation of people and to receive His blessing, having everything they needed to be prosperous and happy in the land He had given them. But He said they must do two things if they were to receive His blessing. What were they? *(Response)* First, they were to wait on the Lord. Waiting *on* the Lord is actually waiting *for* the Lord, fully expecting Him to do what He has promised in His Word. Waiting involves *believing (add BELIEVE)* or trusting God to do something only He can do. Second, they were to keep His way. That means *to obey (lift flap) Him (add OBEY)*.

As long as God's people believed and obeyed Him, God blessed them greatly, making them the greatest nation in the world. When they chose to disobey God by worshiping other gods and ignoring His warning of judgment, God took them away from the land He had given them and took them into captivity. God wants *us* to understand what happens if we do not trust and obey Him. This should help us to choose to follow God's Way, *An Obedient Way,* and receive His blessing rather than His judgment. *(Work on memorizing the verse.* ▲#1

📖 BIBLE LESSON OUTLINE

Daniel Reads the Writing on the Wall

■ **Introduction**

Warning!

■ **Bible Content**

1. Belshazzar becomes king of Babylon.
2. Belshazzar holds a great banquet.
   a. A hand writes on the wall.
   b. Daniel interprets the writing.
3. The Medes and Persians conquer Babylon.

■ **Conclusion**

Summary

Application
Escaping God's judgment by receiving the Lord Jesus as Savior

Response Activity
Choosing to obey by receiving Jesus Christ as Savior

📖 **BIBLE LESSON**

■ **Introduction** ▲#2

Warning!

(Poster board hands)
As you travel along the highway with your parents or other adults, you may see some road signs that say: STOP, CAUTION, SLOW DOWN, WORK AREA AHEAD, SLIPPERY WHEN WET, ROAD CLOSED, and BUMP. *(Display the hands and read the warnings.)* Of course there are many other signs. What do these signs have in common? *(Response)* Yes, they warn us of danger. What will happen if the driver doesn't pay attention or chooses to ignore these warning signs? *(Response)* Yes, he could be stopped by a police officer and be given a ticket and have to pay a fine. Or, he could have an accident, causing everyone to get very badly hurt or even be killed. Listen carefully to our lesson today to find out what happened to a man who deliberately chose to ignore God's warnings.

■ **Bible Content**

1. Belshazzar becomes king of Babylon.

(Nebuchadnezzar 71, Belshazzar 70, Daniel 88; a current world map)

King Nebuchadnezzar *(place 71 on the board)* ruled over Babylon for forty-three years. Daniel *(add 88)* was about sixty years old when the king died *(remove 71)*. After Nebuchadnezzar died, several different kings ruled Babylon during the next twenty-three years, including Belshazzar *(add 70)*, Nebuchadnezzar's grandson. ◁(1) He did not give Daniel the recognition and honor that Nebuchadnezzar had given him, but Daniel continued to trust and obey God as he went quietly about serving King Belshazzar.

During that time the nation of Persia became very strong, conquering all the nations surrounding it, including much of Babylonia. Persia was located to the east of Babylonia and was ruled by King

Variation: Once the children know the verse well, time them to see how quickly they can go through the above procedure of saying the words in the correct order.

▲ **Option#2**

Display pictures of warning signs around the room before the children come in to class. Then refer to them as you talk about the various road signs in the Introduction.

◁ **Note (1)**

Historical records indicate his father, King Nabonidus, who ruled over Babylon, appointed Belshazzar co-regent. Nabonidus was absent from Babylon for a number of years, expanding and restoring the Babylonian Kingdom to where it had been in the glory years of Nebuchadnezzar. Therefore, he appointed his son to be "in charge" of the city.

Sketch 63   Old Testament Map II

▲ **Option #3**

For older children, refer to the statue mentioned in Lesson 9, Part One and note how God's word was being fulfilled with the Medes and Persians. Continue to verify this as the lesson continues and the city of Babylon is conquered.

Cyrus. *(Indicate the location of Persia on the world map, and explain that Iran is ancient Persia.)* Like Nebuchadnezzar, he wanted to rule the world, so he began to conquer the nations around him. ▲#3

Cyrus's army set up camp outside the walls of Babylon and began to attack the city. But the Babylonians were not afraid. Because the walls of the city were very strong and over 300 feet high, Belshazzar and the people felt very secure inside the city of Babylon. In fact, Belshazzar did not order his soldiers to guard the walls, because he was so sure his enemies could not climb over them or break them down. And he stored up enough supplies to take care of the people for twenty years. He trusted in Babylon's strong high walls and stores of supplies to save the Babylonians from Persia. Our story begins in Daniel 5:1. Find it and place your bookmark there.

2. **Belshazzar holds a great banquet. (Daniel 5:1-29)**

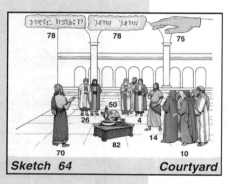

Sketch 64 — Courtyard

a. **A hand writes on the wall.**

(People 4, 10, 14, 26, Belshazzar 70, table 82, dishes 50, hand 76, handwriting 78[2])

During this time King Belshazzar planned a huge banquet in the palace for 1000 of his nobles. *(Place 4, 10, 14, 26 on the board.)* They had much food, wine, and entertainment, and they gave no thought to the Persian army outside the walls of Babylon. As Belshazzar *(add 70)* drank wine with his guests, he remembered the beautiful gold and silver cups that King Nebuchadnezzar had brought from God's temple in Jerusalem. These cups had been used there in worshiping the true and living God.

Belshazzar ordered, "Bring the gold and silver cups out. Everyone may drink from my magnificent cups" *(add 82, 50)*. As his guests drank from the beautiful gold and silver cups they praised their own false gods of wood and stone and iron—gods that could not hear or answer their prayers. How disrespectful Belshazzar was to the true and living God!

▲ **Option #4**

Print the warning message on a transparency and use an overhead projector to project it onto the wall of the classroom at the appropriate time in the story. Or, print it directly on a blank piece of newsprint or poster board that you have attached to the wall ahead of time. Later, as you tell the part of the story when Daniel is interpreting the message, add the words *counted, weighed,* and *divided* next to the appropriate words in the warning.

Suddenly, in the middle of the party, something frightening happened! The fingers of a human hand appeared on the wall *(add 76)*. As everyone watched, the hand began to write a message on the wall *(add 78[2])*. The king was so terrified that he turned pale and his knees knocked together so that he couldn't stand up. ▲#4

This is the message that was written on the wall: MENE, MENE (měn'-ā), TEKEL (těk'-ěl), PARSIN (or UPARSIN [oo-par'-sin]). It was a strange language, which the king could not read or interpret.

Belshazzar shouted for his astrologers and enchanters to come to him. He said, "If anyone can read this writing and tell me what it means, I will give him a purple robe and place a gold chain around his neck. I will make him the third highest ruler in the kingdom."

But his wise men shook their heads. None of them could read it or tell him what it meant. Then Belshazzar became even more afraid. He did not know what to do. Even his noblemen were confused and felt helpless. *(Leave the figures on the board.)*

b. Daniel interprets the writing.

Sketch 65   Courtyard

(Queen 22, Daniel 27)

Just then the king's mother appeared *(place 22 beside 70)*. She had heard all the shouting and confusion about the handwriting on the wall. "O king, live forever!" she said. "Don't be afraid. There is a man in your kingdom who can read this writing and tell you what it means. Your grandfather, Nebuchadnezzar, found him to be the wisest and smartest man in the kingdom. He put him in charge of all the wise men because he could solve difficult problems, explain riddles, and interpret dreams. His name is Daniel, but he is called Belteshazzar. Call for him. He is the one who can tell you what the writing on the wall means."

So Daniel was brought before King Belshazzar. *(Move 22 back; add 27.)* The king asked him, "Is your name Daniel? Are you one of the captives that Nebuchadnezzar brought from Judah? I have heard that you can interpret dreams. If you can read the message on the wall and tell me what it means, I will give you a royal robe and gold chain, and make you the third ruler of this nation."

Daniel trusted God to help him and answered the king in a very bold and courageous way. He said, "You may keep your gifts for yourself and give the rewards to someone else. However, I will read the message and tell you its meaning. The true and living God made your grandfather, Nebuchadnezzar, a very powerful and great king. God took his glory from him when he became proud. His mind became like that of an animal, and he lived with the donkeys and ate grass like an ox. This continued until he learned this lesson: The true God rules over all and controls what happens. He chooses who will be king.

"O king, your ancestor Nebuchadnezzar humbled himself before the true and living God. But you have not done so, even though you knew all about this. You are proud and have gone against God by drinking wine out of cups that were dedicated to Him. You have praised your idols, which cannot see or hear. You did not honor God, but He is the one who has power over your life and everything you do. So God sent the hand that wrote the message on the wall. The message is about your future."

Then Daniel told the king what the words of the message meant, saying, "MENE means God has counted the days until your kingdom will end. TEKEL means you have been weighed on the scales and do not measure up to God's standard. PARSIN (or UPARSIN) means your kingdom is divided and given to the Medes and Persians." **(2)**

What a terrible message! Yet, Daniel did not hold back in giving any of God's message to the king. Many years had gone by since Daniel had an opportunity to speak about his God before the ruling

Note (2)

These are Aramaic words. MENE means *to number or reckon in counting*, as with money. God had counted up the days of Belshazzar and they were done. TEKEL means *to weigh*, as in weighing on a balance or scale. The old scales were a balance—each side had to be equal in weight. If the side containing the product did not match the measured weight of the other side, the product was rejected. God had rejected Babylon because it was evaluated and found to be lacking, not measuring up to God's standard. PARSIN or UPARSIN ("U" means *and*) is the plural of PERES (pā'-res), which means *to break in two or divide*. The Babylonian Empire would be broken up and given to the Medes and Persians.

king. But he trusted God and obeyed Him completely, and spoke boldly to the king. Belshazzar had the right to put Daniel to death if he did not accept his interpretation or like what he said. Why should he believe Daniel? However, an amazing thing happened. The king must have been impressed with Daniel's boldness, for he was faithful to his promise and gave an order for Daniel to be dressed in purple clothes and given a gold chain. Then he announced that Daniel was the third highest ruler in the land. God was truly in all this, protecting and giving Daniel boldness to proclaim His power and word to the king. God blessed him further by allowing him to receive this special honor. (3)

> **Note (3)**
>
> Daniel was the third highest ruler in Babylon, but because Belshazzar was co-ruler under his father, King Nabonidus, Daniel was actually second in command in the city, at least for a short time.

3. The Medes and Persians conquer Babylon. (Daniel 5:30, 31)

(GOD 89; word strips BABYLON, MEDES/PERSIANS; "Statue" visual)

The banquet continued in spite of Daniel's prediction. Probably many wondered if Daniel's words were going to come true. But they didn't have to wait long. That very night God's message *(place 89 on the board)* did come true!

While the banquet was going on inside the palace, the Persian army was very hard at work outside the city. They discovered a way to enter the city of Babylon through the river, which ran through the city. The army changed the direction of the river on the outside of the wall by digging a canal from it to a nearby lake. This lowered the water level in the river, enabling the army to enter the city by following the riverbed under the wall. (4) That very night the Persian army entered Babylon *(add BABYLON)*, taking the king and the people completely by surprise. The Persian army stormed into the banquet hall and killed everyone, including King Belshazzar. Darius the Mede was appointed king over Babylon. (5) The Medes and Persians *(add MEDES/PERSIANS)* were now in control of the Babylonian Empire. God's Word came true, just as Daniel had predicted to Nebuchadnezzar *(add "Statue" visual)* and now to Belshazzar.

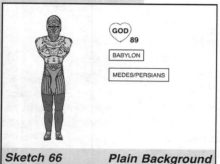

Sketch 66   Plain Background

> **Note (4)**
>
> The record of how the Medes conquered Babylon is taken from Xenophon's *Cyropaedia*, Volume 7, and is found in such reference books as *Barnes' Notes*, Volume 7, pages 302, 303, and *The Bible Knowledge Commentary*, Old Testament, pages 1346, 1347.

■ Conclusion

Summary

(Belshazzar 70, GOD 89, handwriting 78[2], Daniel 88, BELIEVE & OBEY footprints)

Belshazzar *(place 70 on the board)* did not believe *(add footprints)* and obey God *(add 89)*. Even though he knew that Nebuchadnezzar had humbled himself before the true and living God, Belshazzar did not humble himself before God; he deliberately defied God. In what way did Belshazzar do this? *(Encourage response throughout.)* Yes, he drank wine out of the cups dedicated to God; he praised his idols instead of honoring God.

Sketch 67   Plain Background

How did God punish Belshazzar? Yes, Belshazzar was killed when the Persian army conquered Babylon. How did God warn Belshazzar that this was going to happen? That's right; God sent a hand to write a message *(add 78[2])* on the palace wall during a banquet. Who was the only one who was able to read and interpret the message? *(After Daniel is mentioned add 88.)* When did Daniel's prediction come true? Correct, the same night the handwriting appeared and Daniel interpreted its meaning. How did the Persians enter the city? Yes, how clever they were to divert the flow of the river and follow the riverbed under the wall. But it was really God who brought judgment on the Babylonian Empire, and put the Medes and Persians in control.

Application

(Cross 43; word strip YOU)

Belshazzar learned the hard way that you do not get away with rejecting God by ignoring His warning. We need to learn from Belshazzar's mistake. The most important matter of obedience to God has to do with His offer of salvation from sin. Listen carefully as I review God's plan of salvation and see if you have really followed God's Way, *An Obedient Way*, in this matter.

God loves us very much and wants us to obey Him. But we have been born into this world wanting our own way instead of God's Way. The Bible calls this sin, and God must punish sin (Romans 6:23). God sent His Son, the Lord Jesus Christ *(add 43)*, to earth to take the punishment for our sins (Romans 5:8). If we believe that Jesus did this for us and receive Him as our Savior, God will not punish us for our sins (John 3:16). This is good news. However, if we ignore God's warning and continue to go our own way, we will suffer the consequences of our choice and be separated from God forever. Are you *(add YOU)* willing to obey God by submitting to God's Way and receiving the Lord Jesus Christ as your Savior from sin?

Response Activity

*Distribute **"Choosing God's Obedient Way" handouts** and pencils. Encourage the children to carefully consider the responses on the handout as you read them. Then ask the children to check the box that applies to them. Invite any who want to receive the Lord Jesus Christ as their Savior and any who want to make sure they are saved to come and talk with you when the class is dismissed.*

🖎 TAKE-HOME ITEMS

*Distribute **memory verse tokens for Psalm 37:34** and **Bible Study Helps for Lesson 10, Part 1.***

🔼 Note (5)

Cyrus was the king of the Medes and Persians. Since he had conquered many kingdoms, he needed Darius to rule this one.

The Persians Conquer Babylon

Theme: An Obedient Way

Lesson 10

Part Two: God Saves Daniel from the Lions

❋ BEFORE YOU BEGIN...

How many Christians would stop praying if a law were passed forbidding praying to God for thirty days? Probably most of us would respond, "No problem; I'll just adapt to the circumstances and stop praying openly. God doesn't really care whether I pray outwardly or inwardly; I'm still praying. And it's just for thirty days; I'll resume my normal practice next month." Good plan, wouldn't you agree?

Not so for Daniel. He refused to accommodate King Darius' foolish decree. He acted according to principle, not according to expediency. For Daniel, praying to God was a command to be happily obeyed. To pray to any other god or to pretend not to pray was disobedience. So Daniel prayed, willing to face the lions.

What does it take to make us disobey God's Word, whether it be to pray or any other directive? What about your children? Where are they in their level of commitment to "obey God rather than men" (Acts 5:29)? To stand true to the Lord Jesus will require a loyalty to Him that exceeds loyalty to peers and lust for popularity. Make sure your children understand what is at stake. *"Give me understanding, and I shall keep Your law; indeed, I shall observe it with my whole heart"* (Psalm 119:34, NKJV).

☞ AIM:

That the children may

- Know that God blesses His children when they trust and obey Him.
- Respond by choosing to trust and obey God in every circumstance.

📖 SCRIPTURE: Daniel 6

♥ MEMORY VERSE: Psalm 37:34

Wait on the Lord, and keep his way, and he shall exalt thee to inherit the land. (KJV)

Wait for the Lord and keep his way. He will exalt you to inherit the land. (NIV)

MATERIALS TO GATHER

Visual for Psalm 37:34 from *Bible Verses Visualized*
Backgrounds: Review Chart, Plain Background, Council Room, Palace, Plain Dark Background, Cave/Rock Overlays
Figures: R1-R10, R15, R16, 3, 4, 24, 26, 27, 74(1), 77, 79, 80(3), 81, 82, 84, 88, 94
Token holders & memory verse tokens for Psalm 37:34 for any who did not receive them last week
Bible Study Helps for Lesson 10, Part 2
Special:
- **For Memory Verse & Summary:** BELIEVE & OBEY footprints
- **For Introduction:** Poster board lions
- **For Content 3:** Word strips THANKS, HELP
- **For Response Activity:** "I choose to trust and obey" handouts, pencils
- **For Options:** Additional materials for any options you choose to use
- **Note:** *To prepare the poster board lions,* use markers to print the following words, or any others that apply to your group, on lions you have cut from poster board: refusing to go to bed on time, complaining about your lunch, talking when the teacher isn't looking, sharing your candy or video games with others, witnessing to others, bragging about your abilities, doing your homework on time, taking something that doesn't belong to you, forgiving those who hurt you, showing kindness to someone who hurt you.
Follow the instructions on page xii to enlarge and reproduce the lion (pattern P-10 on page 171) to make the poster board lions, and to prepare the "I choose to trust and obey" handouts (pattern P-20 on page 176).

 REVIEW CHART

Display the Review Chart with R15, R16, and R1-R9 in place. Briefly review the theme and the verse of Lesson 10, Part One as a child places R10 on the Chart.

Review Lesson 9, Parts One and Two and Lesson 10, Part One by having volunteers pretend to be the Bible characters given below. Use the suggested questions or questions you and the children write to interview the characters.

SHADRACH, MESHACH, and ABEDNEGO
1. Why did you refuse to bow down and worship King Nebuchadnezzar's statue? *(We could not worship anything or anyone but the true and living God and we trusted Him to help us.)*

▲ Option #1

Reviewing the verse: Hang a clothesline, with clothespins clipped on it, across a wall or a bulletin board or between two chairs. Distribute the verse visual pieces and have the children take turns hanging the visual pieces on the line in the correct order. When all the pieces are on the clothesline, have all the children say the verse together. Then scramble the visual pieces on the clothesline and have other children place them in the correct order. While the children are hanging the pieces on the clothesline, instruct the rest of the class to check to see if the pieces are being put in correct order.

Variation: Hang the verse visual in scrambled order with the words turned away from the class. Have the children, one at a time, choose a piece, look at the words, say the rest of the verse, and then put it in the place where it belongs. Continue until all the pieces have been turned over and put into place.

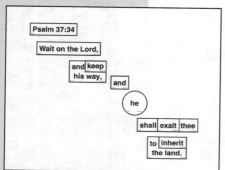

2. What was your punishment for not bowing down to the statue? *(We were thrown into the blazing furnace.)*
3. How did God help you? *(God sent an angel to protect us from burning to death. Our clothes didn't burn, and we had no smell of smoke on us. It was a miracle.)*

KING BELSHAZZAR

1. Since you thought no army could ever capture Babylon, what made you afraid at your banquet? *(I saw a hand writing a message on the wall, but I couldn't read the strange language.)*
2. Why was Daniel brought before you? *(None of the wise men could tell me what the writing said. The queen told me about Daniel and what he had done for Nebuchadnezzar, my grandfather.)*
3. What did you do after Daniel interpreted the message? *(I gave Daniel a gold chain and a royal robe and appointed him as third ruler of the land, but I didn't do anything about the message. I thought that no one could conquer Babylon.)*

DANIEL

1. Why was the message given to King Belshazzar? *(God warned him about his sin and the future.)*
2. What did the handwriting on the wall mean? *(God told Belshazzar that Babylon was going to be taken over by the Medes and Persians because he had not humbled himself before God.)*
3. When did your prediction come true? *(The Medes and Persians took over Babylon and killed Belshazzar that same night.)*

♥ MEMORY VERSE

Use the visual to review Psalm 37:34 and its meaning. Display the BELIEVE & OBEY footprints when indicated. ▲#1

Who can say Psalm 37:34? *(Response)* Did God bless Belshazzar? *(Response)* No. Why not? *(Response)* That's right; he disobeyed God by ignoring Him and choosing His own way. Who did obey God? *(Response)* Yes, Daniel faithfully obeyed God all the time, even when he didn't receive any recognition from Belshazzar. How did God bless Daniel? Yes, God helped Daniel to boldly give His message to Belshazzar. He also allowed Daniel to be rewarded with a gold chain, a royal robe, and the position of third ruler in Babylon.

God wants to bless us too—those of us who have trusted Jesus as our Savior. God blesses us in many ways. ▲#2 He has promised us a home in heaven, where we will live with Him forever. He has given us His Word to help us know what He wants us to do and the Holy Spirit to help us obey Him. He has promised to provide our daily needs and often gives us some of the things we want, even recognition for doing a good job. No matter what our circumstances are—good or bad—we must choose to trust and obey God *(display footprints)*.

📖 BIBLE LESSON OUTLINE

God Saves Daniel from the Lions

■ **Introduction**

Obey or disobey

■ **Bible Content**
1. Daniel serves a new king.
2. Daniel's enemies trick King Darius.
3. Daniel prays to God.
4. Daniel is thrown into the lions' den.
5. King Darius makes a new law.

■ **Conclusion**

Summary

Application
Trusting and obeying God in every circumstance

Response Activity
Choosing to trust and obey this week

📖 BIBLE LESSON

■ **Introduction**

Obey or disobey

(Poster board lions)
As I hold up each lion and read what it says, stand up if you think it is a way to obey God. If it is not, stay seated. *(Let the children respond as you read.)* ▲#3

How do we know what God wants us to do? *(Response)* Yes, the Bible tells us. That is why it is so important to read it and learn what God tells us to do. Daniel knew God's Word very well and chose to obey God, even when others were not watching. Today we will see what happened when Daniel chose to obey God in a very difficult circumstance.

▲ **Option#2**

Have the children discuss or draw on paper ways they have seen God bless them. Allow the children to explain their illustrations, and then hang them up for everyone to see.

▲ **Option#3**

Let children hold the lion visuals or hang the visuals on a wall or a bulletin board for all to see. Discuss why each statement is or isn't a way to obey God.

Bible Content

1. Daniel serves a new king. (Daniel 6:1-3; 9:1)

Sketch 68 — Council Room

(Daniel 88, King Darius 84, men 3, 4, 26, 94)

Daniel *(place 88 on the board)* served King Nebuchadnezzar for about thirty-nine years after being taken from his home in Jerusalem. During all those years Daniel honored God by serving the king well and by speaking for God when he could. In turn, God allowed him to have a place of importance in the Babylonian government. During the reigns of Nebuchadnezzar's son and grandson, Daniel remained faithful to God, trusting and obeying Him as he went about his work.

When the Medes and Persians conquered Babylon, huge changes took place for everyone, including Daniel. He was over eighty years old now. Daniel may have wondered if he would lose his position in the government. Did the new king hate Jews? Was he going to lose his life? How would King Darius treat the people? There were a lot of unanswered questions, but Daniel never stopped trusting God *(remove 88)*.

When Darius *(place 84 on the board)* became king over Babylon, he appointed 120 governors *(add 3, 4, 26, 94)* to help him rule the kingdom. He then appointed three men to supervise the governors. The supervisors were to make sure that no one cheated the king. Daniel was chosen to be one of the supervisors.

Let's read Daniel 6:3 to learn how Daniel did his job. *(Have someone read the verse aloud or have the children read it silently and tell what they learn.)* Even though Daniel was old, he did his work better than the other supervisors and governors. Darius was pleased with Daniel's work and made plans to put Daniel in charge of the whole kingdom. *(Remove 3, 4, 26, 94; add 88.)* That meant that Daniel was going to be next to the king in power, and the other two supervisors would have to report to him. What a great God Daniel served—a God who controls wicked kings and puts the right people in the right place for His own purpose! *(Remove 88, 84.)*

2. Daniel's enemies trick King Darius. (Daniel 6:4-9)

Sketch 69 — Council Room

(King 84, men bowing 74[largest figure only], man 24)

How would you feel if you had been one of the supervisors who had not been chosen to serve next to the king? *(Response)* Would you be jealous and angry? *(Response)* That is exactly how those men felt. But even worse than that, Daniel was a Jew—one of the exiles from Israel—not a Babylonian or a Mede or a Persian. So the men tried very hard to find fault with Daniel so that they could report it to the king and have him removed from his position. Read the end of verse 4 in chapter 6 and tell us what they found. *(Have a child read the last sentence aloud.)* They could find *nothing dishonest or wrong* with Daniel or his work. What a great witness Daniel was for God even in his work! How frustrated and angry those men must have been. Finally they said, "We will never find anything against Daniel unless it has something to do with the way he worships his God." Then it dawned on them. This was the very thing they could use to get Daniel into doing something against the king's law.

Immediately the governors and supervisors went to the king *(place 84 on the board).* They *(add 74[1])* bowed down before him and said *(add 24),* "O King Darius, live forever! We have all agreed that the king should make this law for everyone to obey: No one can pray to any god or man except to you, O king, for the next thirty days. Anyone who doesn't obey will be thrown into the lions' den. Make the law and write it down so that it cannot be changed." ▲#4 The king must have thought this was a great way to have the people honor him. He never suspected what the men were really planning. So he wrote the law and put his seal on it. That meant it couldn't be changed or reversed; it was an official law according to the Law of the Medes and Persians. As the men left, I'm sure they were laughing and thinking, "We can get rid of Daniel now." ◪(1)

3. Daniel prays to God. (Daniel 6:10-15)

(Daniel 77, men 3, 26; word strips THANKS, HELP)

Daniel heard about the king's new law. We don't know what he thought or how he felt, but we do know what he did. Look at verse 10 for the answer. *(Allow a child to give the answer after reading the verse silently.)* Daniel went home and knelt in front of his window to pray to God. *(Place 77 on the board.)* Was this the first time? *(Response)* No! Verse 10 tells us it was Daniel's habit to pray three times a day. *(Have a child read the last half of the verse out loud.)* Do you think Daniel realized what would happen if anyone saw him praying? *(Response)* It certainly would mean death, but Daniel loved God and knew he could trust God in this very difficult situation. So Daniel prayed to God as he always did. He did not let those wicked men force him into disobeying God.

Sketch 70   **Palace**

Verses 10 and 11 tell us some things about Daniel's prayer. *(Have the children find two things Daniel said in his prayer.)* First, he gave thanks to God *(add THANKS).* ▲#5 Would you feel like thanking God if you knew you might die if someone saw you praying to Him? Second, Daniel asked God for His help *(add HELP).* Daniel knew he needed God's power and help to give him victory over the wicked plan of those evil men.

▲ **Option #4**

Write the king's two laws on separate pieces of poster board. Attach the first one to the wall as it is introduced at this time. Cover it with the second law at the end of Bible Content 5.

◪ **Note (1)**

Even though the Medo-Persian Empire was an absolute monarchy and the word of the king was law like the Babylonian Empire, it was different in this way: the government of Medo-Persia was a government of law; its principle was the supremacy of THE LAW. Once the word of the king had gone forth as the law, that law could not be changed or reversed even by the king himself. The king was bound, even against himself, by his own word or decree once it had become the law.

▲ **Option #5**

Discuss some of the things Daniel might have been able to thank God for in his situation.

Sketch 71   Council Room

The governors and supervisors *(add 3, 26)* went as a group and found Daniel praying to his God.

(Men 26, 3, man 24, King 84)
Immediately the men *(place 26, 3, 24 on the board)* went to the king *(add 84)* and said, "Didn't you make a law stating that no one can pray to any man or god except you, O king? Doesn't it say that anyone who disobeys this law during the next thirty days will be thrown into the lions' den?"

"Yes," replied the king, "and the law cannot be changed or cancelled."

Then the men said to the king, "Daniel, the exile from Judah, has not paid attention to the king's law! He still prays to his God three times a day!" When Darius heard this, he became very upset. He realized he had been tricked into signing the law. He respected Daniel very much because he was an honest and fair leader. So the king worked until sunset, trying to find a way to save Daniel.

But the king could not change the law. The men who had talked him into making the law came to him and said, "Remember, O King, the law of the Medes and Persians. It says that no law or command given by the king can be changed."

⌂ Note (2)

Wax seals: Wax was melted and poured over the edge of the lid of the den and then the king's ring was pushed into the hot wax, setting his seal into the wax. If anyone tried to free Daniel, the seal would be broken and all would know it. This was a means of security for this type of situation as well as for sending important letters and special orders.

4. Daniel is thrown into the lions' den. (Daniel 6:16-24)

(King 81, Daniel 79, lions 80[3])

Finally the king gave up trying; he had to obey his own law. He gave orders for Daniel to be thrown into the lions' den. As Daniel was being led away, Darius *(place 81 in the cave opening)* said, " May the God you serve all the time save you." Even at that moment the king showed respect for Daniel's trust in God *(remove 81)*.

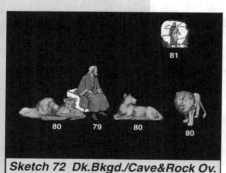

Sketch 72 Dk.Bkgd./Cave&Rock Ov.

Being thrown into the lions' den was a form of punishment used for the king's enemies. The lions were kept hungry and killed prisoners immediately. After Daniel *(add 79)* was thrown into the lions' den *(add 80[3])*, a large rock was placed over the mouth of the den, and the king put his seal on it along with those of all his officials. ⌂(2)

King Darius returned to the palace, but he could not eat or sleep. His servants tried to play music to help him sleep, but all he could think of was Daniel.

At dawn the next morning the king hurried out to the lions' den. Had Daniel survived? What would he find? When he came near to the den *(add 81)*, he called out to Daniel in a loud and worried voice, "Daniel, servant of the living God! Has your God, whom you always worship, been able to save you from the lions?" Would Daniel answer him? It did not seem possible!

But then Daniel answered, "O king, live forever! My God sent His angel to close the lions' mouths. They have not hurt me, because my God knows I am innocent. I never did anything wrong to you, O king." The king was bursting with joy and relief as he gave orders to bring Daniel out of the lions' den. Sure enough, Daniel had no injuries, not even a scratch! It was truly a miracle, something only the true and living God could do. Verse 23 tells us why it happened. *(Have the children turn to verse 23 and have someone read the last phrase aloud.)* Yes, it says that Daniel trusted in his God. Daniel had trusted and obeyed God, and God protected him in the lions' den.

Then the king gave orders for the men who accused Daniel to be thrown into the lions' den. The lions grabbed them before they hit the floor of the den and destroyed them quickly.

▲ **Option #6**

The children may act out this entire story in Chapter 6. Have one person read the narrative as the children act out the parts, or provide copies of the dialogue for individual children to read as they act out the story. Provide costumes and props for interest if possible.

5. King Darius makes a new law. (Daniel 6:25-28)

(King 84, Daniel 79, bench 82)
Then King Darius *(place 84, 79, 82 on the board)* wrote a new law to all people throughout the lands where the Medes and Persians ruled. We can read it in verses 26 and 27. *(Read the verses together or have a child read them aloud.)* Darius said, "I am making a new law that is for everyone in my kingdom. Everyone must fear and respect the God of Daniel." Why did the king do this? *(Response)* Darius saw God's power at work—doing things no man-made god can do.

Sketch 73 — Council Room

Because Daniel trusted and obeyed his God, God made him very successful throughout the reign of Darius the Mede. ▲#6

■ **Conclusion**

Summary

(Daniel 79, bench 82, lion 80[1]; BELIEVE & OBEY footprints, verse visual [optional])

From the time Daniel *(place 79, 82 on the board)* was young he had faced one difficulty after another. What were some of them? *(Add to the children's responses any of the following answers they do not give: He was taken as a captive to Babylon when he was young; he was expected to learn a new language and culture and eat the king's food; he faced death when the wise men couldn't tell Nebuchadnezzar his dream and its meaning; he boldly told Belshazzar of God's judgment; he was put in the lions' den because he disobeyed the king's law.)*

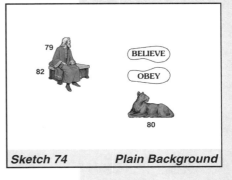

Sketch 74 — Plain Background

Do you think it was hard for Daniel to disobey the king's law forbidding him to pray to God? *(Response)* We don't really know if it was hard for Daniel or not. But we *do know* that Daniel had trusted and obeyed God *(add footprints)* through everything that had happened to him before this. We also know that he experienced God's care and

▲ **Option#7**

Ask the children to name the ways God blessed Daniel, and list them on newsprint or chalkboard.

blessing throughout the difficult circumstances he faced, including the lions' den. How *did* God care for Daniel in the lions' den?" *(Response)* That's right. He sent an angel to shut the lions' mouths. How did God bless Daniel? *(Response)* Yes, He kept him safe in the lions' den and gave him success during the reign of Darius. He is a good example of our memory verse *(say it together; use the visual if necessary).* ▲#7

Application

God wants us to trust and obey Him in every circumstance, too—at home with our families, at school, with our friends in the neighborhood, at church, and Bible Club. Will it always be easy? *(Response)* No, but God has given us His Word so that we will know how to obey Him, and He has given us the Holy Spirit who gives us the power to obey Him. We can trust His promise that He will help us.

We do not know all the circumstances God may allow us to experience, but we need to decide now that no matter what happens or where we are, we *will* trust God and obey Him.

Response Activity

Distribute the **"I choose to trust and obey" handouts** *and pencils. Challenge the children to decide now to trust and obey God no matter where they are or what happens to them. Have them sign their name on the line to show they are making the choice. Lead them in prayer, asking God to help them trust and obey Him this week.*

Invite any who have never received the Lord Jesus as Savior to take the first step of trust and obedience by receiving Him as their Savior.

✍ TAKE-HOME ITEMS

Distribute **memory verse tokens for Psalm 37:34** *and* **Bible Study Helps for Lesson 10, Part 2.**

Esther Becomes Queen
Theme: A God-Planned Way

Lesson 11

❀ BEFORE YOU BEGIN...

This lesson is all about commitment—God's commitment to us to work out His plan and our commitment to Him to follow His plan. In a day when commitment in any area of life is a foreign concept, it is a struggle to communicate it to our children.

The problem begins at home where the mutual commitment of husband and wife should be modeled to their children. That commitment has largely been watered down to be only as long as the marriage is convenient or enjoyable. The high divorce rate is convincing evidence that escaping is too quickly considered and carried out, leaving the family in shambles with devastated children. Even the church is plagued with shallow commitment. Pastors, youth leaders, teachers, and even missionaries cannot commit to long-term service.

Commitment involves a fair amount of hard work plus a generous supply of perseverance, permeated with a solid conviction of God's calling. Can your children develop a commitment to match Esther's and Mordecai's? It's up to you, dear teacher, to lay the foundation that can produce "Esthers" and "Mordecais" for their generation. *"I know the thoughts that I think toward you, says the Lord, thoughts of peace and not of evil, to give you a future and a hope" (Jeremiah 29:11, NKJV).*

☞ AIM:

That the children may

- Know that God wants to use them to carry out His plans.
- Respond by trusting God and committing themselves to do whatever He wants them to do.

📖 SCRIPTURE: Esther 1–4

♥ MEMORY VERSE: Isaiah 55:9

For as the heavens are higher than the earth, so are my ways higher than your ways. (KJV)

As the heavens are higher than the earth, so are my ways higher than your ways. (NIV)

125

📁 MATERIALS TO GATHER

Visual for Isaiah 55:9 from *Bible Verses Visualized*
Backgrounds: Review Chart, Plain Background, Old Testament Map II, Council Room, General Interior, Courtyard, Palace, City Street, City Wall
Figures: R1-R11, R15, R16, 3, 4, 8, 9, 10, 13, 14, 15, 22, 23, 26, 27A, 29, 47, 70, 71, 74(2,) 83, 84, 85, 88, 89(GOD)
Token holders & memory verse tokens for Isaiah 55:9
Bible Study Helps for Lesson 11
Special:
- **For Introduction:** A jigsaw puzzle with its box.
- **For Bible Content 1:** A world map; word strips EZRA, NEHEMIAH, ESTHER
- **For Bible Content 2:** Word strip JEWS
- **For Summary:** A large poster board puzzle
- **For Response Activity:** "God's Plan" handouts, pencils
- **For Options:** Additional materials for any options you choose to use
- **Note:** Follow the instructions on page xii to prepare the large poster board puzzle (pattern P-9 on page 171; directions in Summary) and the "God's Plan" handout (pattern P-21 on page 177). Glue a jigsaw puzzle piece to each handout.

REVIEW CHART

Display the Review Chart with R15 and R16 in place. Place R1-R10 in mixed-up order on the Chart or on a table. Have R11 ready to use when indicated. Have children come one at a time and each place one of the review tokens on the Chart, giving its name and meaning. Then have all the children repeat the corresponding memory verse for each one. Use the questions below to review Lesson 10, Part Two.

1. Who was the new king in Babylon? *(Darius)*
2. Why did the governors and supervisors want to get rid of Daniel? *(They were jealous of Daniel because he had been appointed second in command.)*
3. How did they plan to get rid of Daniel? *(They tricked the king into making a law that anyone who prays to any god or man, except him, for thirty days would be thrown into a den of lions.)*
4. What did Daniel continue to do? *(He prayed to God three times a day as he always did.)*
5. How did God show His power to all the rulers in Babylon? *(He saved Daniel from the lions.)*
6. Why did God do this for Daniel? *(Daniel trusted and obeyed God all the time.)*

Because Daniel trusted and obeyed God, God was able to use him to carry out His plan of making His name known in Babylon. Today we will see that nothing takes God by surprise, for God's Way is *A God-Planned Way* (place R11 on the Chart).

♥ MEMORY VERSE

Use the visual to teach Isaiah 55:9 when indicated.

Have you ever tried to figure how high the sky is or how far away the clouds are? When we ride in an airplane and go above the clouds, there is still sky that goes higher and higher above the clouds. If we traveled into outer space and got closer to the moon and the other planets, the galaxies are still very far away. They are so far and so high that no one can ever really get near them.

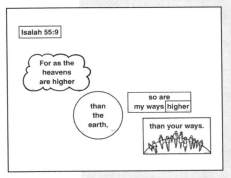

God's ways of doing things are like the sky and galaxies that cannot be reached. His ways of doing things are so far beyond anything we can imagine. That is what our memory verse tells us. Let's read it together. *(Have the children find the verse in their Bibles. Display each visual piece as the class reads the verse together.)* The word *higher* *(flip the word up to reveal the meaning)* is describing God's Way as being *wiser* or *way beyond all our thinking and understanding.* Let's read the verse again and say *wiser* in place of *higher.*

If God were not wiser than each of us, He would not be God. He would be just like us, and we could never trust Him completely. Since God has all wisdom and is in control of all that happens in our world, we can trust him completely. Even though we do not always understand God's ways, we can still trust Him with our lives, because we know He knows what is best for us far better than we do. *(Work on memorizing the verse.)* ▲#1

▲ Option#1

Memorizing the verse: Seat the children in a circle on the floor or on chairs. Stand in the middle of the circle holding a beanbag, beach ball, or soft-textured ball. Throw the ball to one of the children, who should say the first word of the verse and then throw the ball back to you. Then throw it to a second child to say the second word of the verse and throw the ball back to you. Repeat this process until all the words and reference of verse have been said. Give the children an opportunity to take turns standing in the middle of the circle to throw the ball. Encourage all the children to throw the ball gently. If the room is too small for a circle, follow the procedure from the front of the classroom.

📖 BIBLE LESSON OUTLINE

Esther Becomes Queen

■ **Introduction**

Seeing life as a puzzle

■ **Bible Content**

1. Ahasuerus becomes King of Persia.
2. Ahasuerus chooses a new queen.
   a. Vashti disobeys the king.
   b. The king banishes Vashti.
   c. Esther goes to the palace.
   d. Esther becomes queen.

3. Haman plans to destroy the Jews.
     a. Mordecai reports an assassination plot.
     b. Mordecai refuses to bow to Haman.
     c. The Jews receive bad news.
     d. Mordecai begs Esther for help.

■ Conclusion

Summary

Application
    Being used by God at home, at school, and at church

Response Activity
    Making a commitment to do whatever God wants

📖 BIBLE LESSON

■ Introduction

Seeing life as a puzzle

Spread the puzzle pieces on a table. Hide the picture on the puzzle box. Make at least part of the puzzle together. ▲#2

Did you ever put a puzzle like this together? *(Let the children respond throughout.)* How long did it take you to finish the puzzle? Did you have a hard time knowing where to fit some of the pieces? What helped you to know? Yes, seeing the picture on the box. *(Display the picture on the puzzle box.)* Seeing the picture helped you to understand how the pieces all fit together. The person who made the puzzle planned the picture first and then cut the pieces so they would all fit together to make the completed picture.

Sometimes our life seems like a puzzle that is made up of many pieces. God has a plan for each of our lives; in fact, he has a plan for the whole world. We discover God's plan in the Bible. It tells us what God has done to make a way for us to get to heaven and some of what will happen when we get there. But sometimes we don't see how all the pieces of the puzzle are going to fit together. That is why it is so important to read God's Word and do what it says. Even if we don't understand how He wants to use us to carry out His plan in this world, God wants us to trust Him and be willing to do whatever He asks us to do now. This will help us to be ready to serve Him in the future. In our lesson today we will see how God used someone to carry out His plan for the Jewish nation.

▲ **Option#2**

You can use a large floor puzzle as long as it has a box with a picture of the entire puzzle.

Variation: Divide the class into small groups and distribute age-appropriate puzzles. Allow time for groups to try and put puzzles together without seeing the pictures. Discuss the difficulties of doing this and relate them to the lesson as stated.

Bible Content

1. Ahasuerus becomes King of Persia. (Esther 1:1, 2)

(A world map; word strips EZRA, NEHEMIAH, ESTHER)
The Medes and Persians ruled from India to Egypt. Fifty years earlier, during Daniel's time, the Persian Empire conquered the Babylonians. Ahasuerus (Ä-ha´-shoo-ār´us) became king after Darius died. △(1) The capital city was moved from Babylon to Shushan. *(Indicate BABYLON and SHUSHAN; show the approximate location of these cities on the world map.)* Shushan was larger and much more beautiful than Babylon. By this time many of the Jews had returned to Israel, but many more chose to live as free people in Persia. We can read about this in the books of Ezra, Nehemiah, and Esther *(place EZRA, NEHEMIAH, ESTHER on the board)*. Turn to Esther 1:1 and place your bookmark there.

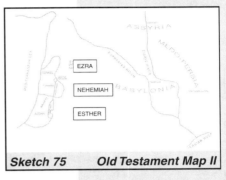
Sketch 75   Old Testament Map II

2. Ahasuerus chooses a new queen. (Esther 1:1-2:20)

a. Vashti disobeys the king.

(King 84, people 3, 4, 26, 9, 14, wise men 47, 71)
After reigning as king for three years, Ahasuerus decided to give a banquet for all the leaders, wise men, and military leaders in all the provinces of the Persian Empire. *(Place 84, 3, 4, 26, 9, 14 on the board.)* For six months the king entertained them and gave tours of his beautiful city and palace and showed off all his wealth. *(If time permits, have the children read Esther 1:6, 7.)*

Sketch 76   Council Room

At the end of the six months the king gave another banquet. All the men in Shushan were invited. They celebrated for an entire week.

Meanwhile, Queen Vashti prepared a great feast for the women of the palace. In that culture, the men and women never ate together. During the banquet the king sent one of his servants with this message to Vashti: "You must come immediately to the king so he can show everyone how beautiful you are." When Vashti refused to come, the king was furious. No one, not even the queen, could disobey an order from the King of Persia!

b. The king banishes Vashti.

Immediately Ahasuerus called his wise men and experts of the law together *(remove 9, 26; add 47, 71)*. Ahasuerus asked them, "What does the law say must be done to Queen Vashti? She has not obeyed my order."

△ Note (1)

In Lessons 11 and 12 we have chosen to use the Hebrew names for the king (Ahasuerus) and the city (Shushan) as they appear in the KJV. The NIV uses the Greek names taken from the Septuagint Version. So if you are using the NIV, you will use Xerxes (Zûrk´-sēz) for the king and Susa for the city to keep from confusing the children.

One adviser answered, "The queen has not only done wrong to the king, but she has done wrong to all the nobles and all the peoples of the kingdom. When all the wives in the kingdom hear what Vashti has done, they will show disrespect for their husbands by refusing to obey them. So, if it pleases the king, make a royal order that Vashti be sent away from the palace forever. Then let the king find a new queen." So, a law was made—a law of the Medes and Persians that could not be changed or reversed—which said that Vashti could never again enter the king's presence.

c. Esther goes to the palace.

(Mordecai 88, Esther 22, GOD 89; word strip JEWS)
In another part of the city of Shushan lived a Jewish man named Mordecai *(Mor´-de-kī; place 88 on the board)* and his cousin Hadassah *(Ha-das´-sa; add 22)*. Hadassah was also called Esther (Esther is a Persian name meaning *star*). Mordecai raised her as his daughter after her parents died. Mordecai's relatives had been captives from Jerusalem. He worked for the Persian government; so he sat at the gate of the palace, where many government affairs were handled. Esther loved and respected him.

Now that Vashti was gone, the king needed a new queen. He sent an order throughout the empire that every young and beautiful girl who had never been married be brought to the palace. The girl that pleased the king the most would be chosen as the next queen of Persia. Those who were not chosen would spend the rest of their lives in a special part of the palace reserved for them, never to leave it for as long as they lived. ◸(2)

The king's soldiers went throughout the empire bringing the girls to the palace. Can you imagine how Esther and Mordecai felt when they came to their home? *(Response)* For many of the girls it was a dream come true, but for Esther it was more like a nightmare. The Jewish law said she was to marry only a Jewish man. She must have been frightened and worried—wondering what would happen to her. Would she have to eat things that were forbidden by God's laws? Would she ever see Mordecai again? Mordecai told her not to let anyone know she was a Jew.

Even though there is no mention of God *(add 89)* in the book of Esther, He was always with Esther. The Jews *(add JEWS)* were God's chosen people, and He had a plan for them. Even though Esther and Mordecai could not understand what was happening, God was in control and was working out His plan for His people.

d. Esther becomes queen.

(Esther 22, girls 8, 13, Hegai 29)
Each girl spent a year preparing for her night with the

Sketch 77 — General Interior

◸ Note (2)

All those girls who were not chosen would then be made to live inside the palace in an area reserved for the king's concubines. They would live hoping the king would ask for one of them sometime to sleep with him when he pleased. Some were never called. All of them lived out their days there, never to go outside the palace again.

Sketch 78 — Courtyard

king. *(Place 22, 8, 13 on the board.)* Let's read what she had to do. *(Have children read Esther 2:12 aloud.)* Yes, she had to complete twelve months of beauty treatments. Then she could choose whatever she wanted to take with her to the king's palace—her own clothes and jewelry. Every day Mordecai came to the gate outside the place where Esther was living to see how she was doing.

But God was at work helping Esther. Look in verse 9 and at the end of verse 15 to see how He did it. *(Response)* Yes, she won the favor of everyone, including Hegai (Hā′-gī), the chief servant *(add 29)*. He gave her beauty treatments, special food, seven servants, and the very best place to live. God was continuing to work out His plan.

(King 84, people 3, 4, 26, Esther 83, people 9, 10)
When it was Esther's turn to spend the night with King Ahasuerus, God worked on her behalf and gave her favor with the king. Verse 17 tells us what happened. *(Have the children read it and respond.)* Yes, Esther pleased the king more than all the other girls. So Ahasuerus made Esther, a Jewish girl, queen over the entire Persian Kingdom. *(Place 84, 83, 3, 4, 26 on the board.)* The king then made a huge feast in her honor and proclaimed a holiday throughout the kingdom *(add 9, 10)*, giving gifts to everyone. I'm sure it

Sketch 79   **Palace**

was not easy for Esther to be the queen of such an evil king, but God was giving her the help and courage she needed. He had a plan for His people; Esther was an important part of it! *(Remove all figures except 84.)*

3. Haman plans to destroy the Jews. (Esther 2:21–4:17)

a. Mordecai reports an assassination plot.

(Esther 83)
One day while Mordecai was working at the palace gate, he overheard two of the king's soldiers making plans to assassinate the king. Mordecai sent word to Esther *(add 83)*. She told King Ahasuerus that Mordecai had discovered the plot. When the report was found to be true, the men were hanged on the gallows and the incident was recorded in the official book. But Mordecai was never rewarded according to the Persian custom.

b. Mordecai refuses to bow to Haman.

(Haman 70, people bowing 74 [2 largest], Mordecai 88, men 4)
Sometime after Esther became queen, the king decided to honor one of his nobles named Haman (Hā′man; add 70). Haman was not a good man and cared only about himself. The king promoted him above all the nobles at the

Sketch 80   **City Street**

palace and then gave the order for everyone to bow down to Haman whenever he rode through the city.

How proud Haman was of himself! As he passed by the people, they *(add 74[2], 88)* would all bow down before him. All but one! Mordecai refused to bow down. This made Haman furious, and he began to hate Mordecai. *(Remove 70, 74; add 4.)*

Some of the royal officials asked Mordecai, "Why don't you obey the king's command and bow to Haman?" Every day they kept talking to him about it, but he refused to obey the order, telling them he was a Jew. God had commanded the Jews not to bow down or worship anyone but Him (Ex.20:1, 2). When Haman learned Mordecai was a Jew, he decided to destroy *all* the Jews in the kingdom. 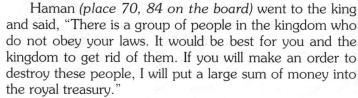(3)

⌂ Note (3)

Satan's strategy was to get rid of God's people completely so that the Savior of the world could not be born. He knew about the prophecy that the Messiah would be born of the tribe of Judah. This was one way to accomplish it.

c. The Jews receive bad news.

(Haman 70, king 84, scroll 27A)

Haman *(place 70, 84 on the board)* went to the king and said, "There is a group of people in the kingdom who do not obey your laws. It would be best for you and the kingdom to get rid of them. If you will make an order to destroy these people, I will put a large sum of money into the royal treasury."

The king gave his signet ring to Haman and said, "Keep your money. The people are yours. Do as you please." So the law was written and sealed with the king's ring and could not be changed or reversed. *(Place 27A in Haman's hands.)* It stated that all the Jews in the kingdom were to be put to death on a certain day. It was determined that the day would be just one year later. Riders traveled across the Persian Empire carrying the dreadful news to everyone. There must have been great sorrow and fear among the Jews when they heard it. Even the people in the city of Shushan were astonished by this horrible news. Many who lived and worked alongside the Jews must have wondered why they were to be killed.

Sketch 81   Palace

d. Mordecai begs Esther for help.

(Mordecai 85, servant 15)

When Mordecai heard the news, he cried very loudly and sadly at the city gate *(place 85 on the board)*. Everyone heard him as they passed by. When Esther heard about her cousin, she sent a servant *(add 15)* to find out why Mordecai was so upset. She hadn't heard the news yet. Mordecai gave the servant the entire report and a copy of the king's law to give to Esther. Mordecai also told him to tell Esther to go to the king and beg for mercy, and plead with him for the lives of her people.

Queen Esther sent a message back to Mordecai, "There is a law that anyone who goes to the king in the inner

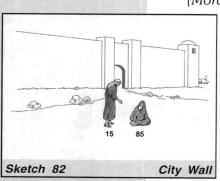

Sketch 82   City Wall

courtyard without being called must be put to death. There is only one exception. If the king holds out his royal scepter, that person will live. The king has not called for me for the past month." Esther realized she could die in obeying Mordecai.

Mordecai sent another message to Esther, this time showing us God's plan and purpose in placing Esther in the palace. He said, "Do you think that you will be saved from death because you are in the palace? Remember, you are a Jew and will die with the rest of us. If you keep quiet, then someone else will save the Jews. But who knows, you may have been chosen queen for such a time as this?"

Mordecai trusted the living God and knew that God would never go back on His plan for having the Savior come through the Jews and that He would save them somehow. God was working out His plan for Mordecai, Esther, and her people to show His power throughout the Persian Empire.

Then Esther sent her answer to her cousin, "Gather all the Jews in Shushan and fast three days and nights for me. My servants and I will do the same. Then I will go to the king. If I die, I die." Mordecai did just as Esther had instructed him. For three days all the Jews in the palace and all over the city fasted. They did not eat, but prayed, which is what the Jews did when they fasted. The Jews believed in a God who could do miracles. They had seen and heard of them throughout their history. Would God do a miracle for them now? Remember His ways are higher and wiser than anything we can imagine. We will see how His plan was carried out in our next lesson.

■ Conclusion

Summary

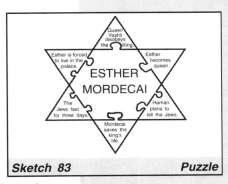

Sketch 83 — Puzzle

Have the following sentences printed on the poster board puzzle pieces, starting with the top center triangle and moving clockwise: Queen Vashti disobeys the king. Esther becomes queen. Haman plans to kill the Jews. Mordecai saves the king's life. The Jews fast for three days. Esther is forced to live in the palace. Place the puzzle pieces on the board or on the floor. The Esther and Mordecai piece should be in the center of the puzzle when it is finished.

Esther's and Mordecai's lives seemed like one great big puzzle without a picture. We can see some of the ways God was working in Esther and Mordecai by looking at the puzzle pieces of their lives. The pieces are all scattered and do not seem to fit together easily. And there *isn't* any picture to look at. But let's look at the pieces and see *if* God was working even when no one could see what God had planned. *(Have the children come one at a time to choose a puzzle piece and tell how they think God was working in that situation. Then have them put their piece in the right place in the puzzle. Continue until the puzzle is completed.)*

God was using Esther and Mordecai to work out His plan for His people, the Jews. Did Esther understand what God was doing? *(Response)* No, probably not. What did she do to show she was trusting God? *(Response)* Yes, she got Mordecai and the Jews to fast and pray for her so she would have courage to go before the king. Esther and Mordecai were not able to see God's big picture yet, but they knew He was the only one who could help them at this frightening and dangerous time.

Application

God wants to use you to carry out His plan. He has placed you in a particular family, neighborhood, school, and church. You may not know how He wants to use you or what He wants to accomplish through your life. But He wants you to live for Him in that place so that others will see their need to trust God and live for Him.

Your life may seem like one big puzzle right now. Are there some things in your life that you do not understand? Maybe someone you love has an illness or has had an accident and is hurting. Or your family is in trouble and splitting up. Maybe you are having big problems with your schoolwork. Maybe there is someone who bullies you or makes fun of you. We always want to know what God is doing and why He allows such things to come into our lives. When we know Jesus as Savior, we have God on our side to help us get through these things, even if we don't see how the puzzle pieces fit together. We can ask God to help us as He helped Esther. This shows we trust God, especially when we cannot understand His plan for us. *(Say the memory verse together.)*

Response Activity

Distribute **"God's Plan" handouts** and pencils. Challenge the children to consider making a commitment to do whatever God wants them to do. Give them an opportunity to sign the commitment handout if they are willing to do so. Remind them that God's ways are higher and wiser than theirs, and He will help them to do whatever He asks them to do, just as He did for Esther. Close in prayer, thanking God that He has a plan for each of them and asking God to help them to cooperate with His plans for them.

Invite any who desire to receive Christ as Savior to speak with you after class. Help them understand that God's plan for them begins with their becoming His children.

✎ TAKE-HOME ITEMS

Distribute **memory verse tokens for Isaiah 55:9** and **Bible Study Helps for Lesson 11.**

God Saves Esther and Her People
Theme: A Courageous Way

Lesson 12

❈ BEFORE YOU BEGIN...

It is easy to miss the significance of Esther's statement to her cousin: "If I perish, I perish." Was she overreacting, overstating the situation to gain maximum sympathy? Or was she really grasping the state of affairs: the heartless protocol of the Persian court; the capricious character of the Persian king; the perplexing status of women in Persian male chauvinist culture. The bottom line was that to go into the king's court uninvited was virtual suicide—one chance in a hundred that she would come out alive.

In such a situation true courage thrives. Esther was convinced there was no other way but to put her life on the line for the sake of her people. And she knew she needed the prayers of God's people to make it through. Certain suicide in God's hand is sure success.

Your children face an unfriendly world that is extremely intimidating to those who want to be godly in daily living. Yet the God of Esther is still granting courage to those committed to His ways and trusting Him for strength to do the right thing no matter what. *"Be strong and of good courage...for the Lord your God, He is the One who goes with you. He will not leave you nor forsake you"* (Deuteronomy 31:6, NKJV).

 AIM:

That the children may

- Know that God gives His children courage to do what is right when they are afraid.
- Respond by asking God for courage when they are afraid to do the right thing.

📖 SCRIPTURE: Esther 5–10

♥ MEMORY VERSE: Proverbs 10:29

The way of the Lord is strength to the upright. (KJV)
The way of the Lord is a refuge for the righteous. (NIV)

📁 **MATERIALS TO GATHER**

Visual for Proverbs 10:29 from *Bible Verses Visualized*
Backgrounds: Review Chart, Plain Background, Palace, City Street, Council Room
Figures: R1-R12, R15, R16, 3, 4, 9, 10, 14, 15, 24, 26, 27, 27A, 27B, 70, 70A, 74(largest only), 82, 83, 84, 84A, 86, 87, 88, 89(2)
Token holders & memory verse tokens for Proverbs 10:29
Bible Study Helps for Lesson 12
Special:
- **For Memory Verse and Summary:** BELIEVE & OBEY footprints
- **For Introduction and Summary:** Word strip COURAGE
- **For Content 6:** Word strips MARCH, FEAST OF PURIM
- **For Application:** Newsprint & marker or chalkboard & chalk
- **For Response Activity:** "Prayer Reminder" handouts, pencils
- **For Options:** Additional materials for any options you choose to use
- **Note:** Follow the instructions on page xii to prepare the word strips and the "Prayer Reminder" handouts (pattern P-24 on page 178).

REVIEW CHART

Display the Review Chart with R1-R10, R15, and R16 in place. Have R11 and R12 ready to use when indicated. Have a child read the name on R11, explain what it means, and place it on the Chart. Have the class say Isaiah 55:9 together. Use the following "Who Am I?" questions to review Lesson 11.

1. I was removed from my throne because I disobeyed the king. Who am I? *(Queen Vashti)*
2. I conducted business by the palace gate every day in Shushan. Who am I? *(Mordecai)*
3. I ordered all the young beautiful women to prepare to be my queen. Who am I? *(King Ahasuerus)*
4. I respected and helped Esther as she prepared to meet the king. Who am I? *(Hegai, the chief servant)*
5. I hated Mordecai and planned to get rid of all Jews in the kingdom. Who am I? *(Haman)*
6. I asked my people to fast and pray before I risked my life to go see the king. Who am I? *(Esther)*

Today we are going to learn that God's Way is *A Courageous Way*. *(Have a child place R12 on the Review Chart.)* This is something Esther and the Jewish people found to be true. It is something you and I will learn as we follow God's way through life. Our memory verse today will help us understand where courage comes from.

❤ MEMORY VERSE

Use the visual to teach Proverbs 10:29 and BELIEVE & OBEY footprints when indicated.

Do you ever find it difficult to live the way God wants us to? Why is it so difficult? *(Response)* Sometimes we are afraid that others will make fun of us, especially when we try to tell them about Jesus or we refuse to go along with those who are doing wrong. But God will help us when we choose to follow His way by obeying Him. ▲#1

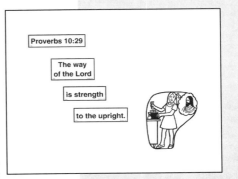

Let's look at God's promise in Proverbs 10:29. *(Have children find it in their Bibles and read it out loud together. Display the verse visual.)* What is the promise in this verse? *(Response)* It tells us that the upright or righteous will receive strength from God (or have God as their place of refuge or safety) when they walk in His way. Who are the upright or righteous? *(Response)* They are those of us who have been made right with God by receiving the Lord Jesus as our Savior. We have the Holy Spirit living in us to give us power to do what is right.

Because God gives us the strength we need, we can trust Him to help us to do the right thing even when we are afraid. This means we will walk in footsteps of faith by believing *(add BELIEVE)* that God will do what He promises and by obeying *(add OBEY)* what God commands in His Word. When we do that, God will give us the courage to do what is right. *(Work on memorizing the verse.)* ▲#2

📖 BIBLE LESSON OUTLINE

God Saves Esther and Her People

■ **Introduction**

Needing courage?

■ **Bible Content**

1. Esther invites the king to a banquet.
2. Haman plans to hang Mordecai.
3. The king rewards Mordecai.
4. Haman is hung on his own gallows.
5. Esther pleads for her people.
6. God saves His people.

■ **Conclusion**

Summary

Application
  Thinking of one way they are afraid to obey God

Response Activity
  Asking God for courage when they are afraid

▲ Option#1

Some of your children will actually face or have experienced physical or emotional harm from family or peers because of their stand for Christ. If there is such a need in your class, give the children an opportunity to share or even illustrate times when they have faced opposition for taking a stand for Jesus. Help them to see that many children in other parts of the world do face such opposition, especially in countries where Christianity is outlawed.

▲ Option#2

Memorizing the verse: Have the children do the following actions as they repeat the words of the verse (NIV in parenthesis). Then have them just do the actions.

The way of
  Walk in place.
the Lord
  Point upward.
is strength (is a refuge)
  Form circle with arms overhead.
to the upright (for the righteous)
  Put hand over heart.

▲ Option#3

Give paper and crayons to the children and instruct them to illustrate a time when they needed courage; invite them to share it with the class.

Or, divide the class into small groups and have each group act out a situation in which courage is needed. Ask the non-participants to tell why courage was needed in each situation.

Sketch 84 — Palace

▲ Option#4

During the Feast of Purim, Jewish families retell the story of Esther. Each time the name of Esther or Mordecai is mentioned, the children cheer and celebrate with party noisemakers. Each time the villain, Haman, is mentioned the children boo and hiss. You may wish to explain this old Jewish custom and allow your students to interact with part of the story in this way.

138   L12

📖 BIBLE LESSON

■ Introduction

Needing courage?

(Word strip COURAGE)

Have you ever needed courage? *(Display COURAGE.)* When did you need it? *(Have children share their experiences.)* You needed to be bold and strong to do what had to be done when you were afraid. ▲#3 That is what courage is. It is the ability to take action even when you are afraid. Where does courage come from? *(Response)* Yes, from God.

Why did Esther need courage? *(Response)* Yes, she knew she could die if she walked into the king's presence without being invited. Listen to our lesson today to see what happened when she went before King Ahasuerus.

■ Bible Content

1. Esther invites the king to a banquet. ▲#4 (Esther 5:1-8)

(King 84, scepter 84A, men 4, 14, Esther 83)

Esther and the other Jews in Shushan spent three days fasting and asking God to give Esther courage to go to the king. What else do you think they prayed for? *(Response)* Yes, that the king would hold out his scepter to Esther and listen to her request for mercy for the Jews. *(Place 84, 84A, 4, 14 on the board.)*

On the third day Esther *(add 83)* dressed in her royal robes and crown. Without regard for her own life and with faith in God, Esther went and stood in the inner courtyard of the palace, which faced the king's hall. The king was sitting on his royal throne facing the doorway. She probably did not feel very courageous as she waited to see what the king would do. Would he hold out his royal scepter and welcome her? Or would he be angry and have her put to death?

Finally, King Ahasuerus looked up and saw her standing there. How do you think Esther felt at that moment? *(Response)* Maybe her heart skipped a beat or she felt afraid, but God helped her to be brave. Chapter 5, verse 2 tells us what the king did. *(Have a child read the verse aloud.)* The king was very pleased when he saw Esther, and he held out his scepter to her. *(Lower 84A toward Esther and move Esther forward to touch the scepter.)* Esther went up to him and touched the end of the scepter. This custom showed she was accepted into his presence. How do you think Esther felt now? *(Response)* She probably was relieved and realized that God had answered the prayers of the people! He had given Esther the courage and strength she needed. He had saved her life!

Then the king asked, "What is it, Queen Esther? What do you want to ask me? I will give you as much as half of my kingdom."

Esther replied, "O King, if it pleases you, come today with Haman to a banquet I have prepared for him." She never mentioned the order against her people.

King Ahasuerus called his servants, "Bring Haman quickly so we may do what Queen Esther asks." So the king and Haman *(remove 84, 84A, 83)* went to the banquet Esther had prepared for them. ◩(1) While they were eating, the king again asked Esther to make her request. But Esther still did not tell the king what she wanted; she was waiting for the right moment to make her request. So she invited both of them to return the next day for another banquet. She told the king she would answer his question then.

◩ Note (1)

It was a huge honor for Haman to be invited by the queen to a private banquet. It probably made him feel that his power was secure.

2. Haman plans to hang Mordecai. (Esther 5:9-14)

(Haman 87, people bowing 74[largest figure], man 15, Mordecai 88)

Haman *(place 87 on the board)* left the palace full of excitement and feeling very important. What an honor it was to be invited to another banquet with the king and queen! The people *(add 74, 15)*, as usual, bowed when he passed by. But when he saw Mordecai *(add 88)* still refusing to bow down to him at the city gate, he became very angry.

When Haman arrived home he called his family and friends together and boasted, "I'm the only person the queen invited with the king to her banquet. And she has honored me again by inviting me, along with the king, to another one tomorrow. But all this does not really make me happy when I see Mordecai sitting at the gate and still refusing to honor me."

Sketch 85   City Street

His wife and friends said to him, "Mordecai has disobeyed the king's order. Why don't you have someone build a gallows? Then in the morning ask the king to have Mordecai hanged on it. Haman was delighted with this idea. So he had a platform built that was seventy-five feet high.

3. The king rewards Mordecai. (Esther 6:1-13)

(King 84, servant 27, scrolls 27A, 27B, Haman 70)

It was no accident that Esther did not tell the king her request at the first banquet. God was working out his plan through this. That very night King Ahasuerus *(place 84 on the board)* could not sleep. So he called for the official record book *(add 27, 27A, 27B)* to be read to him. These records gave great detail of the history of the kingdom, especially about the actions of people who had served the king well. The king listened as the record was read about Mordecai

Sketch 86   Coucil Room

▲ **Option #5**

Have several children dramatize Haman's leading Mordecai through Shushan. Have Haman call out the words from Esther 6:11 as they move about the class. Use simple costumes to enrich the drama.

Or, the children could act out the entire chapter. One or several children could read the Scripture narrative as the others act out the parts.

and how he had saved the king's life from a plot to kill him by some of his own soldiers. The king asked, "What reward and honor was given to Mordecai for this?"

His servants answered, "Nothing has been done for him."

Early in the morning Haman arrived at the palace. He had come to ask the king about hanging Mordecai on the gallows he had built. When he *(add 70)* was brought before King Ahasuerus, the king asked, "What should be done for a man the king wants to honor?"

Haman thought to himself, "Whom would the king want to honor more than me?" Haman was so full of pride, he could only think of himself.

Haman thought about how he would want to be honored and then answered the king, "Let him appear as royalty before everyone, wearing the royal robe and riding a royal horse that the king has ridden. Have one of your most important men help him dress and then lead him on the horse through the city streets, proclaiming to all, 'This is what is done for the man the king wants to honor!'"

Sketch 87 — City Street

(People 9, 10, 3, 4, 26, Haman 87, Mordecai 86)

Then the king ordered Haman, "Go and do everything you have said for Mordecai the Jew. Do not leave out anything you have suggested."

Can you imagine Haman's surprise? How do you think he felt after hearing this? *(Response)* He probably was angry and humiliated that he had to do this for a man he hated. But Haman *(place 87 on the board)* obeyed and put the royal robe on Mordecai *(add 86)* and led him through the city before all the people *(add 9, 10, 3, 4, 26)*. ▲#5

Then Mordecai returned to the king's gate, and Haman hurried home, feeling very embarrassed. He told his wife and friends what had happened. They said to him, "Since Mordecai is a Jew, you cannot win against him. You will surely be ruined." What did this mean? The people of Shushan knew that the Jews worshiped the true and living God. They probably understood that no one could defeat the powerful God of the Jews.

4. Haman is hung on his own gallows. (Esther 6:14–7:10)

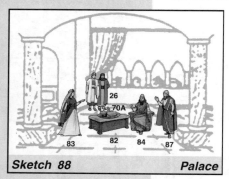
Sketch 88 — Palace

(King 84, Haman 87, Esther 83, table 82, food 70A, servants 26)

Later that day King Ahasuerus *(place 84 on the board)* and Haman *(add 87)* went to Queen Esther's *(add 83)* banquet *(add 82, 70A, 26)*. Once again the king asked Esther, "What is your request? I will give it to you. I will give you as much as half of my kingdom."

This time Esther answered, "O King, if you are pleased with me, let me and my people live. We are going to be killed and completely wiped out."

Immediately the king demanded, "Who has dared to do such a thing?"

"Our enemy is this wicked man, Haman," Esther cried out.

The king got up and went out into the garden in an angry rage *(remove 84)*. Haman was terrified for he knew this meant certain death for him. But he stayed inside and begged Esther to show him mercy. *(Move 87 closer to 83.)* When King Ahasuerus returned *(add 84)*, one of his servants told him, "There is a seventy-five-foot-high gallows near Haman's house. He was planning to use it to hang Mordecai, the man who saved your life."

The king ordered, "Hang Haman on it!" So Haman *(remove 87)* was hanged on the gallows that he had built for Mordecai. God's power won over the evil plans of man in order to save His people. No one can stop God's plan. *(Remove 26, 82, 70A; leave 84, 83 on the board.)*

5. Esther pleads for her people. (Esther 8:1-17)

(Mordecai 88, scroll 27A)

Sketch 89 — Palace

Esther told the king all about her background and how she was related to Mordecai. Then King Ahasuerus gave Haman's position of power and authority in the kingdom to Mordecai, and Esther put him in charge of Haman's property, which had been given to her by the king.

But there was still a huge problem. What do you think it was? *(Response)* Yes, it was the law that Haman had signed into action with the king's ring—the law that sentenced all the Jews to death in a year's time. It could not be changed or reversed.

So Esther spoke to the king again, "O King, if you are pleased with me and you think it is the right thing to do, let another order be written that will cancel the order against my people who are still in danger of being killed. I cannot stand to see this terrible thing happen to them."

The king agreed and gave Mordecai *(add 88, 27A)* the job of writing another order. He was given permission to write whatever he felt was necessary to save the Jews from being completely destroyed. So the new law was written, sealed, and sent to everyone in the province. It gave all the Jews in the kingdom the right to protect and defend themselves, killing anyone who attacked them. The new law also gave them permission to take anything that belonged to their enemies.

The Jews had nine months to prepare themselves for the attack. As the new order was announced throughout the land, there was much rejoicing among all the Jews. Even though it was not going to be easy and there would be fighting and danger, God had worked for them. Now they had a chance to live! *(Remove 84, 27A only.)*

6. God Saves His People.
(Esther 9:1-32)

(Word strips MARCH, FEAST of PURIM)
When the day of the battle finally arrived, the Jews were prepared to fight their enemies. None of their enemies were able to stand against them; they were afraid and backed down. All of the government officials helped the Jews. When the attackers realized this, many decided to not even go out and fight. Those who did attack God's people were killed. Once again God showed that He was more powerful than any king or people or nation. God had used these evil circumstances to work out His plan for His people.

After this great victory all the Jews throughout the land of Persia celebrated with a feast. It was a feast of joy and celebration for all God had done for them. The Jews still celebrate this victory every year in March *(add MARCH)*, usually just before Easter and the celebration of the Jewish Passover. It is called the Feast of Purim *(add FEAST OF PURIM)*. During the celebration the entire book of Esther is read aloud as a reminder of God's wonderful miracle and the courage He gave to Esther and Mordecai.

■ Conclusion

Summary

(Esther 83, hearts 89[2], Mordecai 88, Haman 87; word strip COURAGE, BELIEVE & OBEY footprints)

Sketch 90   Plain Background

Why did Esther *(place 83 on the board)* need courage? *(Allow for response throughout.)* Yes, she was afraid she would be sentenced to death if she entered the king's presence without being invited. Where did she get the courage *(add COURAGE)* to go before the king? Yes, God *(add GOD 89)* gave it to her. What did she do to show she had faith in God's promises and trusted Him to help her? Yes, she asked the Jews *(add 77)* to fast and pray for three days. How did God answer their prayers? *(The children may give the following answers in any order: God gave her courage to go before the king, and he invited her into his presence. Esther was able to expose Haman's plan, and he was put to death. The king gave Mordecai permission to write a law that allowed the Jews to defend themselves.)*

Our memory verse says that God gives strength to the upright. *(Say the verse together.)* Was Esther an upright (righteous) person? Yes, she walked in footsteps of faith, believing and obeying *(add footprints)* God even when she was afraid. Who else was upright? Yes, Mordecai *(add 88)*.

Was Haman *(add 87)* an upright man? No, he had no regard for God and His way. He thought only of himself and what he could get *(add GET 89)* for himself. What did Haman get when he tried to destroy the Jews? Yes, when Esther revealed his evil plan, he was hanged on the very gallows that he built to hang Mordecai on.

Application

(Newsprint & marker or chalkboard & chalk)
Is there anything that you know God wants you to do, but you are afraid to do it? Let's make a list, showing one thing each of you needs courage to do? *(List the name of each child with one thing he or she is afraid of doing.)* Who can give you the courage to do the right thing? Yes, God can. *(Say the memory verse together, using the actions suggested in Option 2.)* What did Esther and the other Jews do to show they were trusting God to give Esther the courage? Yes, they prayed, showing their trust in God. Let's show our trust in God by praying for each other, asking God to give us the courage we need to do the things He wants us to do.

Response Activity

Remind the children that God promises to give courage to those who belong to Him. Give the unsaved children an opportunity to receive Christ as Savior as their first step toward trusting God for courage.

Distribute pencils and **"Prayer Reminder" handouts**. *Instruct the children to choose a child's name from the list and write it on the handout to show they are willing to pray for that child each day this coming week. Suggest that they hang the handout on their bedroom doorknob to remind them to pray. Give them an opportunity to pray aloud or silently in class. Close with a prayer for God to give courage to each of them. Next week ask the children to share how God gave them courage during the week.*

✍ TAKE-HOME ITEMS

Distribute **memory verse tokens for Proverbs 10:29** *and* **Bible Study Helps for Lesson 12.**

Job Is Tested

Theme: A Tested Way

Lesson 13

❋ BEFORE YOU BEGIN...

There are very few of us who did not groan or gripe over tests in school, either because they were too difficult or because we had a dislike for this kind of accountability. Yet tests are still the "in thing" in education today.

Testing must be a good idea, for God utilizes it quite frequently in our lives. Scripture instructs us that God uses tests to give us the opportunity to pass, not to make us fail. God's tests are for positive purposes: to teach about Him and about ourselves; to strengthen our weak areas; to develop our faith.

Job was God's star student, so to speak, and so received probably the severest series of tests known to man. As you present this lesson your children will no doubt think that God was too hard on Job. This will be your golden opportunity to let them know that God is too loving and wise to give bad tests, that they can trust Him fully to give them good tests throughout their Christian lives, and that they should take them without complaining, no matter how much they hurt. *"You, O God, have tested us; You have refined us as silver is refined" (Psalm 66:10, NKJV).*

☞ AIM:

That the children may

- Know that God tests their faith in Him by allowing difficult things to happen in their lives.
- Respond by acknowledging God's right to test them and choosing to trust Him no matter what happens.

📖 SCRIPTURE: Job 1; 2; 38:1–42:16

♥ MEMORY VERSE: Job 23:10

He knoweth the way that I take; when he hath tried me, I shall come forth as gold. (KJV)

He knows the way that I take; when he has tested me, I will come forth as gold. (NIV)

📁 MATERIALS TO GATHER

Visual for Job 23:10 from *Bible Verses Visualized*
Backgrounds: Review Chart, Plain Background, Plain with Tree
Figures: R1-R13, R15, R16, 15, 27, 29, 59, 69, 89(GOD), 90, 91, 92, 93(2), 94(14), 95
Token holders & memory verse tokens for Job 23:10
Bible Study Helps for Lesson 13
Special:
- **For Memory Verse:** Gold or gold tone items, such as a necklace or a vase, or pictures of them
- **For Introduction & Summary:** Name cards ELIJAH, AHAB, DANIEL, JEREMIAH, ESTHER, JOB; large gold stickers
- **For Bible Content 1:** Word strips ESTHER, JOB, PSALMS; a world map; BELIEVE & OBEY footprints
- **For Application:** Newsprint & marker or chalkboard & chalk
- **For Response Activity:** "Name Card" handouts, pencils, gold stickers
- **For Options:** Additional materials for any options you choose to use
- **Note:** *To prepare the name cards*, print ELIJAH, AHAB, DANIEL, JEREMIAH, ESTHER, and JOB on separate 9" x 12" pieces of poster board or card stock. Punch two holes in each card and attach a 24" piece of yarn to it to hang around a child's neck.
  Follow the instructions on page xii to prepare the "Name Card" handouts (pattern P-22 on page 177).

REVIEW CHART

Display the Review Chart with R15, R16, and R1-R12 in place. Have R13 ready to use when indicated. Have the children complete the statements below to review Lesson 12.

1. Haman hated the Jews and wanted to kill them all because _____ *(Mordecai refused to bow to him).*
2. Esther showed her real trust in God when _____ *(she went before the king without being invited).*
3. The king made Haman honor Mordecai by _____ *(putting a royal robe on him and taking him through the streets of Shushan).*
4. Esther invited the king and Haman to a banquet because _____ *(she wanted to ask the king to save her people from death).*
5. The king put Haman to death because _____ *(Esther was a Jew and Haman had ordered the death of the Jews).*
6. God saved the Jews by _____ *(having the king make a new order, allowing the Jews to defend themselves).*

7. The Feast of Purim is celebrated to remember _____ (how God saved His people from being destroyed).

Today we are going to learn that God's Way is *A Tested Way*. *(Place R13 on the Chart.)* How many of you like to take tests? *(Response)* Most of us don't like to take tests because we are afraid we might fail. When you get a good mark on a test, how do you feel? *(Response)* Yes, it makes you feel proud and excited that you have done well. Did you know that God gives us tests? Our memory verse tells us why.

♥ MEMORY VERSE

Use the visual to teach Job 23:10 when indicated. Display gold or gold tone items or pictures of them.

Most things that go into a fire are burned up, but gold is a precious metal that cannot be destroyed by fire. Instead, fire is used to refine gold, making it purer and beautiful. Our memory verse says that we can be like gold. *(Display the verse and read it together.)* (1)

God uses the picture of purifying gold to show us His purpose for allowing difficult things to come into our lives. *Has tried me* means *(flip the word "tried" up to show the word "tested")* has tested me. God does this by allowing us to go through hard things. He tests us to see how strong our faith in Him is when difficult things happen. He wants to be sure we really love Him enough to trust Him through everything that happens in our lives.

God's tests are sometimes painful like being burned by fire. But God knows everything about us and allows only what will accomplish His purpose. If we trust Him, He will take us through the test just as gold goes through the fire, and when the test is over, our faith in Him will be stronger. *(Work on memorizing the verse.)* ▲#1

📖 BIBLE LESSON OUTLINE

Job Is Tested

■ **Introduction**

Who passed God's test?

■ **Bible Content**

1. Job trusts and obeys God.
2. Satan gets permission to test Job.
3. Job passes his first test.
4. Satan tests Job a second time.
5. God blesses Job again.

◸ Note (1)

Gold is purified when it is melted at a high heat until the impurities come to the surface and are skimmed off. Gold is the only metal that does not lose its properties when it is heated at high temperatures. The more it is heated, the purer it becomes.

■ Conclusion

Summary

Application
Recognizing difficult situations as tests

Response Activity
Choosing to trust God no matter what happens

📖 BIBLE LESSON

■ Introduction

Who passed God's test?

(Name cards ELIJAH, AHAB, DANIEL, JEREMIAH, ESTHER, JOB; gold stickers)

As we have been learning to walk God's Way this year, we have met some people whose faith was tested. God tested them to teach them to trust Him through all the circumstances they faced. Let's see if any of these people passed God's tests and came through like gold.

Distribute the name cards (except JOB) to five children to hold up in front of the class. Have each child briefly tell what problem the person faced and if he or she passed or failed God's test. If the person passed, have the child place a gold sticker on the card. Use the statements below to verify and elaborate on each child's comments.

• **Elijah** trusted God to answer his prayer by fire on Mount Carmel. When discouraged, he trusted God and brought the people back to God.

• **Ahab** married wicked Jezebel. He worshiped false gods and led the people of Israel in worshiping false gods. He stole Naboth's vineyard.

• **Daniel** refused to eat the king's food, and he prayed to God, which was against the king's law.

• **Jeremiah** faithfully gave God's message to the people of Judah even though they refused to listen, arrested him, and put him in a cistern.

• **Esther** appeared before the king to ask for the lives of her people, even though she knew the king might refuse to see her and put her to death.

With the exception of Ahab, all these people saw God's power at work on their behalf. Their faith was strengthened as they trusted God to help them through some very difficult situations. Today we will add another name *(hold up JOB)*. Listen carefully to see if Job passes God's test and gets a gold sticker.

▲ Option #1

Memorizing the verse: Have the children say the verse and reference a few times. Then have them choose partners (or assign them). Give the pairs time to say the verse to each other without the visual and to review its meaning. Let one of the pairs volunteer to stand and recite the verse and explain its meaning. Then have them choose another pair to do the same. Repeat until all have had a turn.

Variation: Distribute a sheet of newsprint and a marker to each pair and have them write out the verse from memory. They could also illustrate its meaning or a situation in which God might test their faith. Have them share their pictures with the class.

Sketch 91 Plain Background

Note (2)

While the author has endeavored to arrange the lessons of *Footsteps of Faith* in chronological order generally, an exception was made for this lesson on Job. It appears here in Volume 4, following the book order of the Bible rather than following a chronological order, which would have placed Job in Volume 1 during the patriarchal period.

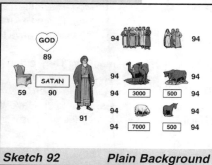

Sketch 92 Plain Background

Note (3)

Satan was thrown out of heaven as his dwelling place, but he still has access to God to accuse sinning Christians. Satan's access to heaven will end when he is bound at Christ's return.

■ **Bible Content**

1. **Job trusts and obeys God.**
   (Job 1:1-5)

(Word strips ESTHER, JOB, PSALMS; a world map, BELIEVE & OBEY footprints; Job 91, people 94[2], animals 94[4], numbers 94[3,000, 500(2), 7,000])
Job was a man who lived many years ago, probably during the time of Abraham. His story is in a book of the Bible named for him. It is between the book of Esther *(place ESTHER, JOB, and PSALMS on the board)* and Psalms. *(Have the children turn to Job 1:1 and place their bookmarks there.)* This book tells the story of Job and the tests God gave him. (2)

Job *(add 91)* trusted and obeyed God and God blessed him. *(Have the children read Job 1:2, 3 and tell what they learned about Job.)* He had seven sons and three daughters *(add people 94[2])*. He was very rich *(add numbers 94[4] and animals 94[4] as you mention them)* because he had many animals—3,000 camels, 500 yoke of oxen, 7,000 sheep, and 500 donkeys. He also had many servants. He was the greatest man among all the people of the Middle East. *(Indicate on the map.)* He was a good businessman—fair, honest, and well respected by many people.

But there is one description of Job that is more important than any of these. Look at verse 1. *(Have a child read the verse.)* Job was an honest man; he honored God and stayed away from evil. He offered sacrifices for sin as God had instructed. Job walked in footsteps of faith, believing *(add BELIEVE)* and obeying *(add OBEY)* God. *(Remove the word strips, footprints; leave the figures on the board.)*

2. **Satan gets permission to test Job.**
   (Job 1:6-12)

(Throne 59, GOD 89, Satan 90)
As Job was trying to live for God every day, something was happening in heaven that he was not aware of. We will let this throne *(add 59, 89)* stand for God. One day the angels came and stood before God. God's enemy was standing there with them. Read verse 6; who was it? *(Response)* Yes, Satan *(add 90)* was once an angel who served God in heaven. But when he became proud and wanted to be like God, God threw him out of heaven. Since then he has tried to get people to follow his way instead of God's Way.

Satan came before God for a specific purpose that day. (3) The name he is called in verse 6 tells us what he came to do. Satan's name means *accuser*. An accuser says that a person has done something bad, or sometimes the accuser just talks against a person.

Do you think God needs Satan to tell Him what we do and the sins we commit? *(Response)* No! God knows everything about us; He hears and sees everything we do. Satan may say something like this to God: "Oh, look at Leah *(use an appropriate name)*. See what terrible thing she has done. She does not deserve to be blessed or to go to heaven." But Jesus reminds him that Leah has received Him as her Savior, believing He died and rose again to forgive her sins. Satan stops from saying anything more because he knows that Jesus has spoken the truth.

God said to Satan, "Where have you been?" Do you think God didn't know? *(Response)* No, but he wanted an answer from Satan.

Satan answered, "I have been wandering around the earth."

God asked, "Have you noticed My servant Job? He is the finest man on earth. He is an honest man. He honors Me and stays away from evil." God was very pleased with Job; he had trusted and obeyed God.

Satan replied, "Of course he is, for a good reason. You have protected him and made him very successful and wealthy. But take it all away from him and then see if he honors You. He will curse You instead."

So God tested Job by giving Satan permission to test him. Verse 12 tells us what God said. *(Have the class read it together.)* God gave Satan permission to take away everything that belonged to Job. Then Satan left God's presence. ▲#2 *(Remove 89, 59, 90; move 91 to the left.)* ◁(4)

3. Job passes his first test. ▲#3 (Job 1:13-22)

(Servants 29, 69, 15, 27)

One day while all of Job's children were having dinner at the home of his oldest son, one of Job's servants *(add 29)* came and reported to him, "While your oxen were plowing the fields and the donkeys were eating grass nearby, some enemy raiders came and stole all the animals and killed all your servants. I am the only one who escaped to tell you." *(Remove oxen, donkeys, and 500[2].)*

The servant was still speaking when another servant arrived *(remove 29; add 69)* and said, "Lightning struck and burned up all your sheep and their shepherds. *(Remove sheep and 7,000.)* I am the only one who escaped. The second servant was still speaking, when a third servant came in *(remove 69; add 15)*. He said, "Three groups of robbers attacked us and stole all the camels and killed all the servants. I am the only one who escaped to tell you. *(Remove camels and 3,000.)*

Poor Job! What terrible news! All his wealth was gone. And if that wasn't bad enough, while the third servant was still speaking, a fourth servant *(remove 15; add 27)* came and told him the saddest and most horrible news of all. "Your sons and daughters were eating and drinking at your oldest son's house. Suddenly a powerful wind came in from

▲ **Option#2**

Dramatize scenes in which God and Satan are talking. Or read Job 1:6-12 aloud, using one child (or half of the class) to read God's part and another child (or the other half of the class) to read Satan's part.

◁ **Note (4)**

Your children need to recognize that Satan is as real as God is and that he is much stronger than they are, but not stronger than God. A biblical view of Satan will be a balanced view that will keep them from either cowering in fear or carelessly discounting his threats. The story of Job clearly indicates that Satan cannot operate outside of God's control.

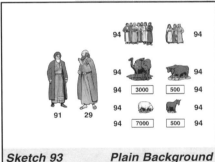

Sketch 93   Plain Background

▲ **Option#3**

Choose a child to play the part of Job and several children to play the parts of his servants and wife. Allow them to dramatize the story of Job as you tell it. Before you start, give Job five index cards listing his blessings: oxen, donkeys, sheep, camels, and children. Have Job sit in the front of the classroom

(Continued)

holding his cards. As the story progresses, have the servants approach him one at a time and remove a card from his hands. Have Job read his response from Job 1:21b. Place red stickers on Job to signify his boils and have Job's wife approach him and read Job 2:9. Have Job read his response from Job 2:10. At the end of the story have Job read his response to God's voice from Job 42:2 and then have the servants return his blessings (cards) to him.

Variation: Have the children dramatize Job 1:13-19 by reading or speaking the parts as the servants might have given the news.

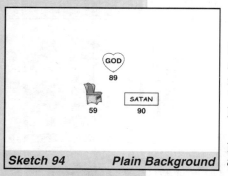

Sketch 94   **Plain Background**

Sketch 95   **Plain with Tree**

the desert. It struck the house with such force that it collapsed, and all your children were killed. *(Remove family 94[2].)* I am the only one who escaped.

What would you have done if you were Job? *(Response)* Maybe we would have cried and screamed and gotten angry, even blaming God for letting it happen. Or we might have just given up. But that is not what Job did. First, he tore his robe and shaved his head to show his great sorrow and grief over the loss of his family—a common custom in those days.

Then verse 20 tells us an amazing thing that Job did. *(Have someone read it aloud.)* Job got down on his knees and worshiped and praised God! How was he able to do that after all the terrible things that had just happened to him? Let's read what he said in verse 21. *(Read it aloud.)* Job knew that God had given him everything he had, and no one could take it away from him unless God allowed it. Job never sinned by blaming God for what happened to him. Satan was wrong about Job. Job passed the test. He did not curse God. His faith in God was very strong. Do you think God was pleased with him? Yes, He was. *(Remove 91, 27.)*

4. Satan tests Job a second time. (Job 2:1-13)

(Throne 59, GOD 89, Satan 90)
Job had proved Satan was wrong and Satan didn't like it. Satan does not give up easily. So he *(add 90)* came a second time and stood before God *(add 59, 89)*. God reminded Satan of Job's faithfulness. But Satan replied, "Job blesses you because You bless him. But take away his health, and he will curse You and turn from You."

So God said, "Job is in your hands to do with as you please, but you must not kill him." Why do you think God allowed this? *(Response)*

(Job 92, wife 95, friends 93[2], GOD 89)
Soon after this, boils or painful sores broke out all over Job's body, making it hard for him to sit or lie down. The boils caused running sores that itched and caused pain. *(Place 92 on the board.)* To soothe the itching, Job sat down in some ashes and rubbed them on his skin. He also used a piece of broken pottery to scrape himself. He was in terrible pain and agony.

Then his wife *(add 95)* asked him, "Are you still trying to live to please God? You have nothing to live for. You should just curse God and die." If you had been Job, how would you have answered her? *(Response)*

Once again Job showed his faith in God by answering, "You are talking like someone who does not know God," he said. "God has given us many good things, and He has the right to take them all away." Did God still love and care for Job? *(Response)* Yes. He did.

In spite of everything that happened to Job, he still trusted God. So much so, that no one could understand him, not even his friends. When three of them *(remove 95; add 93[2])* came to visit Job, they were shocked at his appearance. They hardly recognized him. Then they tore their clothes and cried loudly to show their sorrow for him. For a week they sat quietly, realizing there was nothing they could say to comfort their friend. When Job did speak and told them he was still trusting God, they did not understand it. When they finally spoke, they kept telling him to confess his sins because God was punishing him, forcing Job to defend himself. The more they said how bad he was, the more he said how good he was. ◩**(5)** *(Leave the figures on the board.)*

5. God blesses Job again. (Job 38:1–42:16)

(GOD 89)
Finally, after listening to Job speak and ask questions, God spoke *(add 89)* to him from a whirlwind. He reminded Job (and his friends) that He had made the earth and everything in it and that He guided the stars and kept them in place. God spoke about more of His creation, reminding Job of His great power and control over everything on earth. ▲#4

As Job listened, he began to realize how holy and wonderful God is. Job had believed in God and lived an upright life, but now as he compared himself to God and His holiness, he saw that he was truly a sinner. Job said to God, "Now I know that You can do anything and no plan of Yours can be ruined. I had heard about You before, but now I have seen You with my own eyes. I realize I am not as good as I thought I was and I don't know as much as I thought I did. I'm sorry for my foolish pride." He recognized that all his goodness could never compare to God's holiness.

Then God spoke to Job's three friends and said, "I am angry with you because of the wrong things you have said about My servant Job. Now offer a burnt sacrifice for your sin, and Job will pray for you. I will listen to Job's prayer and forgive you. I will not give you the punishment you deserve." So the men did as God said, and Job prayed for them. I wonder if it was hard for Job to pray for them after all they had said about him. But his obedience in praying for them showed that he was forgiving them. His faith in God was stronger than ever. *(Remove all the figures except 89.)*

(Job 91, wife 95, animals 94[4], numbers 94[14,000, 1,000(2), 6,000], people 94[2])
God restored Job's health and made him successful again. *(Add 91, 95.)* All of his brothers and sisters and friends came to comfort him and bring him gifts of money and gold. *(Have the children read verse 10 and tell what*

◩ **Note (5)**

As you prepare this lesson, read chapters 3-37 for the complete discourse between Job and his friends. It will help you sense how heated the arguing became before God intervened.

▲ **Option#4**

Show some pictures of God's creation as you teach this section. You may want to add other details from chapters 37-39.

Variation: Choose several of the following passages (or others of your choice) to read or illustrate to emphasize what Job learned about God's power as Creator: Job 38:31, 32; 38:34, 35; 38:37, 38; 39:1, 2; 39:19-21; 39:26-29.

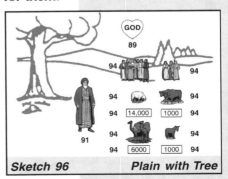

Sketch 96   **Plain with Tree**

happened.) God restored his wealth *(add numbers 94[4] and animals 94[4] as you mention them)*, giving him twice as much as he had before—14,000 sheep, 1,000 yoke of oxen, 6,000 camels, and 1,000 donkeys. God also gave Job and his wife ten more children—seven boys and three girls *(add 94[2])*. Then Job lived for another 140 years. *(Leave the figures on the board.)*

■ Conclusion
Summary

(Name cards from Introduction, gold sticker)
Distribute the name cards to six children to display in front of the class. Have the child displaying JOB step forward.

Did Job pass God's tests? *(Allow for response throughout.)* Yes, how do we know that? Yes, he continued to trust God when he lost everything and his life seemed hopeless. What did Job learn about God? That's right; everything belongs to Him, and He has the right to do whatever He wants. How did God show He was pleased with Job? Yes, He gave him ten more children and doubled his wealth *(point to the visuals on the board)*. Does Job deserve a gold sticker? Yes, he came through the test as gold goes through fire. His faith in God was stronger than it had been before. *(Have the child place a gold sticker near Job's name.)*

Application

(Newsprint & marker or chalkboard & chalk)
If you belong to the Lord Jesus, God will allow your faith to be tested. You won't always know the reason why. The tests may not be as difficult as the ones given to Job, but God will give you tests that He decides are best for you. What are some difficult things you are facing right now? *(List the children's responses on the newsprint or the chalkboard. Mention a few difficulties to help them think: divorce of parents, move to a new town, seriously ill parent.)* Is it easy to go through any of these things? No! Do you believe that God has the right to allow this to happen to you? Are you willing to trust Him no matter what happens?

Response Activity

Distribute the **"Name card" handouts** and pencils. Read the information on the card and explain the response the children are being asked to make. If they agree with what the handout is saying, have them print their name on the top line. Then have them complete the sentence by writing down one of the difficult things they are facing right now.

Close in prayer, asking God to help the children keep their commitment to trust Him this week. If possible, pray for them by name and mention the tests they are facing. Help them to understand that the test may continue for a while or that God may never remove the difficulty, but He will be with them and help them. Distribute the gold stickers and tell the children to put a gold sticker on their card at the end of the week if they were able to trust God throughout the week. Then encourage them to bring their card back and tell how God helped them.

Invite the children who are not ready to make the commitment on the card and would like to talk to you about it to stay after class. Take this opportunity also to lead the unsaved ones to receive Jesus as their Savior.

✍ TAKE-HOME ITEMS

*Distribute **memory verse tokens for Job 23:10** and **Bible Study Helps for Lesson 13**.*

God Frees His People
Theme: A Rejoicing Way

Lesson 14

❦ BEFORE YOU BEGIN...

We readily acknowledge the link between music and emotions. Some musical compositions cause us to be pensive and sad; others cause us to be upbeat and happy. This is no accident, but a deliberate provision from God to help us worship Him. Here's how it works: When we sing praise and thanksgiving from our hearts, God is honored and we are blessed with joy. This is the essence of worship. It is our privilege to practice it, whether alone in the secret of our prayer closet or corporately with the congregation of a church.

Children need to be trained in the art of worship. This includes learning to be thankful, learning to recognize God as ultimate provider, and learning the difference between real needs and whimsical wants.

What a challenge! May this concluding lesson help you to motivate your children to cultivate the art of worship and to sing their way through life with the joy of the Lord as their portion and strength. *"Singing and making melody in your heart to the Lord, giving thanks always for all things to God the Father in the name of our Lord Jesus Christ"* (Ephesians 5:19b, 20, NKJV).

☞ AIM:

That the children may

- Know that God wants His children to rejoice over who He is and what He has done for them.
- Respond by rejoicing through singing praise to God for His greatness and for His kindness to them.

📖 SCRIPTURE: Ezra 1–4; 6:14–7:10; Nehemiah 1:1–6:15; 8:1–9:5

♥ MEMORY VERSE: Psalm 138:5

Yea, they shall sing in the ways of the Lord: for great is the glory of the Lord. (KJV)

May they sing of the ways of the Lord, for the glory of the Lord is great. (NIV)

📁 MATERIALS TO GATHER

Visual for Psalm 138:5 from *Bible Verses Visualized*
Backgrounds: Review Chart, Plain Background, Old Testament Map II, General Outdoor, Council Room, City Wall, City Street
Figures: R1-R16, 3, 4, 5, 8, 9, 10, 15, 16, 17, 18(1), 22, 23, 24, 25A, 25B, 26, 27, 27A, 27B, 29, 36, 36A, 37, 38, 39, 47, 48A, 50, 61, 62, 64, 72, 84, 94(2), 96(2), 96A, 97(5)
Token holders & memory verse tokens for Psalm 138:5
Bible Study Helps for Lesson 14
Special:
- **For Bible Content 1:** Word strips EZRA, NEHEMIAH
- **For Bible Content 3:** Word strips HAGGAI, ZECHARIAH
- **For Summary:** "PRAISE GOD FOR" poster, marker
- **For Response Activity:** A copy of a praise song for each child
- **For Options:** Additional materials for any options you choose to use
- **Note:** Follow the instructions on page xii to prepare the word strips.

    To prepare the "PRAISE GOD FOR" chart, use a marker to print the title "PRAISE GOD FOR" across the top of the poster. Draw 2 vertical lines under the title to make 3 columns, and title the columns JEWS, NATHAN, and ME respectively (see Sketch 104 on page 163).

REVIEW CHART

Place the R1-R13 review pieces on a table in mixed-up order. Have R14 ready to use when indicated. Display the Review Chart; place R15 and R16 on it and review the meaning of each piece. Have the children take turns giving the theme names that describe God's Way, finding the corresponding review pieces, and placing them on the Chart. Then have another child tell what the theme means and name a person from the corresponding lesson who followed or refused to follow God's Way. Then ask a third child to recite the memory verse for that lesson. Use the questions below to review Lesson 13.

1. Job trusted and obeyed God. Why did God allow him to be tested? *(God knew Job would trust Him and not turn against Him.)*
2. What did Satan want to do to Job? *(He wanted to make Job curse God.)*
3. What did Satan need to do before he could take everything from Job? *(He needed to get God's permission.)*
4. What did Job lose? *(He lost all his children, wealth, servants, and health.)*

5. How did Job prove Satan wrong? *(Job never stopped trusting God.)*
6. After seeing God, what did Job realize about himself compared to God? *(God is holy, and he was a sinner.)*
7. How did God reward Job? *(He gave him a new family and twice as many animals and servants than he had originally.)*
8. Why does God test His children? *(He tests them to see how strong their faith in Him is when difficult things happen.)*

Today we are going to complete our journey on God's Way. The last piece on the Review Chart is *A Rejoicing Way*. *(Place R14 on the Chart.)*

God wants us to rejoice, which means to be happy or full of joy. Have you ever felt like this? What made you feel this way? *(Response)* Did you keep it to yourself? Probably you didn't. When we are excited or happy about something that has happened, it shows in our face and voice. ▲#1 Sometimes it is hard to be happy or joyful, but our memory verse tells us why we should always rejoice.

♥ MEMORY VERSE

Use the visual to teach Psalm 138:5. Have music notes 97[5] ready to use when indicated.

The psalms were the songs the Jews used to worship and praise God. King David wrote many of them including Psalm 138, where our memory verse is found today. *(Have the children find Psalm 138:5 in their Bibles.)* David's heart was full of joy because of all that God had done for him. He expressed his joy by singing this praise song. *(Display the visual.)* ▲#2

God wants us to do the same thing. Joy comes from the Holy Spirit who lives in those of us who have received the Lord Jesus Christ as our Savior. *(Place 97[5] on the board.)* Having our sins forgiven and knowing we have eternal life give us great reasons to praise Him. By singing our praise to Him we express our joy for having such a wonderful Savior and for all He has done for us. *(Work on memorizing the verse.)* ▲#3

📖 BIBLE LESSON OUTLINE

God Frees His People

■ **Introduction**

Nathan's joyful heart

▲ **Option #1**

Have the children share or illustrate experiences that gave them joy. Display the pictures for everyone to see.

▲ **Option #2**

Before the children look up the memory verse, review the books of the Bible learned so far. Distribute the word strips for the books used throughout this course. Have the children put them in order on the board or on the floor. Or have the children hold up the word strips for all to see as they arrange themselves in the correct order.

■ Bible Content

1. Cyrus gives the Jews permission to return to Judah.
2. Zerubbabel leads the first group of Jews back to Judah.
3. The Jews begin to rebuild.
    a. The altar.
    b. The temple.
4. Ezra comes to Jerusalem to teach God's Word.
5. Nehemiah comes to Jerusalem to rebuild the walls.
6. Ezra and the Levites read and explain God's Word.

■ Conclusion

Summary

Application

Thinking of things we can praise God for

Response Activity

Rejoicing through singing praise to God

📖 BIBLE LESSON

■ Introduction

Nathan's joyful heart

As Nathan got on the bus Monday morning to go to school he was humming a tune, which soon turned into quiet singing. The song was from Psalm 118:24. *(Have children find the verse in their Bibles. If they know a song with these words, sing it together.)* ▲#4 At each stop, other children got on the bus. It wasn't long before they noticed Nathan's singing. Some were annoyed and said, "Nathan, stop that singing. It's stupid." But Nathan was full of joy and kept right on quietly singing. Others just ignored him.

When school was over, Nathan got on the bus as usual. Sam, one of the younger boys, asked, "Hey Nathan, how come you were singing and humming that song this morning?"

"Well," answered Nathan, "for many months my family has been praying that my dad would get a job. We didn't have much money left, and my dad was getting discouraged. Then, on Friday morning my dad got a phone call from the boss at his old job. He asked him to come back, and he told him he would get a higher salary. I just can't stop thanking God for answering our prayers. I feel so great about it."

"Wow, that's cool!" said Sam. "I was curious because your song made me feel real good about going to school today. I was humming it all day." Nathan had a lot to be joyful about, and it spilled over to the other kids, especially to Sam.

God's people, the Jews, had many opportunities to praise God. Listen to see if you can find the reasons why.

▲ Option #3

Memorizing the verse: Have the children pretend they are a choir. Divide the class into three groups. Have group 1 say the reference, group 2 say the words on the first visual piece, group 3 say the words on the second visual piece, and have the whole group say the words on the third visual piece. Encourage them to say their parts with expression and joy. Reassign the words several times until the children can say the verse without seeing the visual.

▲ Option #4

Visualize Psalm 118:24 and have the children sing it.

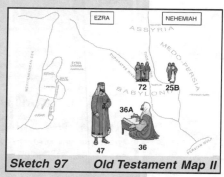

Sketch 97 Old Testament Map II

⌂ Note (I)

King Cyrus and King Artaxerxes still ruled the known world, including Israel/Jerusalem, so they could issue any orders they wished on the Jews, even though the people were free to go. It is amazing to see how God worked in these kings to give orders that would honor Him and enhance their worship of Him.

▲ Option #5

Have the class turn to Ezra 1:2-4 and have several read it with expression as though it were an official proclamation.

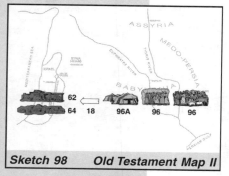

Sketch 98 Old Testament Map II

■ **Bible Content**

1. **Cyrus gives the Jews permission to return to Judah.**
   (Ezra 1:1-4)

(People 72, 25B, king 47, scribe 36, desk 36A; word strips EZRA, NEHEMIAH)

Long before the Jews *(place 25B, 72 on the board)* were taken into captivity, Isaiah and Jeremiah wrote about God's promise to take them back to the land of Judah *(indicate JUDAH)* after spending seventy years in Babylon *(indicate BABYLON)*. God even told them the name of the king who was going to give them the freedom to return. Turn to Isaiah 44:28 to see what God said. *(Have a child read the verse aloud.)* Yes. King Cyrus, one of the Persian kings, was going to let them go.

It seemed like such a long time for those Jews who had spent most of those seventy years in Babylon. Would God really keep the promise He made so long ago? Would they actually be permitted to leave Persia? God did just what He had promised. The books of Ezra and Nehemiah *(add EZRA, NEHEMIAH)* tell us how He did it. *(Have the children find the books in their Bibles. Then have them place their bookmarks in Ezra 1:1.)*

One day King Cyrus had one of his scribes write out an announcement *(add 47, 36, 36A)* and send it throughout his kingdom. It was for all the Jewish captives still living there. Let's read Ezra 1:1 to find out why the king did it. *(Response)* Yes, God caused him to do it. Maybe Daniel, who was still living and serving the king, showed Cyrus what the prophets had written about him. We don't know, but we do know that God was working in the king's heart. He wrote: "The Lord God of heaven has given all the kingdoms of the earth to me. He has appointed me to build a temple for Him in Jerusalem. All of you who are God's people are free to return there. And may God be with you! You may build the temple of the Lord. Those who stay behind should support those who choose to go. Give them silver, gold, supplies, and livestock. Also give them money to rebuild the temple in Jerusalem." Can you imagine how excited God's people must have been when they heard of this amazing thing God had done? How they must have praised Him for this miracle. ⌂(1) ▲#5 *(Remove all the figures.)*

2. **Zerubbabel leads the first group of Jews back to Judah.**
   (Job 1:6-12)

(People 96, choir 96, tents 96A, arrow 18[1], city ruins 64, temple ruins 62)

Now everyone had to make a decision—to go or to stay. Many had made a good life in Babylon and decided to stay there. But thousands were ready to pack up and leave.

God gave them the desire to go. Some of them were very old now and remembered living in Judah. They had dreamed of the day when they would return to live and worship God in their own land. Some of them had been very young when they were taken to Babylon and could not remember living in Judah, while others had been born in Babylon. Because their parents had taught them God's ways and about His promise to take them back to Jerusalem, they too were ready to return to Judah.

There was much to do—packing all the food, supplies, tents, and water for the long trip and their arrival in Jerusalem. There was no guarantee they could obtain food once they arrived in Jerusalem. All their neighbors who were staying behind helped them. They gave them things made of silver and gold, along with supplies, cattle, valuable gifts, and money to build the temple. Cyrus gave them all the gold and silver items King Nebuchadnezzar had taken from the temple in Jerusalem. Can you imagine how joyful the people felt when they saw them? Then everything had to be loaded on carts and donkeys, camels, mules, and horses. Soon everyone was ready to leave. Led by a man named Zerrubabel (Zer-rub'-a-bel), almost 50,000 Jewish people *(place people 96 on the board)* including a choir of 200 people *(add choir 96)*, began the long trip back to Judah *(add 18[1])*.

It took four months for the people to make the 900-mile journey back to Judah. I wonder if the choir led the people in singing praises to God as they traveled each day. It surely would have made the trip more enjoyable for everyone. At night they set up camp and slept in their tents *(add 96A)*. They did not know what to expect on the trip, but they had learned a new lesson in trusting God—He was a God who kept His promise in a wonderful way!

What joy and relief the people must have felt when they finally arrived in Jerusalem *(move 96[2], 96A over to JUDAH)*. However, they were deeply saddened by what they found. The city walls were broken down *(add 64)*, and the beautiful temple built by Solomon was in ruins *(add 62)*! Most of the homes were gone, so the people had to continue living in tents until they could rebuild. Many families traveled outside of Jerusalem to the towns where their fathers and grandfathers had lived many years before. There was much work ahead of them, but the people were very thankful to be back in the land God had given them.

3. **The Jews begin to rebuild.**
   (Ezra 3:1-4:24; 6:14-22)

   a. **The altar.**

   (People 4, 9, 10, 26, priests 37, 38, altar 39, fire 48A)
   All agreed that their first job was to rebuild their own homes and get settled in their towns. After that was completed, they all met in Jerusalem to rebuild the altar.

Sketch 99   General Outdoor

▲ **Option #6**

There are several times in this story where the Israelites stop and praise God—the completion of the altar, the temple foundation, the temple itself, and the city walls. Stop at each of these points in the story to sing a short praise song with your class.

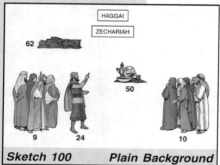

Sketch 100   Plain Background

▲ **Option #7**

Print these words on newsprint or poster board. Instruct the children to say the words as if they were the Israelites rejoicing and praising God.

(Place 4, 9, 10, 26 on the board.) They wanted to worship God and to make sacrifices to Him, something they had not been able to do in Babylon.

Even though the Israelites were afraid of the other people living around them, they still built the altar *(add 39)* where it had been before. The priests *(add 37, 38)* took charge of the construction of the altar and soon had everyone involved with building, or giving gold and supplies. They trusted God to take care of them, since He was the one who had brought them back to the land. Finally the altar was ready. For the first time in over fifty years, God's people offered sacrifices *(add 48A)* and worshiped Him in the way He had instructed. Just imagine what it must have sounded like as they joyfully sang and played their instruments in praise to God! ▲#6

b. The temple.

(Temple ruins 62, people 9, 10, dishes 50, enemy 24, temple 61; word strips HAGGAI, ZECHARIAH)

Now the next job was to rebuild the temple *(place 62 on the board)*, which had been completely destroyed by Nebuchadnezzar. *(Add 9, 10.)* Once again the people gave supplies and gifts *(add 50)* to help with the rebuilding. Large quantities of gold and wood were needed. King Cyrus gave them permission to get logs from Lebanon in the north. Everyone who was able helped in all the areas of construction. After the foundation was laid, the people celebrated. Let's read 3:11 to see what happened. *(Have a child read it aloud or read it together as a group.)* They sang and praised God together with these words: "He is so good! His faithful love for Israel endures forever!" The people sang and some even cried for joy at God's goodness to them. ▲#7

As God's people tried to build the temple, their enemies made many strong attacks and threats to stop them *(add 24)*. They became so scared and discouraged that they stopped building. But after several years God sent two of His prophets, Haggai and Zechariah, to encourage them to finish the work *(add HAGGAI and ZECHARIAH; have the children locate these books)*. We can read what they continually said in their books: "This is God's work and His temple. When it is finished, God will fill it with His glory and presence. It will be greater than Solomon's temple ever was."

Their words encouraged the people to again work on rebuilding the temple. It took them fifteen years to finally complete it. *(Replace 62 with 61.)* Once again there was great joy and celebration as they dedicated it to God! How wonderful that now they could worship God in His temple! Then they celebrated the Passover Feast for the first time in over fifty years.

4. Ezra comes to Jerusalem to teach God's Word. (Ezra 7:1-10)

Sketch 101   **Council Room**

(King 5, Ezra 27, Nehemiah 29)
Some time later King Artaxerxes *(place 5 on the board)*, the next King of Persia, gave Ezra *(add 27)*, a priest and teacher of God's Word, permission to take another group of people back to Jerusalem. The king told him, "Ezra, you are to appoint good leaders who know God's laws to govern the people in the land. You are to teach them God's laws if they do not know them so they can properly lead the people." So Ezra led a group of Israelites to Jerusalem, taking with him the scrolls of God's Word that had been preserved all the years the people were in captivity *(remove 27)*.

When Ezra arrived in Jerusalem, he was disturbed to see that the people who had returned from captivity were not obeying God. As Ezra began to pray and explain God's Word to them, the people began to confess their sins and started to live according to God's Word. *(Leave 5 on the board.)*

5. Nehemiah comes to Jerusalem to rebuild the walls. (Nehemiah 1:1–6:15)

With God's help, the people worked hard and rebuilt their homes and the temple. But there was still one more important task to be completed. We discover what it is in Nehemiah 1:3. *(Have one of the children read it.)* Yes, the walls and gates surrounding the city of Jerusalem still needed to be rebuilt. Why was it important to do this? *(Response)* Yes, the walls and gates of a city protected the people inside by keeping their enemies out.

When Nehemiah, the cupbearer for King Artaxerxes, ⌂(2) received a letter telling him about the broken-down walls in Jerusalem, it made him so sad that he cried. He wanted to do something about it. Where did he go for help? Let's look in Nehemiah 1:4 to see what he did. *(Have children read the verse silently and then give the answer.)* Yes, he fasted and prayed to God. Can you think of someone else who did the very same thing when she needed God's help? *(Response)* Yes, it was Esther. Nehemiah prayed, "O God please hear my prayer. Please give me success today. Allow the king to show kindness to me." *(Add 29.)* God answered his prayer, and the king gave him permission to return to Jerusalem. Not only did he grant permission but also the king sent some of the army to protect him on his trip. Do you remember how long that trip was? *(Response)* Yes. It was about 900 miles, a four-month journey. This must have greatly encouraged Nehemiah and given him joy.

> ⌂ **Note (2)**
>
> The king's cupbearer was a most trusted servant. He had a dangerous job in that he had to taste everything, especially the wine before the king would drink it. If it contained poison, the cupbearer would get sick or die first, and the king would know to not drink it. In those days there were many plots to get rid of kings and people in power by poisoning them.

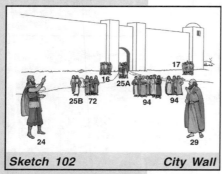

Sketch 102 — City Wall

(Nehemiah 29, people 72, 25B, 94[2], enemies 24, 17, soldiers 25A, 16)

When Nehemiah *(place 29 on the board)* arrived in Jerusalem, he gathered all the leaders together and told them why he had come and how God had answered prayer to get him there. Then he said, "Let's all work together and rebuild the walls."

The people were excited and answered, "Yes, let's do it!" Then everyone helped to do the work. Each family group who lived in the city worked on the part of the wall closest to their homes *(add 72, 25B, 94[2])*. It was hard and dangerous work. Their enemies tried to stop them *(add 24, 17)* by laughing and making fun of them and by spreading rumors and threatening their lives. They even tried to burn and destroy the wall that was already completed. What do you think Nehemiah did when he realized what was happening? *(Response)* Yes, he asked God to help them.

Then Nehemiah called the leaders together and said to them, "Don't be afraid of the enemy. Remember that the Lord, who is great and mighty, is with us. So fight for your families and homes!" *(Add 25A, 16.)* Then he told the men to carry their weapons as they worked. So they did just that. Also, half of the men guarded the wall while the other half worked on building it.

It wasn't easy. But the people prayed and worked, and God helped them finish the walls and gates around the entire city in fifty-two days! When their enemies realized what Israel's God had done, they stopped bothering them *(remove 24, 17)*. Once again the people were full of joy as they sang and celebrated and praised God for helping them to rebuild their city and the temple of their God. ▲#8

▲ Option #8

Nehemiah 12 tells us that when the new wall was dedicated, the Israelites took a praise walk around the city. The company divided into two groups and headed off in opposite directions. They marched around the walls singing praise to God until they met at the midpoint. You may wish to reenact the scene with your children. Give them simple musical instruments and encourage them to make their praise very loud as the Israelites did (12:43).

6. Ezra and the Levites read and explain God's Word. (Nehemiah 8:1–9:5)

Sketch 103 — City Street

(People 72, 25B, 3, 4, 26, 23, 9, 10, Ezra 27, scroll 27A, scrolls 27B, priest 38)

After the walls were built, all those who could understand gathered together in the city square *(place 72, 25B, 3, 4, 26, 23, 9, 10 on the board)* and asked Ezra to read God's Word to them. They stood and listened very carefully as he read to them from morning till noontime *(add 27, 27A, 27B)*. Some of the priests walked *(add 38)* through the crowd, helping the people understand the meaning of what they were hearing. It was the first time that many of them had ever had it read to them. *(Have someone read the last part of Nehemiah 8:9.)* What does it tell us the people did when they heard God's Word? *(Response)* Yes, many of them cried. They cried for joy because they were able to understand what God's Word said, but they cried also because they had sinned and disobeyed God. Ezra told them first to celebrate and find strength in the joy of God. They did this by having a feast and giving gifts to one another as they continued to hear God's Word. They did this for seven days until the entire law of God was read.

On the eighth day the Israelites met again to hear God's Word. This time they came dressed in rough cloth and put dust on their heads to show their sadness. They did not feast and celebrate as before. Instead they stood and confessed their sins. Then they made sacrifices to God.

■ **Conclusion**

Summary

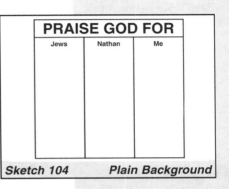

Sketch 104   Plain Background

("PRAISE GOD FOR" poster, marker, verse visual)
God's people were filled with joy because of all He had done for them. On many occasions they expressed their joy by thanking and praising Him. Let's look at this poster and list some things for which the Jews were able to praise God. *(Display the poster, and write the children's responses on the chart. Include the following: for permission to return to Judah, for a safe journey back to the land of Judah, for being back in their own land, for the completion of the altar, for the temple, for helping them rebuild the walls of Jerusalem, for the Word of God, and for those who helped them to understand it.)*

How did the Jews express their thanks and praise to God? *(Response)* Yes, they prayed and sang praises to God. They obeyed Him by giving offerings, by celebrating the feasts as they were instructed to in God's Word, and by giving gifts to each other. ▲#9 ⌂(3)

God's people really put the words of our memory verse into practice. *(Place the verse visual on the board.)* Let's say it together as praise to God just as they would have done. *(Encourage the children to say the verse with expression as they did earlier when learning the verse.)*

Application

At the beginning of our lesson we heard a story about Nathan. What did Nathan praise God for? *(Write the responses on the chart.)* God answered his prayer by giving his dad's job back to him with more money. How did Nathan express his thanks and praise to God? *(Response)* He hummed and sang for joy. He also told someone else what God had done for him.

What has God done for you? Is there something you want to thank and praise Him for today? Let's make a list of some of these things. *(Write the children's responses on the chart under "ME." Suggest the following to help their thinking: for permission to come to the class even though their parents won't go to church; the Lord's help to complete a hard school project and to get a good grade on it;*

▲ **Option#9**

Divide the children into small groups and give each group paper and markers. Instruct them to discuss the things the Jews could praise God for and to write one or two ideas on their paper. As each group shares its ideas, print them on a chart for all to see.

⌂ **Note (3)**

Psalms 113-118 were used throughout the Passover Celebration as songs of praise and are still being used to praise God.

▲ **Option #10**

Print the words of a Psalm, such as Psalm 118:24, 103:1, 115:1, or 118:1, or chorus on poster board or have the children sing the words right from their Bible. Or let the children sing one of the verses from the Psalms to a familiar tune.

◨ **Note (4)**

If your church has a contract with Christian Copyright Licensing, Inc. of Portland, Oregon, permission to make a limited number of copies of a copyrighted chorus for a one-time use should be covered. Otherwise you should contact the copyright owner of the chorus to obtain permission.

salvation; protection and help while babysitting a younger brother or sister for the first time.)

How can we show our thanks and praise to God for these things? *(Response)* Yes, we can thank and praise Him in our prayers. We can also tell someone else what God has done for us as Nathan did. We can also hum or sing to express the joy that is in our hearts. We can sing a praise song or repeat our memory verse or read one of the Psalms out loud to God. Let's say our memory verse again. *(Have the children repeat the memory verse and then have them sing a praise song.)* ▲#10

Response Activity

Give an opportunity for any unsaved children to receive the Lord Jesus Christ as their Savior so that they can also rejoice in God's gift of salvation and join in singing God's praise.

Provide copies of a familiar praise song for the children to take home and sing. (Be sure to follow copyright laws.) ◨**(4)** *Lead the children in singing the song and then close in prayer. Encourage them to sing this song throughout the week as they think about how great God is and the different things God has done for them.*

✎ TAKE-HOME ITEMS

Distribute **memory verse tokens for Psalm 138:5** *and* **Bible Study Helps for Lesson 14.**

RESOURCE SECTION

Use the materials in this section to help your children incorporate the Bible truths they are learning into their daily lives in a practical way.

Reproduce the patterns as handouts for the specific lessons where they are recommended.

Permission granted to reproduce materials in this section for use with **God Guides Us** *lessons.*

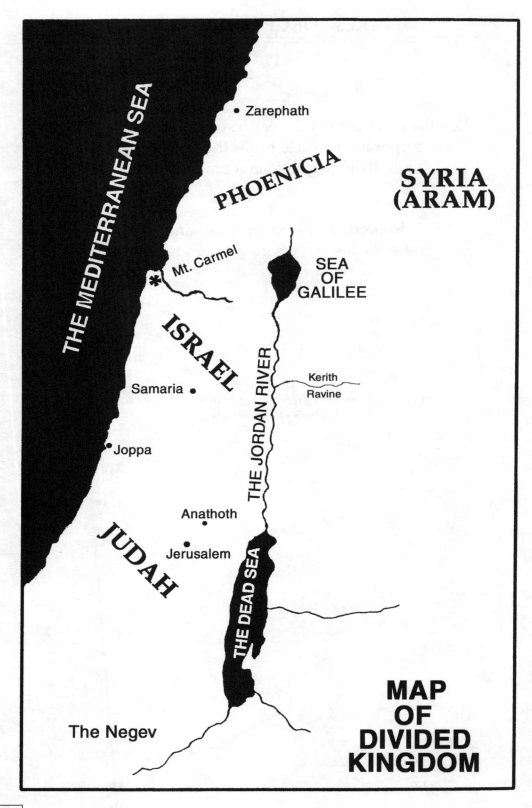

P-3

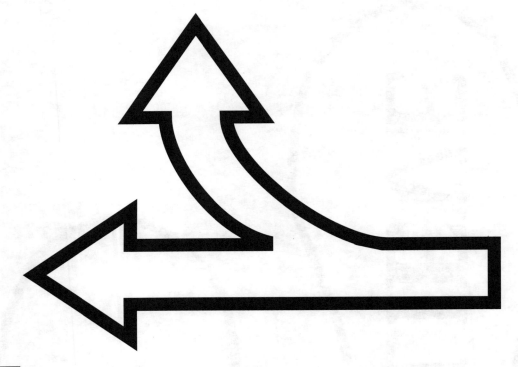

P-4

"God's Word says"

Where?   What?   How?
_____   _____   _____
_____   _____   _____

With God's help, I choose to cooperate with His plans by obeying what He tells me to do in these verses I have chosen.

NAME: _____ DATE: _____

I will obey God's Word.

P–5

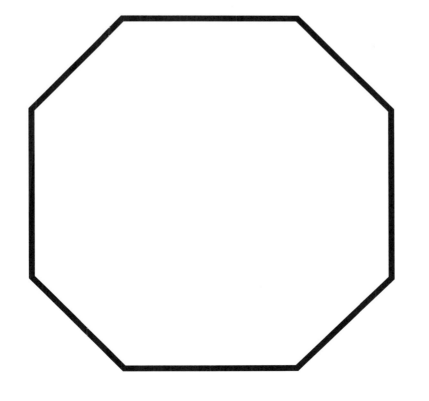

P–6

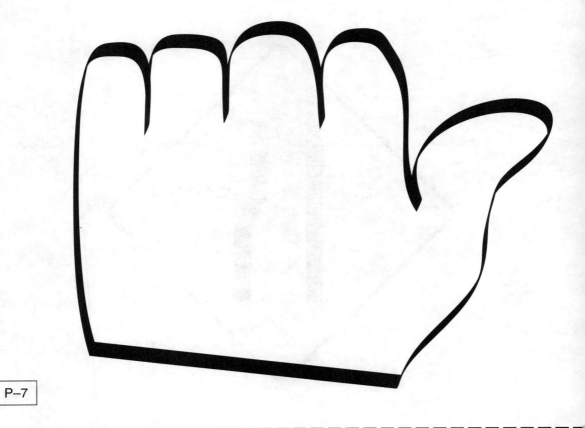

P-7

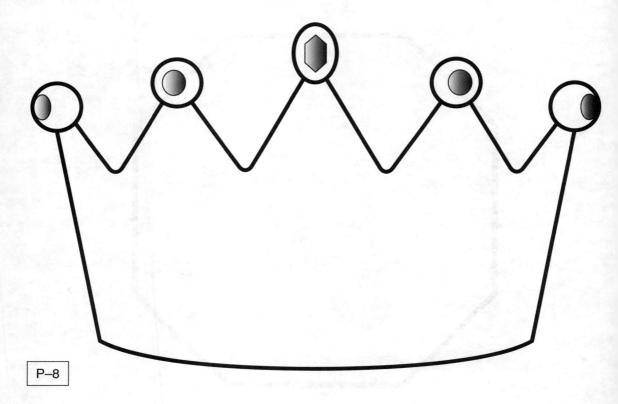

P-8

Cut on bold lines to make puzzle pieces.

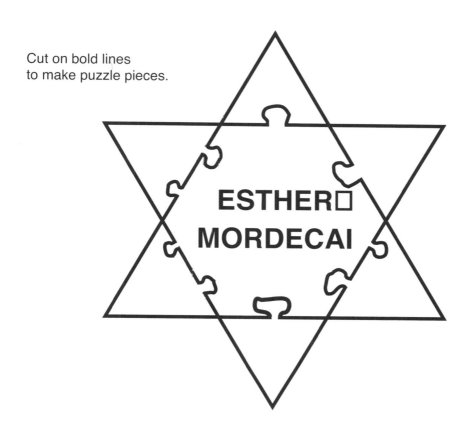

P–9

P–10

P-11

P-12

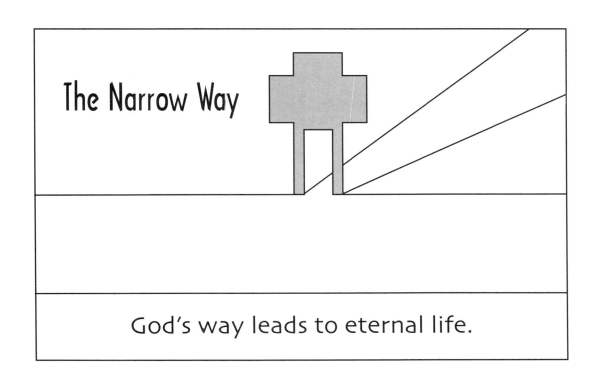

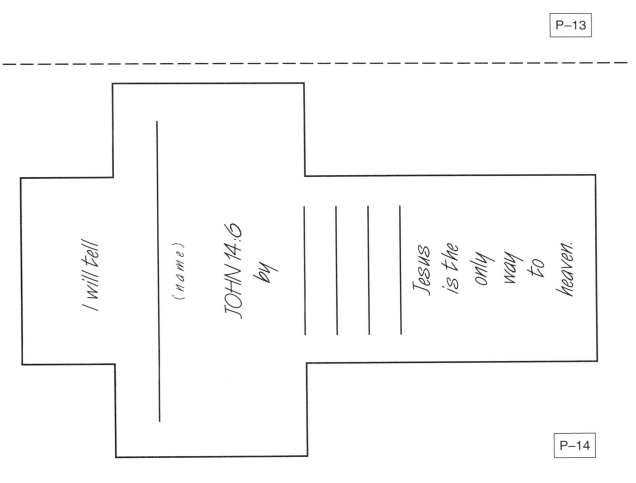

P-15

Today I will live

God's Holy Way

in my

WORDS
ACTIONS
THOUGHTS

God wants me to be holy in everything I think, say, and do.

(Today I will live)

God's Holy Way

in my

WORDS
ACTIONS
THOUGHTS

God wants me to be holy in everything I think, say, and do.

P-16

I have chosen spiritual life and

I choose

to depend on the Holy Spirit to help me obey God.

Signed _____

God gives us a choice of spiritual life or spiritual death.

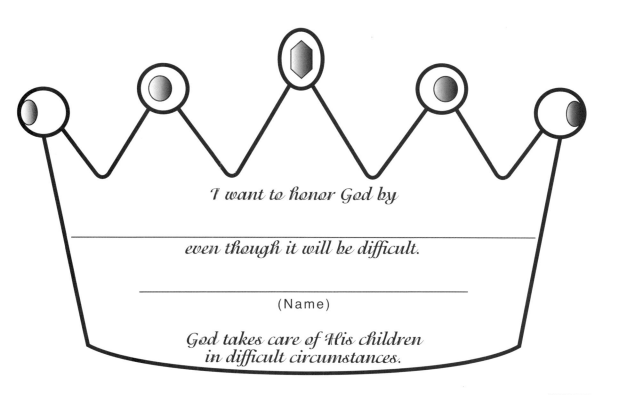

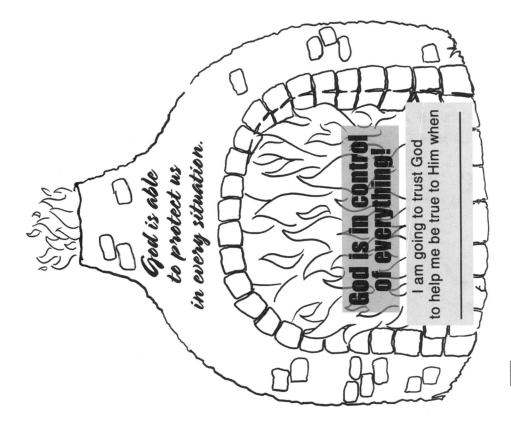

Choosing God's Obedient Way

❑ I choose to follow God's obedient way. I want to receive the Lord Jesus Christ as my Savior.

❑ I have chosen God's obedient way and have already received the Lord Jesus Christ as my Savior.

❑ I want to be sure I have chosen God's obedient way.

God blesses those who obey Him.

P–19

I CHOOSE TO TRUST AND OBEY GOD NO MATTER WHERE I AM OR WHAT HAPPENS.

Name: _____

Trust the Lord and obey what He says.

P–20

God's plan is the BEST for me!

I want God to use me to carry out His plan. I commit myself to doing whatever He wants me to do.

God's ways are higher than mine.

_____
Name

Name: _____

God has the right to test me by allowing

_____ in my life.

I choose to **trust Him** no matter what happens.

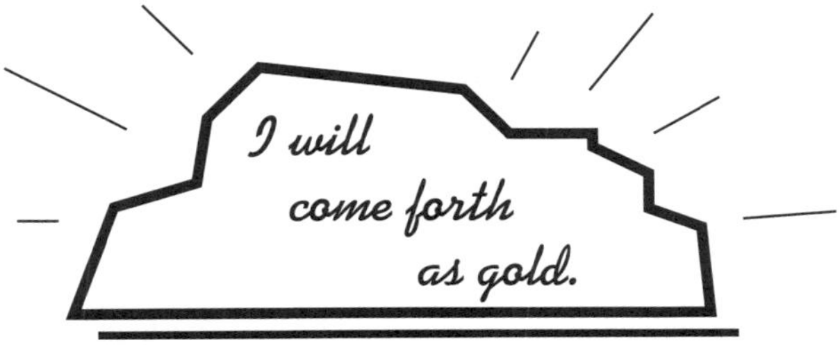

I will come forth as gold.

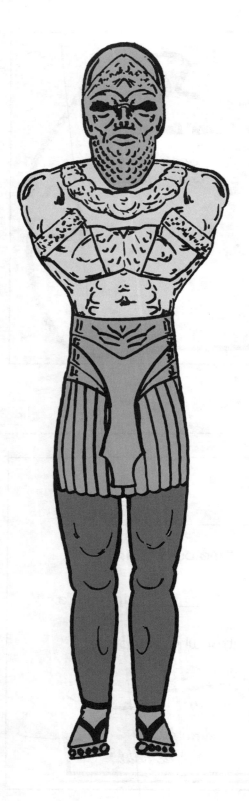

EVERY DAY
I WILL PRAY FOR

_____

_____

TO HAVE COURAGE TO

_____

_____

THE LORD
GIVES HIS CHILDREN
STRENGTH.

P–23

P–24

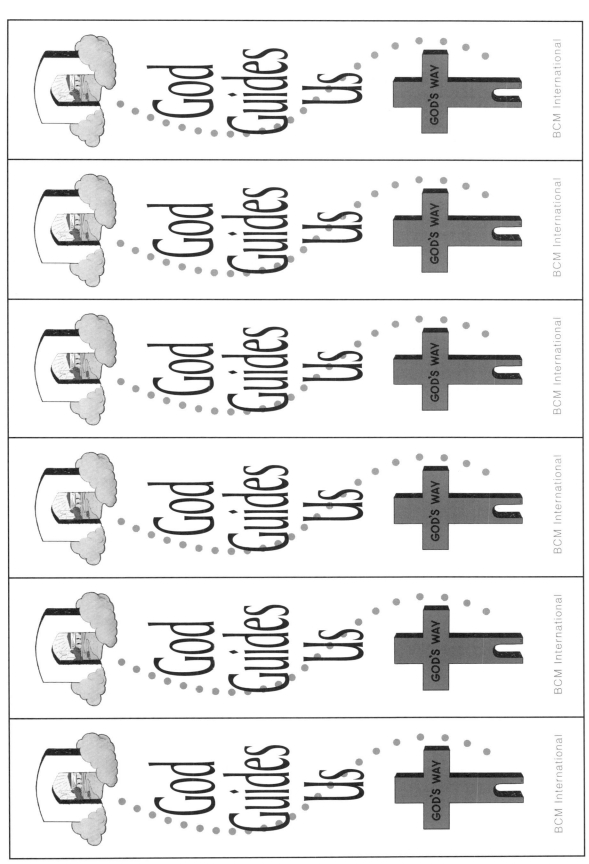

Teaching Materials and Supplies available for
God Guides Us

FO4T	Teacher's Text	
FO4F	Flannelgraph Figures	
	Includes Review Tokens	
FO4R	Review Chart	
	A flannelgraph background designed for displaying Review Tokens	
FO4BK	Basic Teaching Kit	
	Includes Teacher's Text, Flannelgraph Figures, Review Chart	
FO4RCD	*God Guides Us* Resource CD-ROM contains the following:	

> *Bible Verses Visualized*
> Available in King James and New International versions
> Furnishes visual pieces for teaching every memory verse in the course
>
> *Memory Verse Tokens and Holders*
> Individual take-home reminders for children
> Available in King James and New International versions
>
> *Bible Study Helps*
> Uses varied and interesting Bible questions and activities designed to encourage daily study of God's Word
>
> *Creative Idea Menus*
> Provide a wealth of ideas to reinforce and extend learning in programs and learning centers

FO4SK	Starter Teaching Kit	
	Includes Teacher's Text, Flannelgraph Figures, two Flannelgraph Backgrounds, Review Chart, CD-ROM	
FO4V-KJV	Bible Verses Visualized in King James Version only	
	Colorful visuals of every memory verse in the course for flannelgraph	
TGLM	Tract: *God Loves Me*	
	Based on John 3:16; use with younger children	
TCG	*A Child of God*	
	Presents salvation truth and basic teaching for new Christians; use with older children	
FB	Flannelgraph backgrounds	
	Screen-printed black outline on white flannel with instructions for coloring	
EFB	Flannelboard	
	Handmade folding masonite, covered with dark blue flannel (27" x 36")	
EFBC	Heavy-duty Binder Clips	
EFE	Floor Easel	
	Sturdy ABS construction, retracting legs for floor or tabletop use, 62" high	
EFTE	Tabletop Easel	
	Lightweight aluminum, 18" high, folds compactly	

Mailbox Bible Club correspondence Bible studies
Excellent for maintaining contact and continuing guided help after the series is finished

Note: See BCM Publications Catalog for information about price-saving kits.

To request a catalog, order materials, or obtain a Mailbox sample lesson, contact:
BCM Publications
P.O. Box 249
Akron, PA 17501-0249
Phone: 888-226-4685   FAX: 717-859-6914
E-mail: publications@bcmintl.org
or a National Office listed on page xi.